C000311819

STRATEGIC LEADERSHIP AND EDUCATIONAL IMPROVEMENT

Strategic Leadership and Educational Improvement

The companion volumes in this series are:

Effective Educational Leadership, edited by Nigel Bennett, Megan Crawford and Marion Cartwright

Leading People and Teams in Education, edited by Lesley Kydd, Lesley Anderson and Wendy Newton

All these readers are part of a course Leading and Managing for Effective Education (E849) *that is itself part of the Open University Masters programme.*

The Open University Masters Programme in Education

The Open University Masters Programme in Education is now firmly established as the most popular postgraduate degree for education professionals in Europe, with over 3,000 students registering each year. The Masters Programme in Education is designed particularly for those with experience of teaching, the advisory service, educational administration or allied fields.

Structure of the Masters Programme in Education

The Masters is a modular degree, and students are, therefore, free to select modules from the programme which best fit in with their interests and professional goals. Specialist lines in leadership and management, applied linguistics, special needs, and lifelong learning are also available. Study within the Open University's Advanced Diploma can also be counted towards a Masters Degree, and successful study within the Masters Programme entitles students to apply for entry into the Open University Doctorate in Education programme.

OU-Supported Open Learning

The Masters Programme in Education provides great flexibility. Students study at their own pace, in their own time. They receive specially prepared study materials, supported by tutorials, thus offering the chance to work with other students.

The Doctorate in Education

The Doctorate in Education is a part-time doctoral degree, combining taught courses, research methods and a dissertation designed to meet the needs of professionals in education and related areas who are seeking to extend and deepen their knowledge and understanding of contemporary educational issues. The Doctorate in Education builds upon successful study within the Open University Masters Programme in Education.

How to apply

If you would like to register for this programme, or simply find out more information about available courses, please write for the *Professional Development in Education* prospectus to the Call Centre, PO Box 724, The Open University, Walton Hall, Milton Keynes, MK7 6ZW, UK (Telephone 01908 653231). Details can also be viewed on our web page http://www.open.ac.uk/courses

STRATEGIC LEADERSHIP AND EDUCATIONAL IMPROVEMENT

Edited by
Margaret Preedy, Ron Glatter and Christine Wise

The Open University   in association with   Paul Chapman Publishing

Compilation, original and editorial material © The Open
University 2003. All Rights Reserved.

First published 2003

Apart from any fair dealing for the purposes of research
or private study, or criticism or review, as permitted
under the Copyright, Designs and Patents Act, 1988, this
publication may be reproduced, stored or transmitted in
any form, or by any means, only with the prior
permission in writing of the publishers, or in the case of
reprographic reproduction, in accordance with the terms
of licences issued by the Copyright Licensing Agency.
Inquiries concerning reproduction outside those terms
should be sent to the publishers.

Paul Chapman Publishing
A SAGE Publications Company
6 Bonhill Street
London EC2A 4PU

SAGE Publications Inc
2455 Teller Road
Thousand Oaks, California 91320

SAGE Publications India Pvt Ltd
32, M-Block Market
Greater Kailash - I
New Delhi 110 048

Library of Congress Control Number: 2002105579

A catalogue record for this book is available from the
British Library

ISBN 0 7619 4057 X
ISBN 0 7619 4058 8 (pbk)

Typeset by Pantek Arts Ltd, Maidstone, Kent
Printed in Great Britain by Cromwell Press,
Trowbridge, Wiltshire

Contents

Acknowledgements

The Editors and publishers gratefully wish to acknowledge the following for kind permission to use the following copyright material:

Leithwood, K., Jantzi, D. and Steinbach, R. *Changing Leadership for Changing Times*, ch.13, 'Future schools and leaders' values', Open University Press, (1999)

Levin, B. 'Conceptualising educational reform' *Reforming Education: from origins to outcomes*, Routledge/Falmer, (2001)

Glatter, R. 'Governance, autonomy and accountability in education from (eds) Bush T. and Bell, L. *The principles and practice of education management*, Paul Chapman, (2002)

Bottery, M. 'Uses and abuses of quality: the need for a civic version'. Ch. 4 in Bottery, M. *Education, Policy and Ethics,* Continuum (2000)

Dimmock, C. and Walker, A ' Developing comparative and international educational leadership: a cross cultural model', *School Leadership and Management*, Vol 20, no. 2 (2000)

Stoll, L. 'School culture: Black Hole or Fertile Garden for School Improvement', from Prosser, J. (ed) *School Culture*, Paul Chapman. (1999)

Hargreaves, D. 'Helping Practitioners Explore Their School's Culture', from Prosser, J. (ed) *School Culture*, Paul Chapman. (1999)

Foskett, N. 'Strategy, external relations and marketing', from eds. Lumby J. and Foskett N.J., *Managing External Relations in Schools and Colleges*, Paul Chapman, (1999)

Johnson, G. and Scholes, K. part of ch.2 'Strategic management in practice' from *Exploring Corporate Strategy*, 6th ed. *Financial Times* Prentice Hall, Europe, (2002)

Davies, B. and Ellison, L. *Strategic Direction and Development of the School*, ch. 5 'Strategic analysis: obtaining the data and building a strategic view, Routledge, (1999)

Fullan, M. from *The New meaning of Educational Change*, 3rd ed. Teachers College Press, (2001) Routledge/Falmer.

McMahon, A 'Fair Furlong School', from Maden, M. (ed) *Success against the Odds – 5 years on*, Routledge/Falmer, (2001)

Macbeath, J. and Mortimore, P. 'School effectiveness and improvement: the story so far', ch. 1 from their book (eds) *Improving School Effectiveness*, Open University Press. (2001)

Ouston, J. 'School effectiveness and School improvement: critique of a movement', from Bush, T. et al (eds) *Educational Management*, Paul Chapman, (1999)

Martinez, P. 'Effectiveness and improvement: School and college research compared,' *Research in Post-Compulsory Education*, Vol 7, no.1. (2002)

Macbeath, J. et al ch.13 and part of ch.14 from *Self-evaluation in European Schools*, Routledge/Falmer, (2000)

Every effort has been made to trace the copyright holders but if any have been inadvertently overlooked the publishers will be pleased to make the necessary arrangement at the first opportunity.

Introduction

1

Strategic leadership challenges

Margaret Preedy, Ron Glatter and Christine Wise

It is important for educational leaders to establish a shared strategic overview of the future direction of the organisation, clearly focused on the improvement of learning and teaching. This collection of readings explores current thinking and debate on some of the major strategic leadership challenges and concerns facing twenty-first-century educational organisations in undertaking this task. We argue that these challenges are concerned with understanding and responding to the impact of rapidly changing external contextual factors on the organisation, and managing the competing demands of autonomy and accountability. The chapters that follow therefore explore the issues involved in managing the increasingly permeable boundaries between educational organisations and their external contexts, and reconciling the tensions between environmental expectations and internal priorities.

Like its companion volumes, this book does not seek to provide answers but, rather, to contribute to reflection and debate on strategic concerns for educational leaders in schools and colleges, and how these concerns are being addressed. It draws on material taking a range of perspectives and approaches: theoretical overviews, research evidence, application of conceptual frameworks to leadership practice and case examples. Some of the chapters take a generic, cross-sectoral approach; others are based in particular sectors – primary and secondary schools and further education colleges. While most of the readings are set in the UK context, several of them have a broader trans-national focus, exploring themes and issues that span national boundaries and cultures. It is important, we believe, for educational leaders to transcend sectoral boundaries in their thinking; there is much to be learned from reflecting on one's own professional context in the light of insights drawn from other sectors and cultures.

This introductory chapter provides a brief outline of the main themes explored in the book. First we look at the external environment, and societal and organisational cultures, as major influences on the process of strategy development. This is followed by an exploration of some of the main issues confronting educational leaders in developing a strategic overview and managing change. The chapter then explores the major purpose or *raison d'être* of strategy in educational organisations: to promote ongoing improvements in the quality of learning and teaching. This, we argue, entails balancing competing accountability demands and negotiating a shared agenda for educational improvement. We conclude with a short overview of the later chapters contained in the collection.

The External Context

The external environment for schools and colleges is characterised by increasing turbulence and uncertainty as a result of various social and political pressures, including:

- An increase in consumerism and customer orientation, together with growing power and expectations of consumers.
- The impact of the knowledge revolution and the information age on all organisations.
- The major effects of ICT developments on organisational structures, cultures and strategies.
- Growing short-termist, profit-focused practices in both the private and public sectors.
- Increasing globalisation and competition, accompanied by greater global economic turbulence.
- Growing use of private sector principles and practices in public sector organisations such as schools, colleges and hospitals.

At the same time, large-scale legislative changes in the UK and elsewhere have brought increased autonomy for schools and colleges as regards operational decisions, accompanied by requirements making them more accountable for their performance and spending decisions. These requirements include: funding linked to student numbers; prescribed curricula and assessment arrangements; regular publication of comparative performance data; a cycle of regular external inspections in which institutions are assessed against published criteria; and the expectation for public sector organisations to demonstrate year-on-year improvements in performance against measurable targets. These legislative changes have brought about major shifts in the balance of power between the various stakeholders in the work of schools and colleges, and the accompanying accountability relationships.

As well as public accountability pressures, educational leaders also need to be very aware of, and responsive to, market accountability demands. Schools, colleges and other educational organisations operate in a competitive environment where they need to recruit well in order to prosper, since funding and the capacity to resource ongoing improvements are directly linked to student numbers. Success breeds further success – the ability to demonstrate effective performance in terms of student outcomes helps to ensure that the school or college is popular and seen in a positive light by potential clients, and hence maintains high enrolments and the capability for ongoing improvements. Conversely, declining rolls and poor student results lead to negative public perceptions and the prospect of a spiral of decline leading eventually to closure. Thus a key role for educational leaders in managing the boundaries between the organisation and its environment is to take a proactive stance in building effective relationships with external stakeholders.

In developing these relationships, an important prior stage is environmental scanning, to identify stakeholders' needs and expectations, as well as broader social, economic and political trends that impact on the future development of the school or college. Empirical studies of how schools seek to gather and analyse environmental information suggest that this process is often tackled in an informal and ad hoc way, rather than systematically (Levin and Riffel, 1997; Woods et al., 1998). 'School systems do not have good processes for learning about and responding to changes in their environments . . . These limitations are not the result of ill will or incompetence, but of long-ingrained patterns of thought and behaviour that will not be easy to change' (Levin and Riffel, 1997, p. 44). While UK further education colleges have a longer tradition of collecting and using market research information, it is argued by Wearing (1999, p. 191) that they and their clients would benefit from a more systematic approach, developing 'a culture of information, in which the institution is constantly searching for and reacting to developments in its external environment'.

A key issue in environmental scanning is the role of interpretation. The environment is not a fixed and objective reality 'out there' but rather a complex and changing network of agencies, policy initiatives and trends which are perceived and interpreted in different ways by organisation members. It is argued by Senge (1990) and others that ongoing learning, through interacting with environmental information, is important in developing individual and organisation capacities to interpret external events and identify key trends that need to be responded to.

Interpreting external expectations and framing a strategic response are major components of environmental leadership (Goldring, 1997). This form of leadership entails a proactive role – not just reacting to external demands, but playing an active part in shaping the perspectives and expectations of stakeholders. Three main types of strategy for environmental leadership can be identified (ibid.). First, leaders use strategies that seek to *reduce the dependence* of the organisation on its environment. Examples of this form of strategic response are: seeking alternative sources of funding, public relations activities to influence public perceptions about the organisation, and gate-keeping procedures to reduce the access of external groups and individuals to internal activities. A second form of strategic response aims to *adapt the environment*, i.e. to increase joint action and co-operation with stakeholders. Activities here include co-operation and partnerships, for example with other educational organisations, parents and business and community interests, and coalitions with other agencies and groups to achieve a common purpose. A final form of strategic response is to aim to *redefine the environments*, for example by altering organisational goals and mission, or 'rebranding' to attract a different student clientele.

The notion of environmental leadership, and much of the literature generally on schools' and colleges' management of external relations, draws on an open systems perspective of organisations (Scott, 1992). From this point of view, organisations have a two-way, interactive relationship with their environments. Educational leaders seek to maintain an equilibrium in this relationship, by balancing between the organisation's need to be autonomous and to resist excessive demands, and at the same time to maintain linkages and ensure continuing external support. This perspective tends to emphasise the role of human agency, and organisational leaders in particular, in responding to and shaping external demands. It also assumes that we can understand, interpret and make choices in response to external events, in a relatively systematic and logical way.

Other accounts, however, challenge this view, noting the limited capacity of organisations to anticipate and respond purposively to rapid changes in the environment. Thus, drawing on evolutionary theories, some argue that 'environmental change is typically too fast, too unpredictable and too implacable to anticipate and pre-empt' (Whittington, 2002, p. 52). From this point of view, organisational success is often the result of luck or good fortune – being in the right place at the right time – rather than effective strategic choices. Others stress the less-than-rational aspects of organisational decision-making and links with the environment. Thus, for example, Patterson *et al.* (1986) claim that external environmental factors impact on educational organisations in an unstable and unpredictable way, strongly influencing school/college goals, and challenging the autonomy, expertise and decisions of their leaders and staff. Social, cultural and political influences impact on education organisations in multiple and complex ways (Levin, 2001). Such accounts emphasise the limits of human and organisational capacity to understand and predict environmental expectations and make strategic choices. This leaves educational leaders with a more constrained, less proactive role than that described by Goldring – a cautious, gradual and evolutionary approach to strategy development, described by Quinn (1980) as logical incrementalism.

■ Societal and Organisational Cultures

The role of societal cultures in educational leadership has been somewhat neglected (Cheng, 1995) but has now begun to receive more attention. Social values and beliefs about the nature of education and the purposes of schools and colleges exert a strong influence on their activities and goals, shaping what is deemed to be appropriate and legitimate. Societal cultures are not monolithic but diverse and contested, reflecting differing values and interests of various stakeholder groups. One study of educational reform in Hong Kong, for example (Morris and Lo, 2000), identified three distant 'cultural arenas' competing to influence the nature and direction of the reform process: the policy-making arena, dominated by the state bureaucracy; the national policy arena, including the media, teacher unions and politicians; and the schools arena (i.e. the heads and teachers responsible for implementing the changes).

While mediating the influence of diverse external cultural forces, an equally important consideration for educational leaders in developing the organisation's capacity to cope with change is its internal culture, an area that has received increasing attention by organisational analysts. Much of the literature on this topic stresses the importance of a cohesive and collaborative culture in effective organisations, and the role of leaders in maintaining and developing this culture. Indeed, it is claimed by Schein (1985, p. 2) that 'the only thing of real importance that leaders do is to create and manage culture'. Similarly, Hopkins *et al.*'s (1997) work found that the main concern of effective headteachers in school improvement activities was to influence and develop school cultures.

However this normative view of an integrated and unitary organisational culture, shaped by leaders, may be unduly simplistic. Just as societal cultures are not monolithic, organisational cultures, especially in large and complex organisations like many schools and colleges, may be characterised by diversity and heterogeneity, with a number of competing subcultures centred round subject departments or other subunits. Drawing on perspectives that emphasise the less-than-rational aspects of organisational life, organisational cultures may be characterised as ambiguous and anarchic, with a nexus of shifting subgroups, where shared and consistent values are seen as an abstraction, a myth shaped by leaders for the purposes of control. From this point of view, the leader's role in developing an integrated culture may be problematic. There are also issues relating to the long-term and complex nature of cultural change (Schein, 1985), and the nature of the relationship between culture and organisational change. As Hargreaves (1995) points out, this is unclear, culture 'may be a *cause*, an *object* or an *effect* of change' (ibid. p. 41).

While it may pose challenges for educational leaders, the existence of diverse cultural subgroups may have organisational advantages, especially at times of uncertain and rapidly changing external demands. Integrationist organisational cultures may lead to cosy 'groupthink' and failure to perceive and address new external expectations. A range of alternative subcultures, which challenge the dominant organisational perspective, may enable the organisation to be more flexible and responsive in identifying and addressing new external opportunities and threats.

Strategic Leadership and Managing Change

Notwithstanding the problems involved in addressing external demands and cultural issues, in the face of a turbulent and uncertain environment it is essential for educational leaders to be able to manage multiple and ongoing changes, balancing externally initiated innovation with the organisation's own values, purposes and priorities. This entails a strategic overview, looking at the medium and longer-term direction of the organisation, mapping out its future in an integrated way, taking account of expected trends and developments in the environment as well as internally. Schools and colleges need to interpret their environments and their own roles within that context with a clear and shared view of how their organisation will develop and the means of ensuring that development. Strategic planning provides the basis for turning decisions into actions in a proactive rather than reactive way.

Much of the existing literature and indeed the practice of strategic planning and managing external links have been based on the assumption that these tasks are the prerogative of the organisation's senior managers. However, the stance taken in this volume and the course with which it is linked is that strategic understanding and involvement should be a central concern for all organisation members. There are three main reasons for this position. First, as noted above, the boundaries between educational organisations and their environments are becoming more indistinct as stakeholders, including central government and business interests, become increasingly involved in the work of schools and colleges. In these circumstances, the core work of educational organisations is subject to increasing external influence – the environment has a central rather than merely peripheral impact, so it is important for all organisational members to understand and respond to this. Secondly, in order to be effective, strategic planning needs the commitment and ownership of all staff, not just senior managers. Thirdly, there is strong evidence that in successful educational organisations leadership concerns – including strategic thinking – are seen not just as issues for senior managers, but as functions which are widely distributed across the organisational community (see, e.g., Leithwood *et al.*, 1999).

Further education colleges in the UK have considerable experience of strategic planning, as since 1993 they have been required to produce regular strategic plans for funding and accountability purposes. This form of planning in schools, however, is more limited and more recent. Indeed, Davies and Ellison (1999) found that few schools attempted to develop a 'futures perspective' – a long-term view of the future of the school in the light of external trends. School development/improvement plans, they argue, are insufficiently strategic in focus, and would be better titled 'operational target-setting plans', since they are largely concerned with maintaining existing activities in pursuit of short-term performance targets, rather than looking to the future and developing new activities. Much of the literature on strategy development stems from general management ideas and practice, rather than educational contexts. Strategic thinking is crucial to enable businesses to survive in a competitive market economy. A great deal of this literature, in the past and currently, takes a strongly normative position, portraying strategic planning as a rational process, i.e. one that is relatively systematic and logical, and controlled by senior managers. This process comprises gathering external and internal evidence on the current situation and future trends, identifying a range of strategic options, selecting the most appropriate one and implementing it. However, studies of how strategies actually develop have indicated the importance of the less-than-rational aspects of organisations noted earlier. Evidence to form the basis of rational analysis and choice is incomplete and unreliable. Intended strategic plans are often not realised in practice; rather, strategies may emerge as a result of cultural and political processes, negotiation and bargaining, and rational blueprints for the future are frequently rendered useless by the rapid pace of external change.

Similarly, studies of attempted change in educational organisations and systems have shown that the intentions of policy-makers and planners are seldom achieved in practice in school and college classrooms. Bringing about successful educational change is a long-term and socially complex process, where the implementation stage is particularly problematic – requiring scope for practitioners to work out their individual meanings of what the changes involve for their own thinking, beliefs and actions. This recognition of the limits of rational planning models has led to the development of looser, more gradualist approaches to strategic development which take into account the multi-faceted nature of the planning process and the plurality of interests involved. Some accounts emphasise that the process of engaging in strategic planning, generating ownership and commitment, is more important for organisational development than the actual plan. Others have suggested that strategy emerges only after taking action (Fullan, 1999), or that it provides a ritualistic form of security – a comfort blanket that engenders confidence and motivation to take action. Weick (1990) tells the story of a group of people lost in the high Alps in extreme blizzard conditions. Disoriented, frozen and starving, they are preparing to lie down and await death, when one of them finds a map in his pocket. Heartened and reinvigorated by this, the group uses the map to make their way down to safety. It is only then that they discover that the map was of the Pyrenees.

Exploring the complexities of strategy development, Mintzberg *et al.* (1998) suggest that we need to draw on a range of metaphors or lenses to understand the process fully. Thus, in addition to the traditional and still dominant rational planning models, strategy formation may be seen as a learning process, a political or cultural one, or as dominated by environmental forces. For many organisations (e.g. those in the public sector or subunits within large institutions), strategy may be largely imposed by government agencies or head office, leaving little room for choice and manoeuvre. Strategies may emerge from confusion and uncertainty, developing in small steps, their coherence and logic emerging through action, and perceived as a pattern only in retrospect. As Mintzberg *et al.* (ibid., pp. 372–73) argue, these various metaphors need to be used in conjunction, rather than separately to give an overview of the complexity of the strategy process: 'Strategy formation is a complex space . . . And we need to be more comprehensive – to concern ourselves with process *and* content, statics *and* dynamics, constraint *and* inspiration, the cognitive *and* the collective, the planned *and* the learned, the economic *and* the political.'

Educational Improvement: Strategic Concerns

In building and maintaining a shared strategic overview of the future direction of the organisation, leaders need to address a number of key strategic concerns. These include: exploring the influence of societal and organisational cultures, as discussed earlier; balancing competing accountability demands based on differing values and expectations; understanding the complex factors contributing to organisational effectiveness and improvement; and negotiating with colleagues and other stakeholders an agenda for ongoing self-review and action directed towards educational improvement.

As noted above, wide-ranging educational reforms in the UK, North America and elsewhere have made schools and colleges both more autonomous and more accountable. They are accountable to a wide range of stakeholders – parents, governors, education authorities, central government inspectorates, local communities and business interests – in a range of different ways. These various accountability relationships are not necessarily compatible with each other. We have referred above to market accountability, based on consumer choice and competition among educational organisations to attract parents and students. Other forms of accountability (Simkins, 1997; Leithwood, 2001) are as follows:

- *Government control* – educational organisations are responsible to governments agencies for providing appropriate courses and meeting specified performance targets, monitored by inspectorates.
- *Community participation* – responsibilities to be responsive to the needs and expectations of local people and groups – voluntary sector organisations, businesses, other local educational organisations, and so on.
- *Managerial control* – this form of accountability is based on hierarchical lines of authority within the organisation, and directed at organisational effectiveness and efficiency, with an emphasis on clear goals, targets, lines of responsibility and incentives, where teachers are held responsible to the headteacher/principal for contributing to overall organisational performance.
- *Professional* – this approach is based on professional ethics, norms and standards, where teachers are seen as accountable for maintaining these standards to fellow professionals and to clients – students and parents.

These various forms of accountability to which schools and colleges are subject are based on different and competing assumptions about the nature of educational organisations and how they can become more effective. This gives rise to a number of leadership dilemmas. Thus, for example, meeting government control accountability requirements to demonstrate ongoing improvements in students' attainments may lead schools and colleges to focus on boosting the performance of borderline pass/fail students, at the expense of higher and lower attainers. This is likely to challenge professional ethical norms relating to meeting the needs of all clients. As Adams and Kirst (1999) argue, there are particular tensions between external accountability demands focused on students' academic attainment, and internal school/college accountabilities based on professional norms and values, which emphasise broader concerns relating to working collaboratively with colleagues and students as part of an educational community – 'external demands have problematic connections to practice' (*ibid*, p. 485) There may also be problems in reconciling the consequences of particular accountability demands with organisational values. Thus, for example, market approaches have been shown to be inequitable to students, privileging those whose parents have the social and cultural capital to choose successful schools, and disadvantaging those less privileged students who are relegated to less successful schools (Lauder and Hughes, 1999). This outcome challenges organisational and professional values concerned with professional collaboration and partnership with other educational organisations, and those concerned with equity of provision for all students. As Leithwood (2001, p. 228) suggests in an analysis of accountability dilemmas facing educational organisations, 'leaders can be excused for feeling that they are being pulled in many different directions simultaneously. They *are* being pulled in many different directions simultaneously'.

Our next leadership theme is organisational effectiveness and improvement. There is a great deal of literature – largely focused on schools rather than colleges – stemming from these two once separate areas of work which later moved closer together. School effectiveness studies have sought to identify the factors associated with 'effective' schools – usually defined as those where student outcomes (particularly focusing on academic achievements) are better than those of schools with similar intakes, in terms of students' prior attainment and socio-economic backgrounds. This work has been widely used by governments, local education authorities and schools and colleges in seeking to promote greater effectiveness. School effectiveness studies focus largely on quantitative data, measuring the value added by the organisation by measuring the differences between inputs and outcomes. Work in the school improvement field has examined the *processes* involved in bringing about educational change, drawing on qualitative evidence. One group of researchers defines this area of work as 'a distinct approach to educational change that enhances student outcomes as well as strengthening the school's capacity for managing change' (Hopkins *et al.*, 1994, p. 26).

This body of literature provides much useful evidence and guidance on promoting organisational effectiveness, as discussed later in this volume. 'What is of value to managers in existing effectiveness research is in providing clues and in preventing having to reinvent the wheel from scratch' (Davies, 1997, p. 40). However, as researchers in this area acknowledge, such studies need to be approached with caution. As discussed above, there are no 'quick fixes' or recipes for successful change and improvement. Evidence that factors such as purposeful leadership and a focus on learning and teaching are found in effective schools does not provide guidance on *how* organisations become and remain effective. In Rosenholtz's (1989) terms, how demotivated, underperforming 'stuck' schools become dynamic, high-achieving 'moving' schools is unclear. There has been little research on ineffective schools and how they can improve. Effectiveness studies also use very limited indicators of effectiveness, focusing on students' academic performance, to the neglect of broader aspects of their educational experiences and achievements. There is a need for educational leaders to address effectiveness in broader terms, concerned with wide aspects of life in school/college, not just for students but also for staff members of the organisational community. Effectiveness studies have also been criticised for neglecting contextual factors – the interplay of local environment and circumstances and the culture and structure of the school or college – that combination of factors which makes every school or college unique. What works in one context may not work in another. Cultural factors have been shown to be particularly important in bringing about a focus on continuing improvement but, as noted earlier, are particularly difficult to interpret and change. It is argued by Davies (1997, p. 39) that schools and colleges should take charge of the effectiveness and improvement agenda, focusing on their own contextual circumstances and priorities with the collection and use of evidence as a joint enterprise, '[educational] communities must themselves investigate what constitutes effectiveness for all the participants'.

Similar arguments can be put forward about *evaluation*, our final leadership theme here. Schools and colleges are subject to stringent external evaluation of their activities by means of regular inspections with published reports on their performance. This form of evaluation is concerned with accountability purposes – *proving* the quality of a school or college's provision. Another important purpose for evaluation activities is enhancing the quality of provision – evaluation for *improvement*. It is important for educational leaders to ensure that the requirements of meeting external evaluation do not lead to a neglect of ongoing internal evaluation activities directed towards the organisation's own priorities for development, with a clear agenda for self-evaluation in the light of organisational values (Preedy, 2001). Data collected for accountability purposes, inspection visits and post-inspection action planning, and student performance data, provide valuable evidence for development work. As suggested earlier, it is important also to evaluate broader aspects of student and staff experiences of their life and work in educational organisations, not just academic performance.

In the past, self-evaluation by schools and colleges has been somewhat limited. The long tradition of teachers' classroom autonomy tended to promote a view of evaluation in negative terms as a top-down process imposed on teachers, thus inhibiting such activities as classroom observation by peers. There is now much greater recognition that self-evaluation is an important and necessary task, a prerequisite for improving learning and teaching provision. Schools and colleges are increasingly analysing the large amount of performance data now available and using this evidence to inform and improve practice. Studies of school improvement (e.g., Hopkins *et al.*, 1997; Southworth, 1998) show that successful school development depends on setting up and maintaining a culture of inquiry and reflection, and a commitment to ongoing collaborative self-review, where evaluation activities are seen as a routine and unthreatening aspect of teachers' work. An important component in organisational self-review is seeking and responding to the perspectives of students and parents on strengths and areas for improvement. One approach to self-evaluation which builds in the perspectives of students and parents, as well as staff, is outlined later in this volume.

Overview of later Chapters

We now turn to look at the later chapters in this collection in relation to the major themes of the book discussed above. The four chapters in Part 1 explore the environmental context and the complex impact of external influences on strategy development in educational organisations. Chapter 2, by Kenneth Leithwood, Doris Jantzi and Rosanne Steinbach, may be quite challenging to those in schools who are in sympathy with the earlier discussion of the reluctance of schools to become engaged in 'futures' thinking. In this chapter the authors engage in the process of considering changes in society and the demands that these will place on schools. They assess how those changes might be accommodated by schools and the implications that will have for their leaders. Their three visions, however, are very different, and the authors go on to discuss how they might be combined by considering the underlying values that each espouses. As discussed earlier in this chapter, strategic plans are not always implemented in practice. This can be for a range of reasons, often that 'something better' comes along. In Chapter 3 by Benjamin Levin, the author considers the path of government educational reform from its origins to its implementation. He considers the prizes and pitfalls of politics and their effect on policy. In Chapter 4, Ron Glatter presents a set of models for analysing the governance of education with particular, but not exclusive, reference to schools, as well as degrees of autonomy and forms of accountability. He argues that institutional leaders generally face not a single model of governance but several, as a result of which they face a series of tensions and dilemmas. He concludes that they need to analyse their own settings closely in developing their approach to the management of external relations.

Leaders also need to recognise that different external stakeholders may have differing views about what constitutes educational quality. Quality has been a major educational concern for some time now but Mike Bottery challenges the common use of the word in Chapter 5. He proposes that what is meant by quality depends on one's values and beliefs about society and how it should be organised. He looks at seven different definitions of quality as they might be applied to educational organisations, and discusses their assumptions, challenges their ethical application to public sector organisations and reaches a conclusion about which fits most comfortably.

Part 2 examines societal and organisational cultures and the ways in which they impact on organisational decision-making and development. A good idea in one context may not work in another. This is so obvious as to be almost common sense, but what changes in the context are likely to affect what parts of the reform? Do we need to look at all of the context? In Chapter 6, Clive Dimmock and Allan Walker develop a model for comparing educational leadership and management across cultures. They consider what components of the culture of a school it is important to understand before comparisons can be made. This model can equally well be applied to schools within a similar societal culture which may be operating with different organisational cultures.

Chapter 7, by Louise Stoll, begins by considering a range of educational initiatives at school level which have had varying degrees of success. This, she contends, is because the culture of the organisation was not considered before the change was attempted. The change strategy was not in line with 'the way things were done there'. She puts forward various definitions of culture and provides some useful models to help our understanding of the role of culture in organisational improvement. She recognises that there is unlikely to be a single culture (this is in fact one of the problems that can prevent the acceptance of change).

David Hargreaves' Chapter 8 is designed to offer practical help to senior staff in schools in understanding, changing and managing the school culture. He reviews a range of diagnostic tools, emphasising that the choice between them will be influenced by the individual's values. He offers advice on how to move the school in a desired direction, for example under what conditions rapid change can be expected and when a slower rate of progress is likely. On charismatic leadership, he cautions: 'unless you have powerful evidence to the contrary, assume charisma is not your strongest card.'

Part 3 of this collection looks at some of the major issues involved in strategic development and managing planned change successfully. In Chapter 9, Nick Foskett explores the role of marketing in linking the external environment and organisational strategy. He relates marketing to a broader view of external relations management and accountability. He presents a model indicating that student recruitment is only one aspect of marketing, and explains key terms such as strategic analysis and strategic choice, asserting that 'no organisation needs to be entirely the victim of external circumstances'. The chapter concludes with illustrative case studies of a primary and a secondary school and a further education college.

In Chapter 10, Gerry Johnson and Kevan Scholes use various perspectives or 'lenses' in exploring how strategies develop in organisations. They put forward various models of the strategy process, contrasting orthodox, rational approaches with those that acknowledge the impact of constantly changing and unpredictable environmental influences, and the less-than-rational aspects of organisational decision-making. The authors argue that it is important to see strategy development as a complex and multi-faceted process; we need to draw on a range of perspectives to understand it fully, and different participants will interpret the process in differing ways.

Brent Davies and Linda Ellison in Chapter 11 get down to the 'nuts and bolts' of strategic analysis. They present a range of techniques and tools for analysing an institution's market position and defining alternative directions for its future development. Some of the frameworks they present, such as the Boston Consulting Group matrix, are well known in the general marketing literature but rarely applied to education contexts. The authors exemplify through case studies how such models can be used in settings rather different from those for which they were originally devised.

Much of the literature on strategic development focuses on the planning stage. The next chapter explores the often-neglected problems involved in implementing strategic plans. In Chapter 12 Michael Fullan draws on his extensive study of the process of change over many years to give cautionary guidance to policy-makers, institutional leaders and teachers. He emphasises the crucial need to focus on how an innovation will be perceived by those who are intended to implement it, given the cultures, structures and norms within which they operate. Drawing on chaos and complexity theory, he acknowledges the creative role of conflict and resistance in the change process. 'Solving today's educational problems is complex,' he asserts, 'it *is* rocket science'.

The final contribution in Part 3 examines some of the issues in managing sustained change for organisational improvement. Chapter 13, by Agnes McMahon, reports the findings of a follow-up visit to a case study school, which, five years previously, was deemed to be highly successful. The author discusses the problems encountered by the school since the departure of its highly effective headteacher, and the factors that may help to explain these problems.

Part 4 of this collection explores strategic leadership concerns in promoting organisational effectiveness and improvement – the main rationale for strategic planning in educational organisations. Chapter 14, by Tim Simkins, looks at competing models of accountability and how they impact on strategic choices for educational organisations. The author examines current challenges to the traditional professional model of accountability, and proposes that these challenges may be seen as metaphors or images that illuminate different notions of educational organisations and their relationship with the environment, based on different underlying values.

The next three chapters in this part, Chapters 15–17 by Peter Mortimore and John MacBeath, Janet Ouston, and Paul Martinez, explore the findings from educational effectiveness and improvement studies and their implications for organisational development in schools and colleges. Mortimore and MacBeath provide an overview of the literature in this area, summarising what we have learned so far, from a large body of research. Ouston sounds a note of caution, identifying the limitations of this research and arguing that organisational improvement is a long-term, complex and context-specific activity. She emphasises that there are no instant recipes for organisational development and suggests that much of the literature is too simplistic and unduly rational in its assumptions about the potential for rapid improvements in educational organisations. Martinez compares improvement and effectiveness research on schools and colleges, highlighting the implications for further work in this area in both sectors.

The final chapter illustrates the essential role of self-evaluation in organisational improvement. John MacBeath with Michael Schratz, Denis Meuret and Lars Jakobsen in Chapter 18 provide case studies of two schools involved in a large-scale European project which sought to help schools to develop skills in self-review. The case studies explain how the schools undertook the self-evaluation process, the issues they faced and the impact of the project on their policies and practice.

Conclusion

This chapter has outlined some of the main leadership challenges currently facing educational organisations. Increased autonomy and accountability have made it particularly important for educational leaders to build a shared overview of the future of the organisation, directed towards ongoing educational improvement. Much of the literature suggests that this is a relatively straightforward and logical process. The position taken here, however, is that while systematic strategic development is both urgent and essential, it needs to be undertaken within a frame of reference which takes into account the complexity, ambiguity and less-than-rational features of the environmental context and organisational decision-making.

Finally we should acknowledge that this collection is inevitably partial, with many omissions. This book is one of three readers linked to Open University course E849, *Leading and Managing for Effective Education*, and many important themes and issues not covered here are addressed in the course materials or the two companion readers. It is hoped that this volume will contribute to reflection and debate on the leadership challenges which it explores.

References

Adams, J. and Kirst, M. (1999) New demands and concepts for educational accountability. In J. Murphy and K.S. Lewis (eds.) *Handbook of Research on Educational Administration*. San Francisco, CA: Jossey-Bass.

Cheng, K. (1995) The neglected dimension: cultural comparison in educational administration. In K. Wong and K. Cheng (eds.) *Educational Leadership and Change*. Hong Kong: Hong Kong University Press.

Davies, B. and Ellison, L. (1999) *Strategic Direction and Development of the School*. London: Routledge.

Davies, L. (1997) The rise of the school effectiveness movement. In M. Barber and J. White (eds.) *Perspectives on School Effectiveness and School Improvement*. London: University of London, Institute of Education.

Fullan, M. (1999) *Change Forces: the sequel*. London: Falmer Press.

Goldring, E. (1997) Educational leadership: schools, environments and boundary spanning. In M. Preedy *et al.* (eds.) *Educational Management: Strategy, Quality and Resources*. Buckingham: Open University Press.

Hargreaves, D. (1995) School culture, school effectiveness and school improvement. *School Effectiveness and School Improvement* 6(1): 23–46.

Hopkins, D., Ainscow, M. and West, M. (1994) *School Improvement in an Era of Change*. London: Cassell.

Hopkins, D., Ainscow, M. and West, M. (1997) School improvement: propositions for action. In A. Harris *et al.* (eds.) *Organisational Effectiveness and Improvement in Education*. Buckingham: Open University Press.

Lauder, J.H. and Hughes, D. (1999) *Trading in Futures*. Buckingham: Open University Press.

Leithwood, K., (2001) School leadership in the context of accountability policies. *International Journal of Leadership in Education*, 4(3): 217–35.

Leithwood, K. Jantzi, D. and Steinbach, R. (1999) *Changing Leadership for Changing Times*. Buckingham: Open University Press.

Levin, B. (2001) *Reforming Education: From Origins to Outcomes*. London: Routledge/Falmer.

Levin, B. and Riffel, J. A. (1997) School system responses to external change. In R. Glatter *et al.* (eds.) *Choice and Diversity in Schooling*. London: Routledge.

Mintzberg, H., Ahlstrand, B. and Lampel, J. (1998) *Strategy Safari: A Guided Tour through the Wilds of Strategic Management*. New York: Prentice Hall.

Morris, P. and Lo, M.N. (2000) Shaping the curriculum: contexts and culture. *School Leadership and Management* 20, (2).

Patterson, J., Purkey, S. and Parker, J. (1986) *Productive School Systems for a Nonrational World*. Alexander, VA: Association for Supervision and Curriculum Development.

Preedy, M. (2001) Curriculum evaluation: measuring what we value. In D. Middlewood and N. Burton (eds.) *Managing the Curriculum*. London: Paul Chapman Publishing.

Quinn, R. (1980) *Strategies for Change: Logical Incrementalism*. Homewood, IL: Irwin.

Rosenholtz, S. (1989) *Teachers' Workplace: The Social Organisation of Schools*. New York: Longmore.

Schein, E. (1985) *Organisational Culture and Leadership*. San Francisco, CA: Jossey-Bass.

Scott, R.W. (1992) *Organisations: Rational, Natural and Open Systems* (3rd edn). New York: Prentice Hall.

Senge, P. (1990) *The Fifth Discipline*. NewYork: Doubleday.

Simkins, T. (1997) Autonomy and accountability. In B. Fidler *et al.* (eds.) *Choices for Self-Managing Schools*. London: Paul Chapman Publishing.

Wearing, S. (1999) Finding your place: sensing the external environment. In J. Lumby and N. Foskett (eds.) *Managing External Relations in Schools and Colleges*. London: Paul Chapman Publishing.

Weick, K. (1990) Cartographic myths in organisations. In A. Huff (ed.) *Mapping Strategic Thought*. London: John Wiley.

Whittington, R. (2002) Theories of strategy. In M. Mazzucato (ed.) *Strategy for Business*. London: Sage.

Woods, P., Bagley, C. and Glatter, R. (1998) *School Choice and Competition: Markets in the Public Interest?* London: Routledge.

Part 1

External Influences

2

Future Schools and Leaders' Values

Kenneth Leithwood, Doris Jantzi and Rosanne Steinbach

Changing times demand different leadership. The purpose of this chapter is to raise our sights above the present horizon, to imagine what schools might be like in their 'post-restructuring' phase and to consider what the consequences of this future might be for leaders.

Developing defensible visions or images of what those schools should be is an important step in their creation. The purpose of this chapter is to examine some of the more salient aspects of schools and their wider social contexts and to begin to consider some of their implications for those who would exercise leadership in the development of future schools. The chapter examines, as well, some important assumptions about how schools change, since the task of those providing leadership entails not only helping to formulate an image of future schools but also assisting in the transformation of present schools.

Attempting detailed predictions about either the change processes or the nature of future schools clearly would be foolish. There are simply too many variables of which to take account. So the picture of each painted in this chapter is done in broad strokes. Inferring the detailed implications for leadership practice of approaches to change and images of future schools would also be foolish. What does seem within reach, however, is the identification of values to which those exercising leadership will need to adhere in order to help transform schools.

Source: Leithwood, K., Jantzi, D. and Steinbach, R. (1999) *Changing Leadership for Changing Times*. Buckingham: Open University Press. Edited Version.

Broad Trends Stimulating the Evolution of Schools

The social, economic, technological and political contexts within which schools find, and anticipate finding, themselves are obviously crucial considerations in the design of future schools. Such considerations, however, are seriously complicated by the conflicting implications for schools of many such contexts. None the less, the implications of context, including conflicts in the directions they suggest for future schools, provide much of the basis for future school design.

While there are many contextual forces impinging on the direction of future school designs, the six to be examined here illustrate the problems for which designers of future schools must seek solutions. Many dimensions of schooling are touched by these forces, but the focus of this analysis will largely be restricted to their influence on the allocation of power and decision-making authority, and more generally to school structure. Two of these forces press schools towards greater centralization, and two towards greater organizational decentralization. The final two forces fundamentally challenge the institutionalization of schooling as it has been conceived traditionally.

Centralizing forces

End of the 'borrow now: pay later' school of public finance

In the 1990s, developed countries around the world found themselves seriously challenged by debt. Furthermore, there is enough public concern for the long-term consequences of ignoring public debt to make both deficit and debt reduction politically attractive goals. Many countries are experiencing noticeable increases in the proportions of their populations that are aging. They are less willing to allocate their taxes to schools and are in greater need of medical and other social services. (Ng 1992).

The combined effects of government debt-reduction programmes and increased competition for public funding by other social services is significantly eroding the resources allocated to public schooling. This is creating pressure on schools towards greater centralization. Such centralization, it is argued, will allow more efficient use of available resources through so-called economies of scale.

End of the belief that all non-traditional family structures are rare enough to be safely ignored by schools

Few teachers still feel confident in assuming that their students come from two-parent nuclear families and possess the psychological robustness that is at the core of Coleman's (1987) meaning of social capital. While many children still do, evidence concerning the widespread existence of alternative family structures has become too pervasive to ignore (Oderkirk 1994). We are seeing the erosion of the kinds of familial educational cultures built on an unqualified acceptance of the child's worth, which include high value awarded to education in the home, encouragement and direct help available from adults in the home for children with their schoolwork and physical space available for study and homework.

However, it is not alternative family structures themselves that are responsible for an erosion of family educational cultures. Rather, the erosion is due, in part, to the enormous amount of time that many parents now have to devote to work and to further developing work-related skills in order to make certain that their children are provided for (Scherer 1996). The erosion is also a product of the economic disadvantages that often accompany some forms of the postmodern family structure. For example, a very large proportion of single-parent families do suffer undue financial hardship (Oderkirk and Lochhead 1992).

What a great many teachers and other educators now believe, that they did not believe before, is that development of social capital is something for which they must take some responsibility. This has become a force for engaging, for example, in partnerships with social agencies to better position their students for success at school. Various forms of service coordination in which schools play a role (Smylie and Crowson 1996) indicate how this has become a centralizing force for schools.

Decentralizing forces

End of society's willingness to assign major decision-making authority to professional expertise

While the status and autonomy in decision-making awarded to school professionals never matched that of medicine or law, for example, professionals of all types have been experiencing a rapid decline in the public's willingness to continue ceding such power. This is a consequence of, for example, generally higher levels of public education, greater access by the public to information previously possessed largely by members of the professions, and a growing perception that many professionals have betrayed the public trust.

Widespread initiatives by governments around the world to award parents more direct control over schools by establishing either advisory or decision-making roles for parents on school councils (Murphy and Beck 1995) are the most obvious manifestations of this decentralizing force on schools.

End of the public school's technological naïvety

A second decentralizing force is evident in the recent trend among schools to more rapidly adopt current electronic technology and to more fully integrate it into the educational and administrative work of the school. Serious use of electronic technology has been a long time coming and until quite recently seemed anything but inevitable. Even now, many mature technologies (televisions, video recorders) have achieved only marginal status in schools.

The computer, however, has become ubiquitous in our society and such widespread use has brought pressures and incentives for schools to adopt it in a meaningful way from many sources. Increasingly, schools report on their own work to make use of microcomputer technology to achieve existing and new educational goals (Weiss 1996).

While providing access to information is by no means all that schools do, it is a significant part of their current function. And mostly they bring 25 or 30 students together at the same time and in the same place to do it. The reasons for such an arrangement are no longer compelling, however. As video conferencing technology becomes more available and of higher quality, the reasons for students always to be in the same place at the same time will erode even further. This is one of the reasons that conventional classroom structures should not be an assumed feature of future schools.

De-institutionalizing trends

Contemporary understandings of how learning occurs

Constructivism is the label most often used to describe understandings of learning that have emerged from the work of contemporary cognitive scientists (McLaughlin and Talbert 1993). A good many curriculum and instructional initiatives are based on constructivist theory.

As long as constructivist theory is applied to the teaching of literacy and numeracy, its implications are largely restricted to increasing the size and changing the nature of teachers' instructional repertoires. But the implications are much more profound as such theory is brought to bear on the teaching of domain-specific knowledge especially in secondary schools. Such schools are frequently criticized because they provide their students with 'inert knowledge' (Bransford 1993).

Inert knowledge is acquired in contexts separate from those in which it is expected to be applied. As a consequence, those who possess it have considerable difficulty even recognizing instances in which it would be relevant to use, never mind having the capacity to use it to guide their actions. To be of actual use, cognitive scientists suggest that knowledge needs to be both 'situated' and 'proceduralized'.

When people learn in the context in which their knowledge is subsequently to be used, they acquire much more than the explicit knowledge that is part of the planned curriculum. They also acquire the 'tacit' (Polanyi 1967) or everyday knowledge that, in combination with the explicit knowledge, provides the depth of understanding and the skill required for practical problem solving. Authentic learning of useful knowledge, then, depends on involvement in solving real problems within some domain of practice.

Many of the school-to-work transition initiatives associated with the 'new vocationalism' (Goldberger and Kazis 1996) also entail the provision of significantly more workplace contexts for formal education.

Widespread recognition of the need for lifelong learning

In her proposed new agenda for education, Chapman refers to 'the learning society and knowledge economy' (1996: 1) as the broad policy context within which future schools must be designed. This is a context that acknowledges lifelong learning as instrumental to a rapidly changing job market. (Chapman 1996: 3). According to Chapman, future schools must be designed in recognition of a context that privileges those with the capacities to access, make sense of and use both sources and quantities of information unimagined until quite recently.

Widespread commitment to lifelong learning is a de-institutionalization force on schools since it clearly implicates people in systematic education at all stages in their lives. Present school designs, in contrast, respond to a set of requirements that were relevant (and to some extent remain so) for those at pre-adult stages in their lives. These requirements include, for example, custodial care, physical security, limited life experiences, uncertain motivation for learning the formal curriculum and immature levels of cognitive development. To the extent that meeting such requirements is irrelevant in the education of adults, the traditional design of schools cannot be justified. Furthermore, many adults do not depend on formal institutions of any kind for their learning, relying instead on personal reading, practical experience, deliberation with other colleagues and the like. So just redesigning existing school organizations is not obviously a solution.

▎ Images of Future Schools

Taken together, these conflicting forces for change suggest at least three criteria that future school designs ought to meet; inclusiveness, efficiency and effectiveness, and adaptability. First, future schools will need to be more inclusive in their decision making and more comprehensive in the dimensions of student growth (social and emotional as well as intellectual) for which they consider themselves at least partly responsible. This criterion responds to the diversity of student needs arising from alternative family structures, and the desire for greater non-professional control of schools. An image of future *schools as communities* begins to address this criterion.

A second design criterion for future schools is that they will need to become more efficient and effective in accomplishing the outcomes for which schools traditionally have been held accountable. This criterion emerges most obviously from the sometimes dramatic reductions in public funding allocated to schools, reductions likely to continue for some time into the future, along with persistent calls for greater public accountability. Imagining *schools as high reliability organizations* is a response to this criterion.

As a third criterion, future schools will need to be increasingly capable of adapting productively to changing expectations about what they are to accomplish and changing knowledge about best practices. These changing expectations are being accompanied by new instructional practices which teachers must master and which school organizations need to determine how to support both structurally and culturally. These changes in expectations and practices recommend the design of *schools as learning organizations*.

School as community

A school modelled as community, according to Bryk and Driscoll, 'is a social organization consisting of cooperative relations among adults who share common purposes and where daily life for both adults and students is organized in ways which foster commitment among its members' (1988: 2). As Selznick (1992: 369) further explains, its function 'is to regulate, discipline, and especially to channel self-regarding conduct, thereby binding it so far as is possible, to comprehensive interests and ideals'.

These conceptions of schools as communities begin to indicate the ways in which they might provide students with the social capital that, in the past, schools could more safely assume was being provided to their students through some combination of their immediate families and the networks of relationships available in the lives of students outside their immediate families. Social capital consists of the norms, obligations and trust that are developed among people through such relationships (Coleman 1987), and the sense of stability, security and positive self-concept typically engendered in individual children who participate in such relationships.

Implications for leadership

Several forces shaping the evolution of schools warrant more attention to inclusivity in the design of future schools. In this context, inclusivity is a broad category of values encompassing such related values important to reflect in school leadership as:

1 *Caring and respect for others*: As Starratt explains, caring requires 'fidelity to persons, a willingness to acknowledge their right to be who they are, an openness to encountering them in their authentic individuality, a loyalty to the relationship . . . This value is grounded in the belief, that the integrity of human relationships should be held sacred' (1991: 195).
2 *Participation*: This encompasses Hodgkinson's (1978) values of consensus It also reflects the concerns for freedom, equality and social justice in schools rooted in Dewey's concept of the democratic school.

School as high reliability organization (HRO)

While much has been written about the appropriateness of school as community, a conception of school as a highly reliable organization has not yet received much consideration.

Like efforts to develop more 'effective' schools the motivation for exploring how school could become more reliable can be traced to concerns about the development of basic skills. This concern is focused especially on those young students' development of reading skills, in particular, where this is retarded and so, as a consequence, is their opportunity to master other aspects of the school curriculum that depend on the application of such skills.

Stringfield (1992) uses hydroelectrical power grids and air traffic control systems as examples of HROs to demonstrate some of the characteristics that schools would need to acquire in order to be more reliable. HROs of this sort accomplish their goals more or less *all of the time* and the failure to do so would be considered a disaster by the public. Until quite recently the public has not considered failure to learn to read to be such a disaster.

Stringfield argues (personal communication) that there is growing public awareness of the significant negative financial consequences of a failure to successfully complete school for both individuals and for society.

From the dozen or more attributes associated with HROs (Stringfield 1995), one example serves to illustrate one of the small but significant changes that would be required of a traditional school for it to qualify as an HRO. HROs are alert to surprises or lapses. The experience of HROs is that small failures can cascade into major system failures and so such failures are monitored carefully. Yet schools rarely conceive of young students' off-task behaviour as a potential future disaster and so rarely either track it very closely or take extraordinary steps to reduce it.

Application to schools of the full set of HRO characteristics would result in an organization with many of the structural features of a traditional school but with, for example: more flexible, varied and task-dependent sets of professional relationships; greater commitment by staff to a clearer and more precisely focused set of goals; much greater attention to evidence about the effects of selected teaching practices; and meticulous attention to the maintenance of the equipment and technology considered important for achieving the instructional purposes of the school.

Implications for leadership

As a broad category of values, efficient reliability encompasses such specific values important to reflect in school leadership practices as:

1 *Equity*: In this context equity means equal access to knowledge on the part of students rather than equal access to educational resources. The goals of a high reliability school will only be achieved through inequitable distributions of those resources.
2 *Knowledge*: In this case the knowledge of greatest concern is about the effectiveness of educational practices used by the school in accomplishing the purposes for which they are intended, in the context in which they are used.
3 *Dependability*: Valuing dependability means rewarding people for unfailingly implementing the practices that the school judges to be most effective for its purposes.
4 *Persistence*: This value recognizes the failure of initial attempts to accomplish some of the school's goals and being willing to change one's approach and try again, perhaps many times.

School as learning organization

In a future context of declining resources, escalating expectations and turbulent environments, schools will need to be designed so that changing is considered an ordinary activity. At the heart of an organization's capacity to change is the individual and collective learning of its members. There is literature that has popularized some of these ideas in the concept of the 'learning organization' (Senge 1990; Watkins and Marsick 1993).

A learning organization has been defined as 'a group of people pursuing common purposes (individual purposes as well) with a collective commitment to regularly weighing the value of those purposes, modifying them when that makes sense and continuously developing more effective and efficient ways of accomplishing those purposes' (Leithwood and Altken 1995: 63).

The principal challenge facing those designing schools as learning organizations is to determine the organizational conditions that foster individual and collective learning and to build these conditions into the school. Leithwood *et al.* (1995) report that such conditions include: a widely shared vision of what school is trying to accomplish; a professional culture that encourages considerable collaboration among staff on matters of teaching and learning, with strong norms of continuous professional growth; structures that allow for frequent interaction and authentic participation in key decisions in the school; and policies and resources that support professional learning initiatives.

An image of future schools as learning organizations is particularly attractive because it does not require especially accurate predictions about the circumstances that future schools will face or the practices that would be most functional in response.

Implications for leaders' values

As a category of values associated with schools as learning organizations, a propensity to produce new ideas encompasses at least such specific values as:

- *Openness to new ideas*: Learning is fostered as organizational members discard preconceived beliefs about where useful ideas might come from.
- *Tolerance for divergent points of view*: Too much consensus leads to groupthink (Janis 1983). Learning organizations need just enough consensus to carry out their work and no more.
- *Tolerance for strategic failure*: Valuing failure as a source of learning rather than something to be avoided.
- *Questioning of basic assumptions*: Argyris and Schön (1978) refer to this as 'double loop' learning.
- *Speculative thinking*: Encourages people to imagine plausible future states, anticipate the challenges that those future states may create, and prepare to address them.
- *Personal mastery*: As Senge (1990) defines it, this values the effort of individual members to become as skilled and knowledgeable as possible about their individual responsibilities in the organization.
- *Interconnectedness*: Senge's (1990) fifth discipline, interconnectedness or systems thinking, encourages organizational members to appreciate the complex nature of the relationships among different aspects of the organization.

■ Towards a Comprehensive Image of Future Schools

The three images of future schools that have been described are based on quite different assumptions; each image, nevertheless, contains a partial solution to the dilemmas future schools are likely to face, and a synthesis of these images is both possible and desirable.

To illustrate some of the differences in these three images, consider how they differ in their assumptions about human learning, motivation and organizational mission and goals. With respect to learning, a community image of organization is based on developmental views. Members of the community, it is assumed, learn what they need to know and be able to do 'naturally' and relatively effortlessly from participation in a suitable community setting. HROs, on the other hand, reflect an information-processing view of learning, one in which there are clear learning goals and a set of powerful procedures available for their achievement. Finally, learning organizations assume that: learning and problem solving is both an individual and a collective act (Leithwood *et al.* 1996); such learning is often aimed at unclear goals; and knowledge is socially constructed through interactions.

The three images of future schools also vary considerably in their assumptions about human motivation. Using Maslow's (1954) needs hierarchy as an illustration, schools as communities most obviously fill people's affiliation needs. HROs appear to address people's achievement needs most directly, whereas self-actualization needs are most obviously met within the context of a learning organization.

As a final illustration of just how different are the assumptions underlying the three images of future schools, consider the most likely mission and goals each type of organization would be capable of realizing. With their overriding concern for inclusion and diversity, schools designed as communities are most likely to view *equity* as their mission and place considerable emphasis on social-emotional goals; the main instrument for change is likely to be organizational members' commitments to students, and to the school and its mission. A widely distributed version of *excellence* appears the most obvious mission to be addressed by HROs along with a core set of traditional goals for schools. Continuous quality improvement would be a likely contender for the primary mission of the learning organization where 'quality' is eventually judged in terms of services to students. Continuous improvement would be focused especially on higher order, more complex student outcomes; those for which well codified processes do not already exist.

These examples of different assumptions underlying the three images of future schools illustrate two important points. First, and most obviously, these three images really do represent fundamentally different school designs. Less obviously, but central to the purposes of this chapter, there is an important sense in which all of these assumptions can be justified at some point in time, for some people, in some contexts.

School-as-community acts as a foundation for the organization by providing the psychological stability and sense of mutual trust required for organizational members to be willing to risk making changes in their practices. *School-as-HRO* offers the conditions to ensure that students achieve the basic capacities or gateway achievements that parents and the wider community have always expected, and continue to expect, schools to develop. Finally, *school-as-learning organization* works to accomplish those ambitious and/or novel student outcomes for which schools have not, as yet, developed reliable and effective practices.

School Change and Implications for Leadership

The problem of imagining the design of future schools includes the problem of how they will get to be future schools. They will evolve into something different from, but connected to, today's schools, on a broken front, over a very unpredictable timeline and without any sense of ever completing that evolution.

Incremental approaches to change neither spark the imagination of educational reformers nor offer much leverage to policy makers. But as much as we may wish that we are entering a brave new world in which many things (including schools) will somehow behave differently, the wisest bet is that incrementalism will prevail.

First, there is no evidence of significant non-incremental change having occurred in schools in the past. Indeed, most evidence suggests that at least a five-year period of time has been required for changes considerably less ambitious than the comprehensive and systemic reforms currently being proposed.

A second reason why it is safe to assume that schools will evolve incrementally is that most non-regulatory types of changes proposed for schools require significant new learning on the part of teachers and administrators. Contemporary understandings of how such learning occurs suggest that it is an unavoidably messy and protracted process in which existing cognitive resources are used to construct new understandings and further develop one's repertoire of practices.

A third reason for assuming that schools will evolve gradually has to do with their location, largely within the 'institutional' as opposed to 'technical' sector of organizations, with ambiguous and contested goals. Institutional sector organizations must also take account of the interests of multiple legitimate stakeholders when establishing their goals and procedures. Unlike most other employee groups, teachers begin being socialized into their professional roles when they first enter school at the age of 6 or 7. This creates deeply rooted sources of resistance to rapid acceptance of new school designs. Such resistance is likely to be overcome only gradually as teachers have opportunities to understand, experiment with and find satisfaction in new ways of working with their students. So the present design of most schools, unlike many private enterprises, is 'overdetermined'. There are many interests to be satisfied before a significant change in their design can be even adopted, much less implemented.

A final reason for assuming gradual evolution of schools takes as its premise not its inevitability but its desirability. Incremental approaches, as Davis (1996) explains, avoid the debilitating and, finally, destructive 'rhetoric of excess' that has typically accompanied previous reform efforts.

Given the improbability of non-incremental or revolutionary change, future school designs must be ones that we 'can get to from here'; they must be images of organizations whose main features are capable of growing out of the seeds of today's school designs. From this perspective, success means eventually having these seemingly trivial changes add up to something worthwhile. Quite probably this will not be what was originally envisioned.

Implications for leaders' values

Three sets of values underlie incremental orientations to change and are an important part of the value system of those who would exercise leadership for incremental change.

Carefulness and a constructively critical perspective

This set of values fosters incrementalism by eschewing premature initiatives and initiatives that have not been developed to the point where their implications for practice are clear. Such values give rise to demands that the claims made for new initiatives be demonstrated under real-school conditions before adoption.

Respect for the capacities and commitments of past and current educators

This set of values manifests itself in a willingness to build on the insights about how to educate large numbers of children that are embedded in the collective memories and structures of existing school organizations and educational practices. At the minimum, these insights take account of the imperatives in schools that many reformers are neither aware of nor interested in.

Continuous improvement

This value encourages one to build on the existing strengths of the school, and to use those strengths as a means of responding to initiatives for change. Such a value would, for example, give rise to the use of the existing skills of teachers in computer technology to make more manageable aspects of the new student assessment system based on the development of student portfolios.

A continuous improvement value encourages the seizing of as much local control as central mandates and regulations allow, the determination of manageable priorities for change that make local sense, and systematic, focused initiatives for the improvement of schools through achieving such priorities.

Summary and Conclusion

From the consideration of clearly independent images of future schools has emerged a more comprehensive image: the school as *high reliability learning community*. This image responds well to the requirements or criteria that we have asserted to be critical in the design of future schools. Such schools should be inclusive, efficient and effective, and adaptable. They should also be capable of growing out of the design of today's schools, since the most likely process through which future schools will develop is an incremental one.

The high reliability learning community, then, appears to be a plausible design for future school organizations because it addresses quite directly the forces for change currently impinging on schools and because it takes into account critical constraints on the implementation of school change. To create and sustain such a school design requires the practices of stakeholders in the school, especially the practices of those offering leadership, to be governed by a complex array of values, which we have identified in this chapter.

Such values, we think, have never been more important to school leaders as they face the swampy problem of moving their present schools towards a defensible vision of future schools. Transformational leaders understand the importance of values – they are the leadership tools of postmodern organizations.

References

Argyris, C. and Schön, D.A. (1978) *Organizational Learning: A Theory of Action Perspective.* Reading, MA: Addison-Wesley.

Bransford, J.D. (1993) Who ya gonna call? Thoughts about teaching problem solving, in P. Hallinger, K. Leithwood and J. Murphy (eds) *Cognitive Perspectives on Educational Leadership.* New York: Teachers College Press.

Bryk, A.S. and Driscoll, M.E. (1998) *The High School as Community: Contextual Differences and Consequences for Students and Teachers.* Madison, WI: National Center for Effective Secondary Schools, University of Wisconsin–Madison.

Chapman, J. (1996) A new agenda for a new society, in K. Leithwood, J. Chapman, D. Corson, P. Hallinger and A. Hart (eds) *International Handbook of Educational Leadership and Administration.* Dordrecht: Kluwer.

Coleman, J.S. (1987) Families and schools, *Educational Researcher*, 16(6): 32–8.

Davis Jr, O.L. (1996) The pursuit of marginal improvements, *Journal of Curriculum and Supervision*, 11(3): 201–4.

Goldberger, S. and Kazis, R. (1996) Revitalizing high schools: what the school-to-career movement can contribute, *Phi Delta Kappan*, 77(8): 547–54.

Hodgkinson, C. (1978) *Towards a Philosophy of Administration*. Oxford: Basil Blackwell.

Janis, I.L. (1983) *Groupthink*, 2nd edn. Boston, MA: Houghton Mifflin.

Leithwood, K. and Aitken, R. (1995) *Making Schools Smarter: A System for Monitoring School and District Progress*. Thousand Oaks, CA: Corwin Press.

Leithwood, K., Chapman, J., Corson, D., Hallinger, P. and Hart, A. (eds) (1996) *International Handbook of Educational Leadership and Administration*. The Netherlands: Kluwer.

Maslow, A.H. (1954) *Motivation and Personality*. New York: Harper.

McLaughlin, M.W. and Talbert, J.E. (1993) Introduction: new visions of teaching , in D. Cohen, M. McLaughlin and J. Talbert (eds) *Teaching for Understanding: Challenges for Policy and Practice*. San Francisco, CA: Jossey-Bass.

Murphy, J. and Beck, L.G. (1995) *School-based Management as School Reform: Taking Stock*. Thousand Oaks, CA: Corwin Press.

Oderkirk, J. (1994) Marriage in Canada: changing beliefs and behaviors, 1600–1990, *Canadian Social Trends*, 33(Summer): 2–7.

Oderkirk, J. and Lochead, C. (1992) Lone parenthood: gender differences, *Canadian Social Trends*, 27(Winter): 15–19.

Polanyi, J. (1967) *The Tacit Dimension*. Garden City, NY: Doubleday.

Scherer, M. (1996) On our changing family values: a conversation with David Elkind, *Educational Leadership*, 53(7): 4–9.

Selznick, P. (1992) *The Moral Commonwealth: Social Theory and the Promise of Community*. Berkeley, CA: University of California Press.

Senge, P.M. (1990) *The Fifth Discipline*. New York: Doubleday.

Smylie, M.A. and Crowson, R.L. (1996) Working within the scripts: building institutional infrastructure for children's service coordination in schools, *Educational Policy*, 10(1): 3–21.

Starratt, R.J. (1991) Building an ethical school: a theory for practice in education leadership, *Educational Administration Quarterly*, 27(2): 185–202.

Stringfield, S. (1992) Research on high reliability organizations: implications for school effects research, policy, and educational practice. Paper presented to the International Congress for School Effectiveness and Improvement. Victoria, British Columbia, January 2–5.

Stringfield, S. (1995) Attempting to enhance students' learning through innovative programs: the case for schools evolving into high reliability organizations, *School Effectiveness and School Improvement*, 6(1): 67–96.

Watkins, K.E. and Marsick, V.J. (1993) *Sculpting the Learning Organization*. San Francisco, CA: Jossey-Bass.

3

Conceptualizing Educational Reform

Benjamin Levin

The word 'reform' often has a positive normative character, implying something desirable. In this chapter the term is used to refer to programs of educational change that are government-directed and initiated based on an overtly political analysis. The changes examined are driven primarily by the political apparatus of government rather than by educators or bureaucrats, and justified on the basis of the need for a very substantial break from current practice. In other words, for our purposes here, reforms are those changes in education governments have undertaken to make. I do not claim that these reforms are necessarily desirable. This definition of reform also stresses the political element in education reform in contrast, for example, to reforms that may emanate from within the school system itself.

The Four-Element Model

The main theoretical frame for this study is a stage theory of policy. There are many of these, all of which involve some series of stages moving from the identification of a problem, through the identification or adoption of particular strategies, to issues of implementation and impact. To an extent, any specific delimitation of stages is arbitrary and a matter of personal preference. For this study I define four elements or phases of the reform process – origins, adoption, implementation and outcomes.

Source: Levin, B. (2001) *Reforming Education*. London: Routledge Falmer Press. Edited version.

1 Origins. The focus here is on the sources of reforms as initially proposed
   by governments, the role of various actors and forces in originating
   reforms, and the assumptions about education and reform (explicit or
   implicit) contained in these proposals. Where did particular proposals
   come from? How did they become part of the government agenda, when
   so many ideas do not?
2 Adoption. Here the interest is in what happened to reforms between their
   initial proposal and their actual passage into law or regulation in each
   jurisdiction. Policies as finally adopted or made into law often differ from
   those originally proposed. I wanted to examine the politics of the reforms,
   and the factors that led to any changes between proposals and approval.
3 Implementation. A considerable body of research in education and other
   policy fields lays out the difficulties of moving from policy to practice.
   My interest was in the model of implementation, if any, that
   governments used to move their reforms into practice. What steps were
   taken to implement reforms? What 'policy levers' were used? What model
   of implementation, if any, informed the reform process in each setting?
4 Outcomes. Interest here is on the available evidence as to the effects of
   reforms. Any political action may have a number of results, some which
   were intended by policy-makers and others which were not. Because the
   reforms under study are about education, I wanted to give particular
   attention to what may be known about how the reforms have affected
   student outcomes and learning processes in schools.

There is nothing inevitable about this particular organizational frame.
Other schemes have been defined in the literature. Each categorization
scheme draws attention to somewhat different aspects of reform, and each
can be useful.

Though I find a four-part categorization useful for analytic purposes, they
are in practice overlapping and interactive. In political analysis, discrete categories and periods are devices of the analyst, not the experience of those
directly involved. Policy intentions are important, but must be seen in the
light of political practicalities that may substantially change preferences, and
in light of the actual consequences that are provoked by any given policy.
But one cannot simply read back from outcomes to intentions. Some policies
may be substantially rhetorical, with little thought given to actual outcomes.
In other cases outcomes are not those that were anticipated, especially in
complex policy systems such as education. If policy intentions are resisted,
then outcomes are likely to be shaped by the resistance as well as the intentions. No one element of the process is necessarily predominant.

Planning and Contingency in Policy Thinking

The common view of reform tends to assume that a given political or ideological analysis leads to a reform program that in turn leads to changes in practice leading to particular outcomes. Some work embodying these assumptions operates at a high level of abstraction, concerned with such matters as the changing role of the state and the impact of globalization as determining forces in political events. Educational reform in these works is often treated as the implementation of a set of well-defined political views arising from a belief in the reduced role of the state or the primacy of markets over public provision.

These analyses are important and rightly draw our attention to the links between education policy and broader issues of power and social policy. However, few would now uncritically accept a model that posits analysis leading to choice leading to action leading to results as a complete formulation of how the political world works. Political action may be characterized, by both proponents and opponents, as the result of careful thinking and well-laid plans, but such analysis may overstate the logical and understate other aspects of the political world. Politics is intentional, but it is also frequently provisional and ad hoc, and may be shaped as much by the vicissitudes of the moment as by well-defined intentions. At every step, multiple and conflicting influences come to bear, purposes change or are worn down by existing structures and processes, and circumstances change in ways that require modification of plans and actions. As Ball puts it:

> National policy making is inevitably a process of bricolage: a matter of
> borrowing and copying bits and pieces of ideas from elsewhere, drawing upon
> and amending locally tried and tested approaches, cannibalising theories,
> research, trends and fashions and not infrequently flailing around for anything
> at all that looks as though it might work. Most policies are ramshackle,
> compromise, hit and miss affairs, that are reworked, tinkered with, nuanced and
> inflected through complex processes of influence, text production,
> dissemination and, ultimately, re-creation in contexts of practice.
>
> (1998, p. 126)

Thus the view, often expressed, of politics as an irrational activity.

Yet an account that places too much stress on the contingent risks understating the importance of power and the significance of longer-term changes in institutional structures, organizational roles and power relationships.

The approach used here values both a means–ends rationality and a sense of the chaotic.

Coming to grips with these issues is not easy. After all, one is essentially trying to give a coherent account of something that can look pretty much like incoherence. As Ball puts it, a good account should

> capture the messy realities of influence, pressure, dogma, expediency, conflict, compromise, intransigence, resistance, error, opposition and pragmatism in the policy process. It is easy to be simple, neat and superficial and to gloss over these awkward realities. It is difficult to retain messiness and complexity and still be penetrating.
>
> (1990, p. 9)

Alternative Perspectives on Policy Formation

Literature from several disciplines suggests that an adequate account of policy-making should take account of the following points:

- Political decisions are shaped by many considerations, including the requirements of staying in office and the vicissitudes of the moment as well as the beliefs and commitments of policy-makers and their advisors.
- Politics is substantially shaped by symbolic considerations that may have little to do with the real effects of policies.
- Human abilities to understand problems and generate appropriate solutions are limited and often inadequate to the complexity of the problems. The entire process of policy development and implementation takes place in a context that is constantly changing, multi-faceted, and very difficult to read.
- Strategies for reform may focus on elements that are politically salient but that cannot produce the kinds of changes we really want or, to put it another way, the focus may be on what can be done instead of on what might really make a difference.
- Institutions such as schools or governments possess considerable ability to resist or alter policies to fit their own dynamics.
- History and culture are very powerful influences on policy and practice.

What shapes political decisions?

Any understanding of large-scale education reform should be rooted in a sense of how government actually works.

Many accounts of policy-making in education seem to assume that politics are primarily about policy – that governments are there primarily to define and implement a program. Especially among critics of policies, governments are often viewed as being fundamentally interested in particular policy outcomes based on a priori ideological commitments. Of course, policy is important in government, but the evidence would certainly seem to indicate that it is only one factor, and often not the pre-eminent one. Governments are also fundamentally about politics, and politics involve getting elected and staying in office as well as accomplishing goals while there. Governments and individual politicians must please enough voters and supporters to be able to maintain themselves. This leads, as is well known, to all kinds of devices designed both to assess and to influence public opinion and especially the views of key supporters.

To complicate matters still further, governments are subject to all the internal politics of any organization – currying favor, trying to increase one's own power, jockeying for future rewards, pleasing one's own constituency, and so on. Colleagues in a government may dislike each other intensely, for example, while still having to work together closely and put on a public face of collegiality and mutual support. One has only to read any political auto-biography to see just how important factors other than policy are in the politician's life.

Politicians also change positions frequently. Even when there are not changes in government via elections, ministers move from one portfolio to another every few years, making it difficult to sustain a political program.

In the world of politicians and those who work closely with them, everything occurs in an atmosphere that is extremely intense and fast-paced. There are a huge number of pressures and very little time, so that almost everything is done more quickly than might be wished. Senior politicians and staff have to deal with an enormous range of policy issues, so they can never be very knowledgeable about most of what is on their agenda. In this atmosphere, time for planning or reflection is at a premium.

Another fundamental reality of government is that unexpected events occur frequently, divert attention and change political priorities. Crises emerge that require attention and an event halfway across a country or around the world can completely rearrange the priorities of a government for days or weeks. Much of political life is a struggle between having an agenda that one tries to move forward and simply responding to all the things that end up on government's plate. Politicians are also often under intense pressure from competing interests.

Symbolic politics

Murray Edelman is a political scientist who was among the first to argue the view that politics should be understood as being as much a symbolic activity as a practical one. In other words, political talk and action are intended to shape and to respond to people's ideas as much as to their practical interests.

In this view of politics, words and other symbolic activities are of critical importance, but not in any straightforward sense. Instead, they are designed to achieve emotional and symbolic purposes as much as anything else. 'The propagandist whose verbalizations are most intensely embraced is the one who finds a formulation that evokes and synthesizes a large number of the experiences of concern to his audience' (Edelman, 1964, p. 124). Specificity of meaning is not necessarily desirable. Words are intended to be ambiguous as a way of allowing a range of people to project their own feelings and opinions on to what has been said.

Edelman also argues that politicians use symbolic responses as a substitute for dealing with real interests 'which permits the organized to pursue their interests effectively' while others are being satisfied with what is largely rhetoric (1964. p. 40). In other words, the political spectacle is also used to hide policies and actions that do have material advantages for some groups over others.

In symbolic politics, events are used to create legitimations for political actions. As Edelman puts it, 'A crisis, like all news developments, is a creation of the language used to depict it; the appearance of a crisis is a political act, not a recognition of a fact or of a rare situation' (1988, p. 31).

Deborah Stone (1988) describes problem definition as the strategic representation of situations: strategic in shaping a course of action, and representational because the representation of problems necessarily relies on interpretation by both speakers and listeners. Another important aspect of problem representation concerns the attributed causes of problems.

Stone also provides a fascinating discussion of some of the vehicles that are used to create particular representations of problems, including stories (that are told as if they are typical), synecdoche (again assuming, that one instance stands for many), metaphors as well as the selective use of data to support a particular point of view. She stresses the importance of ambiguity in allowing people to see what they need in a given commitment or event, thereby making it possible to build political support or coalitions (1988, p. 123).

The limits of capacity – fuzzy gambling

Political imperatives are not the only source of limits on government capacity to create and sustain reform. Human capacities to understand and solve problems are also limited. Dror (1986) provides a thorough and thoughtful account of both the potential and the limits of government action, Dror describes what he calls 'policy adversities', or the factors that make policy-making difficult. Policy issues themselves can be very complex, may include many interacting and dynamic factors, often seem to be highly intractable, may be outside the sphere of government, and can involve inherent contradictions (1986, pp. 38–45). But these are not the only difficulties. Human problem-analysis and problem-solving capacities are themselves limited in important ways. For example, people tend to overestimate the influence of immediate or visible causal agents, to give credence to the obvious instead of the important. We tend not to see the importance of subtle and long-term changes, to infer causality when events are connected only fortuitously, to give too much weight to what we have seen or been told most recently, and to be powerfully influenced by preconceptions and stereotypes (Kiesler and Sproull, 1982).

The result, Dror argues, is that policy-making may best be viewed as what he calls 'fuzzy gambling', a situation in which not just the odds but the rules themselves change as the activity progresses. In such a context, policy is far from a straightforward matter of calculating costs and benefits.

Focusing on the wrong issues

Another critique of policy-making in education has been based on the claim that reform does not address what really matters, partly because it is so hard to change what really matters.

Cohen (1995) points out that changes in student performance, which is surely what most educational reform at least purports to care about, depend fundamentally on what teachers and students do in classrooms. Yet many reforms are not primarily aimed at teaching and learning but focus instead on school organization, governance, finance, curriculum and assessment. Reform advocates make the assumption that changes in the latter will result in changes in the former. However, Elmore is one of many who have noted that 'Changes in structure are weakly related to changes in teaching practice, and therefore structural change does not necessarily lead to changes in teaching, learning and student performance' (1995, p. 15).

However, focusing on changing teaching and learning is easier said than done. Governance or curriculum changes can be put in place through legislation and can be pointed to as real changes. Altering teaching and learning practices is much more difficult because these depend on the decisions of so many individuals and are so difficult to alter.

Yet even if the focus is on the right policy variables, policy-makers may well overestimate their influence.

The nature of institutions

Policy changes inevitably have to work their way through institutions. Governments, school systems, political parties, labour markets – all are institutional structures with a history and sets of understandings that may affect the way in which policy takes shape. Neo-institutionalism is a subset of organization theory that has provided a renewed focus on the important role institutional structures and processes play in shaping and containing policy. Neo-institutionalists argue that characteristics of institutions and institutional systems have strong effects on organization functioning, independent of rational analysis or self-interest.

Although organizations of all kinds are strongly affected by changing external conditions, the dominant view among researchers is that organizations try wherever possible to maintain the status quo and to avoid changing in response to external demands. Kaufman writes that organizations have two main responses to uncertainty 'incorporation of the source of the uncertainty within the organization – that is, expanding the boundaries to include it – thereby making it subject to the norms and controls of the system' and 'reduction of exchanges across boundaries in an effort to satisfy most needs internally – withdrawal from the source of uncertainty as it were' (1985, p. 43).

Organizations try to manage uncertainty by creating standard ways of thinking about and acting on issues and problems. These standard practices come to shape what people see as possible or desirable.

A particularly interesting variant of neo-institutionalism is what is called 'the logic of confidence' argument (Meyer and Rowan, 1977). The argument is that institutions do not necessarily have to be successful to survive; they only have to appear to be doing the things that people expect such an institution to do. In other words, it is often their appearance that engenders trust rather than their results.

Wilson (1989) shows clearly the degree to which government action is affected by the institutional nature of government and bureaucracy as well as by political factors. Far from chastizing public sector managers for their weaknesses – though he recognizes that such weaknesses exist – Wilson concludes that 'Given the constraints on the managers of public agencies, it is a wonder that there is any management at all . . . often, goals are hopelessly vague, activities sadly ineffectual, and powers sharply limited' (1989, p. 154).

Neo-institutionalism gives a theoretical expression to the common empirical finding that policies are transformed by those who have to turn them into action. It is clear that policies do not move neatly into practice, and that some of these alterations are inherent in the nature of large organizations.

Organizational learning

A more optimistic vein of work concerns the ways in which organizations come to change their practice through learning. A number of writers (e.g. Senge, 1990) have argued that in the face of increasingly complex environments, organizations must be oriented to learning as a way of coping with change.

Although organizational learning is an appealing concept, it has some serious conceptual difficulties. For example, it is not clear whether an organization can learn, as distinct from the people who make it up. What does organizational learning actually look like? The idea of organizational learning also inevitably has a normative character in that it assumes that some kinds of learning are desirable while others are not.

James March (1991) has developed the distinction between the *exploration* and *exploitation* of knowledge in organizations. He argues that organizations will tend to do what they already know: to exploit accumulated skill and knowledge. This is sensible in that it is through exploiting knowledge that efficiencies can be produced. Looking for new approaches and methods is expensive and often wasteful. At the same time, organizations that do not seek new knowledge and new ways of doing things will eventually face problems as the situation around them changes and their ways of doing things become less and less functional. The problem is to find the appropriate balance between these two elements. It might well be argued that school systems have focused very heavily on exploitation, and that relatively few resources have been devoted to finding new ways to educate people. Certainly the formal investment by governments in research and development in education remains very small almost everywhere in the world (Guthrie, 1996).

History and culture

The most important determinant of present arrangements is usually past practice. What has gone before and how people think about their present situation shape what is either desirable or possible at any given point in a jurisdiction. All of the overarching elements discussed earlier in this chapter will themselves have different manifestations in each concrete setting. Elements of social structuring, such as issues of social class, language, religion and ethnicity, are especially significant in influencing education policy. Each of these elements is in turn shaped by unique historical events.

Consider first issues of social structure. Family background continues to be the single most important predictor of educational and life outcomes, but its role in education policy debates varies a great deal across the settings. In England, with a long history of social class divisions, class and elitism are defining elements in all debates about education policy. Edwards and Whitty (1995) have argued that in Britain the entire structure of education policy and provision can only be understood within a framework in which rankings are what matter, and most people's objective is to have their children as high on the academic ladder as possible. Certainly, questions of class were a key part of the debate over reform in Britain. In New Zealand and Canada, on the other hand, social class has historically been less prominent than in Britain, and class issues figured much less prominently in debates over education. In the United States a strong history of individualism means that social class tends to be largely absent from mainstream political debates.

Differences in history and culture are also affected by the differing geographic and demographic situation in each country. Thus Scotland, though nominally part of the British system, continues to have quite different education policies for various historical reasons (Raab *et al.* 1997).

Geography matters, too, even in our digital age. It is far easier to get key people together in a small country such as Britain or New Zealand than in a large and dispersed country such as those in North America. Where people meet less often, certain kinds of political and organizational relationships are less likely to develop.

Both Canada and the United States are federal states, while Britain is largely unitary and New Zealand entirely so. Canada's history and geography have led to a highly decentralized system of education in which the national government has a very limited role. However, Canadian decentralization is quite different in spirit from that in the United States. In Canada, governments have historically been seen as positive and important instruments for achieving social purposes, unlike the United States, where local control is fuelled by a strong orientation towards individual rights and concomitant suspicion of all things done by governments. Canadian provincial governments have always been important actors in education.

The structure of political institutions is also a vital factor. Unitary states such as Britain and New Zealand can take actions that are impossible in federal states such as Canada and the United States. Parliamentary systems provide a quite different set of political opportunities and constraints than does an American-style system with its separation of the legislative and executive functions. The separation of executive and legislative control in the United Stares creates dramatic differences in political practice – for example, in the ability of an executive to implement its program.

All of these factors shape the range of options that policy-makers will even contemplate, as well as the strategies they might use to pursue an issue. No country is the result of a process of rational planning, so the net effect of context is to increase the complexities and contingencies that surround education policy.

Conclusion

These strands of analysis provide useful ways of thinking about policy creation and implementation. They direct our attention both to the promise and to the limits of public policy. Governments are inevitably involved with shaping public policy and activity. This is an important task. At the same time, governments, especially in open political systems, have only limited ability to create the world as they might wish it. Although the analysis in this chapter gives considerable emphasis to the limits of government action, it does also suggest that we can learn from our efforts and improve our capacity to analyze and act on important matters. Public policy remains, whatever its limits, a central way for societies to shape themselves.

References

Ball, S. (1990) *Politics and Policy Making in Education*. London: Routledge.

Ball, S. (1998) Big policies/small world: an introduction to international perspectives in education policy, *Comparative Education* 34(2), 1999–29.

Cohen, D. (1995) What is the system in systemic reform? *Educational Researcher* 24(9), 11–17, 31.

Dror, Y. (1986) *Policy Making Under Adversity*. New York: Transaction Books.

Edelman, M. (1964) *The Symbolic Uses of Politics*. Urbana: University of Illinois Press.

Edelman, M. (1988) *Constructing the Political Spectacle*. Chicago: University of Chicago Press.

Edwards, T. and Whitty, G. (1995) Marketing quality: traditional and modern versions of educational excellence. Paper presented to the American Educational Research Association, San Francisco, April.

Elmore, R. Structural reform in educational practice, *Educational Researcher* 24(9), 23–6.

Guthrie, J. (1996) Evolving political economies and the implications for educational evaluation, in *Evaluating and Reforming Educational Systems* (pp. 61–83). Paris: OECD.

Kaufman, H. (1985) *Time, Chance and Organizations: Natural Selection in a Perilous Environment*. Chatham, NJ: Chatham House.

Kiesler, S. and Sproull, L. (1982) Managerial response to changing environments: perspectives on problem sensing from social cognition, *Administrative Science Quarterly* 27(4), 548–70.

March, J. (1991) Exploration and exploitation in education, *Organizational Science* 2(1), 71–87.

Meyer, J. and Rowan, B. (1977) Institutionalized organizations: formal structure as myth and ceremony, *American Journal of Sociology* 83(2), 340–63.

Raab, C., Munn, P., McAvoy, L., Bailey, L., Arnott, M. and Adler, M. (1997) Devolving the management of schools in Britain, *Educational Administration Quarterly* 33(2), April, 140–57.

Senge, P. (1990) *The Fifth Discipline*. New York: Doubleday.

Stone, D. (1988) *Policy Paradox and Political Reason*. New York: HarperCollins.

Wilson, J. (1989) *Bureaucracy*. New York: Basic.

Governance, Autonomy and Accountability in Education

Ron Glatter

Introduction: A Hazardous Enterprise

To write about concepts such as those in the title for an international audience is a hazardous enterprise. It is easy to become over-impressed by apparent similarities between 'reforms' in various countries and to neglect continuing deep differences at the level of implementation and practice. For example, Levin (1999; 2000) has conducted research into education reform in national contexts which, in global terms, might seem very similar to one another – Canada, England, New Zealand and the USA. Yet he concludes that even across contexts with such close cultural affinities, reforms such as changes in governance exhibit considerable variation: 'The official commitment to decentralisation and parent involvement is ubiquitous, but within this frame policies and practices are highly variable' (Levin, 1999: 136). This observation is likely to have even greater force where the national contexts being compared are more diverse.

In this connection it is important to distinguish different dimensions of change. Green (1999) conducted an analysis of changing education and training systems in a group of distinctive European and East Asian settings. He found that, as a result of the impact of common global forces, there was clear evidence of convergence around broad policy themes, such as lifelong learning, decentralisation of governance and the growing use of quality control and evaluation measures. 'However this does not appear to have led to any marked convergence in structures and processes' (Green, 1999: 69) nor in the details of policy. Indeed, the different models underlying the operation of the various systems appeared to be as distinctive as they were a

Source: Bush, T. and Bell, L.A. (eds.) (2002) *The Principles and Practice of Educational Management*. London: Paul Chapman Publishing.

decade earlier. Rather than simply concentrating on the discourse of policy, he calls for more attention to be given to structural analysis to enable us to understand better the impact of common trends on particular settings.

As Bottery (2000) indicates, global trends in each nation are strongly mediated by factors such as:

■ its central values, for example its orientation towards an individualist or collective ethos
■ its long political and social history as embodied in current educational structures
■ the particular personalities holding power when reform is being attempted, their beliefs, objectives and political strength.

The combination of such factors may create a highly constrained situation for policy-makers so that often 'reforms focus on what can be done instead of on what might really make a difference' (Levin, 2000: 8).

The lack of attention to culture and context in existing models and theories is criticised by Dimmock and Walker (2000: 159) for being ethnocentric and assuming 'a false universalism'. This assessment leads them to develop a model for cross-cultural comparison in educational leadership and management, covering both system-level and school-level cultural characteristics, 'in order to present holistic and contextualised accounts' (ibid.: 159).

The present chapter seeks to avoid the assumption of a false universalism by presenting a set of models which can be used in different contexts:

■ to analyse the governance of school education, as well as degrees of school autonomy and forms of accountability
■ to consider the possible impact of proposed changes in this area.

The term 'school' is used throughout this chapter. However, the analysis presented is believed to be widely applicable across different types of educational institution, including those designed for older adolescents and adults, called 'colleges' in some countries. The emphasis may sometimes be different and reference is made to this later.

Governance

Studies of educational management and administration too often neglect the framework of governance within which school leaders operate. The notion of 'governance' itself is contested. Rhodes (1997) has identified six distinct uses of the term. A common contemporary approach is to speak of 'governing without government' to suggest that the task of governing has now outrun the capacity of governments to perform it. Consequently, it is increasingly undertaken by complex external networks of groupings from the private and volluntary sectors, professional 'experts', lay people and others. This leads to difficulties of 'steering' and monitoring and to 'opaque accountability' (Rhodes, 1999: xxiii). A characteristic definition of governance within this approach is as follows: 'a concern with . . . achieving collective action in the realm of public affairs in conditions where is not possible to rest on recourse to the authority of the state' (Stoker, 2000: 3). Jessop (2000) speaks of the state being forced to share power in order to secure its objectives. Dowling et al. (2000: 109) apply this thinking to local government: 'Governance implies interconnectedness and mutual dependency between a variety of organisations both inside and outside the local authority.'

Such writers adopt the classification of governing structures in terms of markets, networks and hierarchies (Rhodes, 1999; Thompson *et al.*, 1991) but tend to equate 'governance' with networks alone. The related though highly ambiguous concept of 'partnership' attains considerable importance within the perspective (Raab, 2000). However, it is not clear why 'governance' should be conceived in such specific terms, even if, under the so-called New Public Management, government has increasingly adopted the roles of enabler, contractor and regulator (Arnott, 2000). Levin (2000) has drawn attention to the range of 'policy levers' which governments have at their command, including mandates, inducements, capacity-building, system changing and opinion mobilisation (see also Levin, 2001). Increasingly governments in many countries are employing a range of regulatory and monitoring devices such as audits, inspections, target-setting and performance measurement.

These forms of system management are more indirect than the traditional ones based on command and direction, but their overall impact in terms of the distribution of power is an open question, a matter for empirical investigation in each context. Has there been a dispersal of power, as the 'governing without government' approach would suggest, or has there simply been a shift from one form of control to another (Jacobs, 2000)? How successful are governments in 'steering at a distance', or in what Jessop (2000: 23) calls 'metagovernance': 'the process of managing the complexity, plurality and tangled hierarchies characteristic of prevailing modes of co-ordination'? For example, what have been the effects of governments privatising parts of public services and creating arm's length agencies in an attempt to cope with overload by cutting down on direct service provision? Hirst (2000) considers such structural changes have increased not reduced fragmentation and complexity through the requirements they create for enhanced supervision, regulation and co-ordination.

Pending further detailed investigations in different settings, it seems appropriate to adopt more open definitions of governance than Stoker's given above. The *Concise Oxford Dictionary* defines the term simply as 'the act or manner of governing', which would embrace markets, networks and hierachies and any mixes of them found in particular contexts. Hirst (2000) follows this approach but extends it to include the contemporary concern with results, defining governance as 'the means by which an activity or ensemble of activities is controlled or directed, such that it delivers an acceptable range of outcomes according to some established social standard' (ibid.: 24).

Martin et al. (2000: 121) refer to 'a system of rule which constitutes the form and process of the public sphere' which emphasises the formal rather than the behavioural aspects of governance, though they add that it will 'not be neutral but driven by the values of the dominant institutional or political order'. As Rhodes (1997) argues, altruism between levels of government is rare. Governance must be conceived in political (including micropolitical) and not simply in legal or procedural terms. Also, although the idea of governing *without* government is questionable, the concept of governance clearly encompasses *more than* government.

The changing governance of school systems exhibits a series of tensions which will become evident in the analysis below. These include tensions between:

- integration and fragmentation
- competition and co-operation
- central and local decision-making.

The processes involved are delicate ones, and the balances struck at any point in time (for they will frequently change) will impact significantly on the character of the schooling made available.

Models of Governance in School Education

The argument presented here is that governance, provided that it is defined in an 'open' manner as suggested above, can be viewed as an overarching concept to establish a framework within which other common concepts relating to structure and process, such as autonomy and accountability, can be located. This should help to promote conceptual coherence and avoid partial and misleading assessments of these other ideas when considered outside their broader context.

Table 4.1 offers a tentative framework (developed from Glatter and Woods, 1995) for understanding and applying models of governance in school education. It is undoubtedly a crude and oversimplified analysis. Four models are distinguished: competitive market (CM), school empowerment (SE), local empowerment (LE) and quality control (QC). These models should be seen as ideal types. They are separated here for analytical purposes. In practice each governance system or jurisdiction is likely to operate on some composite of these models. Sometimes they may complement and reinforce each other as they impact on localities and schools but their interaction is also likely to cause tensions which participants must seek to resolve.

Table 4.1 *Models of governance in school education*

Models	Competitive market (CM)	School empowerment (SE)	Local empowerment (LE)	Quality control (QC)
Indicative policies	Pupil number-led funding e.g. by vouchers More open enrolment Published data on school performance Variety of school types	Authority devolved to school on finance, staffing, curriculum, student admissions Substantial powers for school council/ governing body	Authority devolved to locality on finance, staffing, curriculum, student admissions Substantial powers for local community council/ governing body	Regular, systematic inspections Detailed performance targets Mandatory curriculum and assessment requirements
Main perspective(s)	Commercial	Political and/or managerial	Political and/or managerial	Bureaucratic
How the individual school is viewed	As a small business	As a participatory community	One of a 'family' of local schools	As a point of delivery/ local outlet
Main focus within the system	The relevant competitive arena	The individual school	The locality as a social and educational unit	Central or other state bodies
Nature of schools' autonomy	Substantial	Devolved	Consultative	Guided
Form of accountability	Contractual; consumerist	Responsive; 'dual'	Responsive; community forum	Contractual; hierarchical
Purpose of performance measurement	Inform consumer choice	Provide management information	Benchmarking across units	Monitor and develop system
Key school leadership role	Entrepreneur	Director and co-ordinator	Networker	Production manager
Function of intermediate authority	Minimal	Supportive, advisory	Strategic co-ordination	Production supervision as agent of controlling body

Competitive market

Examples of policies characteristic of each model are shown first, and then specific features of each of them are identified against a number of issues of structure and process. Thus, the major perspective underlying the CM model relates to the analogy with the commercial marketplace. Under this model, the school is viewed as a small or medium-sized business with a high degree of autonomy and few formal links with the governmental structure. The main focus within the system is placed not on the individual school but on the relevant 'competitive arena' (Woods et al., 1998), which will contain a group of (generally) adjacent schools in competition with each other for pupils and funds. The nature of this arena will vary widely from context to context, depending on factors such as the socio-economic character of the area, including access to private transport, and the relative density of the population – where the population is very thinly spread, there may be no arena at all.

School empowerment

The next model is called 'school empowerment' (SE) because policy-makers often claim that they are seeking to empower school-level stakeholders, in particular the headteacher or principal and other staff as well as parents. The delegation of functions to school level has been 'legitimised by a discourse of empowerment' (Arnott, 2000: 70). The perspectives underlying this model might be either or both 'political' (in the broad sense of dispersing power) and managerial. In some national contexts the emphasis has been purely managerial, on the principle that decisions are best taken as close as possible to the point of action, while in others the argument has also been couched in terms of freedom and choice. Although the SE model is often in practice combined with CM, it is analytically distinct and the picture of the school which is implied in the model is different. The focus is more on the institution itself and the way it is run than on its competitive activities 'against' other institutions. It encompasses ideas of participation, identification and partnership – the school conceived of as an extended community and in this respect it seems to provide a contrast with the CM model. The unit within the system which provides its main focus or 'centre of gravity' is the school itself.

Local empowerment

Some countries have been more concerned with devolution to local and municipal authorities than to schools, and it seemed important to represent this model explicitly within the current version of the framework. Although the LE model shares the term 'empowerment' with SE, and there are a number of commonalties, there are also significant differences between them. As with SE, the justification for this form of empowerment can be in either or both political or managerial terms. However, the perception of the individual school is different. The school is here viewed more explicitly as one of a 'family' of schools, as part of a local educational *system* and as a member of a broader community in which there are reciprocal rights and obligations. The contrast with the CM model is particularly evident here. Martin et al. (2000) have developed a framework which 'contrasts a system of local education devolved according to the principles of community governance as against those of the market' (ibid.: 122): they compare 'consumer democracy' with 'local democracy'. Within the LE model, the main focus is on the locality as a social and educational unit and its representative bodies, though numerous difficulties have been found in practice with implementing representative local democracy satisfactorily.

Quality control

Finally, under the pressures of global competition and growing demands on public expenditure, governments are increasingly seeking control over the quality of key school processes and products even in highly devolved and/or market-like systems. The major underlying perspective in the QC model is likely to be bureaucratic, that is involving laid-down rules and requirements and operating through set procedures, controls and monitoring arrangements. The picture of the school implied here is of a kind of 'point of delivery', with many of the 'goods' on offer and the targets established – the 'product mix' and 'product quality' – having been determined at either the central or state level, depending on the constitutional arrangements. Under the QC model, the units within the system which provide the main focus or 'centre of gravity' usually tend to be located within, or closely connected to, central or regional government.

The four models are by no means comprehensive and the framework could well be formulated differently, but it provides a useful instrument through which to examine some key issues of structure and process in the governance of school education.

■ School Autonomy

The framework suggests differences in the nature of schools' autonomy under each of the four models. Before discussing these, some consideration of the idea of school autonomy is needed. The concept is connected with the trend to devolve power to lower levels in many countries. As Green (1999) points out, such devolution can take many different forms: 'Decentralisation has variously meant devolving power to the regions, the regional outposts of central government (deconcentration), the local authorities, the social partners and the institutions themselves' (ibid.: 61). He suggests that there are still clear differences between countries where most power lies at the centre (such as France and Japan), those where regional control is strongest (such as Germany and Switzerland), those where local control now predominates (the Nordic countries) and those where substantial power has been devolved to schools and the marketplace (Netherlands and the UK).

The term 'autonomy' is often used in a rhetorical sense and to guard against this it needs to be examined closely (Maden, 2000). Two key questions are: autonomy for whom and over what? Bullock and Thomas (1997) distinguish between the autonomy of the individual learner, the educator and the institution, arguing that the level of autonomy might be increased for one of these while at the same time being reduced for the others. The fact that autonomy is a relative concept is also seen when we consider the domains in which autonomy might be given to schools. Writing from an Australian perspective, Sharpe (1994) presents a 'self-management continuum' from total external control to total self-management, and attempts to identify movements along four sub-continua in Australia over a 20-year period. These are concerned with *input* variables, such as finance, staff and students, *structure* variables, such as decisions about the patterns of provision, *process* variables, such as the management of curriculum and *environment* variables, to do with reporting and marketing. His conclusion was that increased government control in some areas had modified or even nullified the impact of enhanced self-management in others.

Bullock and Thomas (1997) examined decentralisation in 11 very diverse countries, including China, Poland, Uganda and the USA, along four dimensions: curriculum and assessment, human and physical resources, finance and access (pupil admissions). They found movements towards both more and less autonomy, and concluded that 'Taken as a whole, the impact of decentralisation – and centralisation – on the general principle of autonomy appears uncertain and problematic' (ibid.: 213). They, also noted that in some countries, such as England and New Zealand, the 'paradox' of simultaneous centralisation and decentralisation was evident, the centralisation relating particularly to the curriculum and, to some extent, funding regimes, with governments tending to take greater powers to define educational priorities and schools having scope to decide how best to implement them. Simkins (1997) distinguishes between *criteria power*, concerned with determining purposes and frameworks, and *operational power*, concerned with service delivery. Karlsen (2000) also refers to such a distinction in his analysis of educational governance in Norway and British Columbia, Canada: 'We are looking at a decentralisation dynamic in which initiating is a central task, but in which implementation and accountability are local duties' (ibid.: 531).

Despite this paradox of 'decentralised centralism', (Karlsen, 2000: 529), substantial autonomy has been accorded to schools in England in recent years. Indeed, the government has claimed that 'No other education service in the world devolves as much power and responsibility to schools as we do' (DfEE, 2001: 16). It is therefore worth briefly noting some key research findings from this experience. The process has led to a much larger role for headteachers (principals), particularly in relation to resources. The external pressure for enhanced performance and for the implementation of curricular changes has increased the scope and intensity of the work, and the head's role is now commonly exercised together with a group of senior staff including the deputy head (Levačić, 1998; Wallace and Hall, 1994). The autonomy of other teaching staff has arguably declined as a result of the advent of the National Curriculum and the impact of school-based budgeting on many teachers' employment position (Bullock and Thomas, 1997).

The evidence that devolution has had any impact on pupil learning is extremely thin, but this is due at least in part to the complexity of the processes involved and the inherent difficulty of investigating them. However, there is evidence that devolution has significantly enhanced the quality of schools' internal planning capacities and processes (Levačić, 1998). Enhancing school autonomy in some respects while extending central control in others, in the context of a limited 'market', has had another somewhat paradoxical effect. Schools have not on the whole tended to differentiate themselves in order to focus on a specific *niche*, but rather have sought to appeal to a broad grouping of parents and pupils. Nor have the structural arrangements tended to promote innovation at school level: instead schools have sought to emulate the dominant model of the high-status school (Woods et al., 1998). At the time of writing the government is seeking to introduce measures to deal with these issues (DfEE, 2001).

Key issues in any move towards devolution are the effectiveness of support systems, including development opportunities: 'Unless there is local capacity for management, there is no advantage to making decisions where action takes place. The Principle of Subsidiarity argues not just for moving decisions to the site of action, but also making local decision-makers competent' (McGinn and Welsh, 1999: 66–7).

An OECD study of 14 national school systems (OECD, 1995) sought to distinguish three modes of decision-making: full autonomy; made after consultation with another authority at an adjoining level; made within guidelines set by another authority, generally at the top level. In Table 4.1 we have adapted this (admittedly crude) classification to our ideal-type framework of models of governance. In a 'pure' CM model the autonomy of schools would be very substantial. We have not used the term 'full autonomy' here since this is virtually unimaginable: there are always constraints, not least from the law, even for a highly unorthodox independent school (Sharpe, 1994). A key purpose of the SE model is to maximise schools' autonomy within an overall system, so here we have suggested that 'devolved' is the most appropriate descriptor. The LE model places emphasis on the school as a member of a co-operating family of institutions, so here we use 'consultative' from the OECD study's typology. In the QC model, however, the role of the senior authority at central or state level is more pronounced, so the appropriate form of autonomy here is 'guided', again based on the OECD typology.

Accountability

Writing about school-based management (SBM) in the USA, Wohlstetter and Sebring (2000) comment: 'An underlying premise of SBM is that school-level participants trade increased autonomy for increased accountability' (ibid.: 174). Accountability is a contested concept, not least, as an Australian writer suggests, 'because it is often the engine of policy: what is held to account is what counts' (Cotter, 2000: 12). It is also complex. There is not space here for a full discussion (see, for example, Adams and Kirst, 1999; Feintuck, 1994; Kogan, 1986; Scott, 1989). I will seek to relate different forms of account-ability to the four models of governance.

An important distinction is that between *contractual* and *responsive* accountability (Halstead, 1994). Contractual acountability is concerned with the degree to which educators are fulfilling the expectations of particular audiences in terms of standards, outcomes and results. It is based on an explicit or implicit contract with those audiences. It tends to be measure-ment driven with the factors to be measured – whether educational, financial or other – selected by those audiences in line with their perceived preferences and requirements. Responsive accountability refers to decision-making by educators after a process of taking into account the interests and wishes of relevant 'stakeholders'. It is more concerned with process than outcomes, and with securing involvement and interaction to obtain decisions which meet a range of needs and preferences.

Such a distinction should not, of course, be drawn too sharply, but it indi-cates different emphases between conceptions of accountability. Thus in the CM model the provision of schooling is analogous to a commercial service and so the predominant form of accountability is contractual. In the SE model with its focus on the school as a participatory community the dimension of respon-siveness is uppermost. In LE the broader local community is the pivotal unit, so responsiveness to stakeholders is even more pronounced here. Finally in the QC model the contractual form will be the significant one, with the 'contract' being specified by governments or their agents rather than by parents or con-sumers as in CM. The method will tend to be drawn from the accounting model of accountability that has pre-specified categories and accounts in terms of discrete scales of measurement . . . The accounting dimension is entrenched at government level and is much loved by ministers who want a simple way of demonstrating good news to the electorate. This will often drive the bureaucracy to organise the tests and deliver the numbers.

(Cotter, 2000: 4, 12)

Two other aspects of accountability are relevant to the models. First, each of the models implies a different mode of accountability. In the case of CM the mode is consumerist (Halstead, 1994), with power in principle being placed in the hands of consumer-surrogates, in the form of parents or guardians, to decide whether to choose the school for their child or to keep them there. The position is more complex in the case of SE. Many formulations (for example, Halstead, 1994; Kogan, 1986) refer to professional accountability but in school empowerment models such as SBM professionals often have to share authority with school boards or councils which include parents and community members. These are often regarded as relatively weak bodies with unclear roles and the 'agenda' firmly set by the professionals particularly the principal and other senior staff (Levačić, 1995), but the SE model as such incorporates the possibility of a significant element of non-professional as well as professional participation. This may be especially relevant, for example, in 'colleges' for older students where employment interests may be represented on governing boards. Hence we characterise the mode of accountability in this model as 'dual'. Within LE we identify the accountability mode as 'community forum'. This indicates that the ultimate authority within this model will lie at a local level beyond the school, though there are many variations in respect of the size and socio-geographical nature of this unit and the extent to which it operates on collegial or directive principles. The possibility of 'network' or 'partnership' arrangements with their tendency to produce fragmentation and 'opaque accountability' (Rhodes, 1999: xiii), referred to earlier, arises here. The mode in QC will be hierarchical, in that accountability will be owed to the body with power to define and control quality, located generally at national or state level.

A final aspect of accountability to be considered in relation to the models concerns the purpose of performance measurement. Although, as indicated earlier, measuring performance will be more prominent in contractual than responsive versions of accountability, the rise of target-setting, performance management and the 'audit society' (Bottery, 2000; Power, 1997) has been a central feature of public service operations in many countries in recent years. However, the prime purpose of such measurement will vary depending on the model. Thus in CM the chief purpose will be to inform consumer choice. In SE performance measurement and analysis will be conducted in order to provide management information to facilitate organisational improvement. In the LE model a key purpose will be to provide comparative 'benchmarking' information across organisational units to promote local system enhancement. Under QC the main purpose will be to seek to monitor, control and develop the system as a whole.

School Leadership

The governance models imply distinct and somewhat contrasting roles for school leadership. In CM, school leaders are expected to provide the kind of education the consumers – and in particular their surrogates, the parents/guardians – want. This means that 'the identification and stimulation of parent demand for the kind of education the organization can produce most efficiently, becomes a primary task of the manager' (McGinn and Welsh, 1999: 47). This requires primarily an entrepreneurial style of leadership. In the SE model the school leader has to draw together the many different educational, managerial and financial threads in the work of the school, as well as to stimulate and if possible inspire the professionals to greater achievement. The evidence suggests that under devolved school management both the roles of chief executive and educational leader attain greater significance (Levačić, 1998). In addition, there is a testing external dimension: 'although headteachers have gained more autonomy, they also have to meet increasingly diverse demands from all sides and are often caught in conflict. Headteachers get headaches' (Hernes, 2000: 2). Thus both a directing and a co-ordinating style are required.

In the LE model, there is a key requirement for school leaders to become effective networkers, both to promote the school's interests within the local system and to collaborate productively in a partnership mode with their peers. Under QC the school leader's role is more akin to that of a production manager, organising the school and its staff to deliver products or outcomes of the requisite quality.

Clearly this analysis is oversimplified. In practice school leaders will interpret and enact their role in a variety of ways depending on their individual personalities, the cultures of their schools and other factors. The analysis is intended to suggest that the governance context is an important and often neglected influence on school leadership. Generalisations are frequently made about the features associated with effective school leadership without taking into account the specific and diverse frameworks of policy and governance within which it is exercised. For example, as Cotter (2000) points out: 'The current exhortations to principals to be transformational do not sit easily beside narrow forms of accountability' (ibid.: 7–8). He argues that such forms, in which principals are expected to accept given categories without reflection, are more consonant with transactional forms of leadership, as in our analogy above with the role of production manager.

However, the position in practice is more complex still. School leaders generally face not a single model of governance but several. So elements of the CM model are combined with others from SE and QC for example. As Leithwood (2001) suggests, in the face of this 'policy eclecticism', school leaders 'can be excused for feeling that they are being pulled in many different directions simultaneously. They *are* being pulled in many different directions simultaneously' (ibid.: 228). From this a series of tensions and dilemmas (Glatter, 1996) arises for school leaders, for example the dilemmas that, within their school 'The principal is required to be both a member of the cast and the star' (Wildy and Louden, 2000: 180) and within the wider system they are expected both to collaborate and to compete. School leaders have the task of successfully managing these tensions and ambiguities – by, for instance, skillful buffering of the staff from external pressures that conflict with the school's goals without insulating them from legitimate influences for improvement (Goldring, 1997; Leithwood, 2001). It is perhaps the most important and difficult task faced by school leaders in many contexts today.

■ Function of Intermediate Authority

The key functions and roles of the intermediate authority (where such a level exists) differ significantly between the four models of governance. In a pure CM model its functions are minimal, covering perhaps the provision of information to parents and support for pupils with additional educational needs. In the SE model the intermediate authority's role will be primarily supportive and advisory. Under LE much will depend on whether the geographical scope of its responsibility fits with the 'local system of schooling' concept underlying the model. In some contexts it does: in others 'cluster' arrangements have been developed (for example, the Education Action Zones in England [DfEE, 1999] based on areas which are smaller and more 'local' than those covered by the relevant intermediate authorities. (By their size intermediate authorities in some countries, for example the municipalities in Sweden and many school districts in the USA, come closer than their counterparts in other countries to a model of 'community governance'.) For simplicity we have disregarded this important distinction in Table 4.1 and suggested that in the LE model the intermediate authority's key function is strategic co-ordination. By contrast, in QC the authority becomes more of a production supervisor as an agent of the central controlling body. The reality of 'policy eclecticism' in many national contexts sets up major tensions and dilemmas for intermediate authorities just as it does for schools and their leaders.

Conclusion

Structures of governance vary widely between different national contexts. Also, as a result of the high level of 'reform' activity in many countries, these structures are often in considerable flux. Practitioners need to analyse their own contemporary settings closely and take this analysis into account in developing their approach to the management of external relations. It is hoped that this chapter will have helped in this challenging process.

References

Adams, J.E. and Kirst, M.W. (1999) 'New demands and concepts for educational accountability: striving for results in an area of excellence', in J, Murphy and K.S. Louis (eds), *Handbook Of Research on Educational Administration, Second Edition*, San Francisco: Jossey-Bass.

Arnott, M.A. (2000) 'Restructuring the governance of schools: the impact of "managerialism" on schools in Scotland and England', in M.A. Arnott and C.D. Raab (eds), *The Governance of Schooling: Comparative Studies of Developed Management*, London: Routledge/Falmer.

Bottery, M. (2000) *Education, Policy and Ethics*, London: Continuum.

Bullock, A. and Thomas, H. (1997) *Schools at the Centre? A Study of Decentralisation*, London: Routledge.

Cotter, R. (2000) 'Accountability in education and beyond', paper presented at the Annual Conference of the British Educational Management and Administration Society (BEMAS), Bristol, September.

Department for Education and Employment (DfEE) (1999) *Meet the Challenge: Education Action Zones*, London: Department for Education and Employment.

Department for Education and Employment (DfEE) (2001) *Schools: Building on Success*, Cm 5050, London: Department for Education and Employment.

Dimmock, C. and Walker, A. (2000, 'Developing comparative and international educational leadership and management: a cross-cultural model', *School Leadership and Management*, 20(2): 143–60.

Dowling, K., Dunleavey, P., King, D., Margetts, H. and Rydin, Y. (2000) 'Understanding urban governance: the contribution of rational choice', in G. Stoker (ed.), *The New Politics of British Local Governance*, London: Macmillan.

Feintuck, M. (1994) *Accountability and Choices in Schooling*, Buckingham: Open University Press.

Glatter, R. (1996) 'Managing dilemmas in education: the tightrope walk of strategic choice in autonomous institutions', in S.L Jacobson, E.S. Hickox and R.B. Stevenson (eds), *School Administration: Persistent Dilemmas in Preparation and Practice*, Westport, CT: Praeger.

Glatter, R. and Woods, P.A. (1995) 'Parental choice and school decision-making: operating in a market-like environment', in K.C. Wong and K.M. Chang (eds), *Educational Leadership and Change: An International Perspective*, Hong Kong: Hong Kong University Press.

Goldring, E.B. (1997) 'Educational leadership: schools, environments and boundary spanning', in M. Preedy R. Glatter and R. Levačić (eds), *Educational Management: Strategy, Quality and Resources*, Buckingham: Open University Press.

Green, A (1999) 'Education and globalisation in Europe and East Asia: convergent and divergent trends', *Journal of Educational Policy*, 14(1): 55–72.

Halstead, M. (1994) 'Accountability and values', in D. Scott (ed.), *Accountability and Control in Educational Setting*, London: Cassell.

Hernes, G. (2000) 'Editorial: headway for headteachers', *IIEP Newsletter*, 18(4), October–December, Paris: International Institute for Educational Planning.

Hirst, P. (2000) 'Democracy and governance', in J. Pierre (ed.), *Debating Governance*, Oxford: Oxford University Press.

Jacobs, K. (2000) 'Devolved management in New Zealand schools', in M.A. Arnott and C.D. Raab (eds), *The Governance of Schooling: Comparative Studies of Devolved Management*, London: Routledge/Falmer.

Jessop, B. (2000) 'Governance failure', in G. Stoker (ed.), *The New Politics of British Local Governance*, London: Macmillan.

Karlsen G.E. (2000) 'Decentralized centralism; framework for a better understanding of governance in the field of education', *Journal of Educational Policy*, 15(50): 525–38.

Kogan, M. (1986) *Education Accountability: An Analytical Overview*, London: Hutchinson.

Leithwood, K. (2001) 'School leadership in the context of accountability policies', *International Journal of Leadership in Education*, 4(3): 217–35.

Levačić, R. (1995) 'School governing bodies: management boards or supporters' clubs?', *Public Money and Management*, April–June: 35–40.

Levačić, R. (1995) 'Local management of schools in England: results after six years', *Journal of Education Policy*, 13(3): 331–50.

Levin, B. (1999) 'An epidemic of education policy: (what) can we learn from each other?', *Comparative Education*, 34(2): 131–41.

Levin, B. (2000) 'Conceptualizing the process of education reform from an international perspective', paper presented to the Annual Meeting of the American Educational Research Association, New Orleans, April.

Levin, B. (2001) *Reforming Education: From Origins to Outcomes*, London: Routledge/Falmer.

Maden, M. (2000) *Shifting Gear: Changing Patterns of Educational Governance in Europe*, Stoke-on-Trent: Trentham Books.

Martin, J., McKeown, P., Nixon, J. and Ranson, E. (2000) 'Community-active management and governance of schools in England and Wales', in M.A. Arnott and C.D. Raab (eds), *The Governance of Schooling: Comparative Studies of Devolved Management*, London: Routledge/Falmer.

McGinn, N. and Welsh, T. (1999) *Decentralisation in Education: Why, When, What and How?*, Paris: UNESCO International Institute for Educational Planning.

Organisation for Economic Co-operation and Development (OECD) (1995) *Decision-Making in 14 OECD Education Systems*, Paris: Centre for Educational Research and Innovation, Organisation for Economic Co-operation and Development.

Power, M. (1997) *The Audit Society: Rituals of Verification*, Oxford: Oxford University Press.

Raab, C.D. (2000) 'The devolved management of schools and its implications for governance', in M.A. Arnott and C.D. Raab (eds), *The Governance of Schooling: Comparative Studies of Devolved Management*, London: Routledge/Falmer.

Rhodes, R.A.W. (1997) *Understanding Governance*, Buckingham: Open University Press.

Rhodes, R.A.W. (1999) 'Foreword: governance and networks', in G. Stoker (ed.), *The New Management of British Local Governance*, London: Macmillan.

Scott, P. (1989) 'Accountability, responsiveness and responsibility', in R. Glatter (ed.), *Educational Institutions and their Environments: Managing the Boundaries*, Buckingham: Open University Press.

Sharpe, F. (1994) 'Devolution: towards a research framework', *Educational Management and Administration*, 22(2): 85–95.

Simkins, T. (1997) 'Autonomy and accountability', in B. Fidler, S. Russell and T. Simkins, (eds), *Choices for Self-Managing Schools*, London: Paul Chapman Publishing.

Stoker, G. (2000) 'Introduction', in G. Stoker (ed.), *The New Politics of British Local Governance*, London: Macmillan.

Thompson, G., Frances, J., Levačić, R. and Mitchell, J. (eds) (1991) *Markets, Hierarchies and Networks: the Co-ordination of Social Life*, London: Sage, in association with the Open University.

Wallace, M. and Hall, V. (1994) *Inside the SMT: Teamwork in Secondary School Management*, London: Paul Chapman Publishing.

Wildy, H. and Louden, W. (2000) 'School restructuring and the dilemma of principals' work', *Educational Management and Administration*, 28(2): 173–84.

Wohlsetter, P. and Sebring, P.B. (2000) 'School-based management in the United States', in M.A. Arnott and C.D. Raab (eds), *The Governance of Schooling: Comparative Studies of Devolved Management*, London: Routledge/Falmer.

Woods, P.A., Bagley, C. and Glatter, R. (1998) *School Choice and Competition: Markets in the Public Interest?*, London: Routledge.

5

Uses and Abuses of Quality:
The Need for a Civic Version

Mike Bottery

Introduction

'Quality' is one of the buzzwords of the last decade. It is a term which has infiltrated most official publications and management agendas, and the suggested need to achieve 'better quality' has been used to underpin many of the major policy moves in education over the last few years. Yet it is not a neutral term. There are different meanings to it besides 'officially' favoured conceptions, and an understanding of its uses by those in power says a great deal about the extent of policy inheritance from the Reagan and Thatcher era. It also says a great deal about the colonization of educational concepts and practice by the private sector. It is therefore a very important area and word to examine.

'Quality' is a word with both 'external' and 'internal' meanings. Its 'external' meaning is normally derived from other people, organizations or legislation, when individuals are persuaded by them to adopt an interpretation of the term not personally held. An 'internal' meaning of quality, however, is adopted when it stems from a personal value belief system, or when an individual's own value system coheres with external recommendations. With an external location, then, people create quality things because they are told to do so. With an internal location, however, people create quality things or perform quality acts because, basically, this is the way they approach the world.

This chapter will argue that while there may be a need for some form of external quality, the best kinds of quality initiatives are internally generated, and in the public sector should be a natural outgrowth of a civic culture value system.

Source: Bottery, M. (2000) *Education, Policy and Ethics*. London: Continuum. Edited version.

A second way of looking at these policy inheritances is through the distinctions that Feigenbaum *et al.* (1999) make between different types of privatization, for these distinctions suggest that a particular external version of quality has entered consciousness at a systemic level. The authors identify 'systemic privatization', which is intended to reshape an entire society by altering the practices and thence the conciousness and values of those within it. It is possible that systemic privatization may have led to the infiltration of private sector concepts into thinking about public policy-making. A key test of this is the extent to which public sector values have been marginalized, the public sector having first been infiltrated then dominated and finally absorbed by the private.

The concept of 'quality' fits this 'systemic privatization' agenda very well, for the concept of 'quality' is being widely used to pursue particular (privatized) agendas in education, and in other areas of the public sector as well. By using 'quality' in this way, an attempt is being made, once again, to 'capture the discourse' – to suggest that there is only one way of looking at this issue, and that therefore education must, logically, be carried out in accordance with such precepts. There is a pressing need, then, to be aware of the different meanings, the different origins and the different implications of the concept, not only to have a clearer understanding of the wider political context of educational changes, but also to be in a better position to choose the most appropriate meaning, or combination of meanings, for the work of an education system devoted to more than wealth production and nation-state legitimacy.

Quality, Politics and the Public Sector

Because changes in the meaning and uses of the concept of quality in the provision of state education are historically bound up with changes in attitude to the role and function of the welfare state, it is important to mention some of these changes. As welfare states in advanced western industrial democracies came under increasing pressure and criticism the problem was perceived by some as primarily an economic matter. These approaches have been underpinned by a combination of different arguments:

■ that, due to an ageing population, there are fewer tax contributors, and so there is less taxation coming in;
■ that the proportion of those requiring benefits is increasing (again, particularly the elderly);
■ that there continues to be an increased demand for such services;
■ that increased competition from overseas means that there is not the economic growth to sustain demand;
■ that the globalization of capital and labour mean that states no longer have the power or legislative reach to supply such services.

(See, for instance, McRae, 1994).

Some, however, see such issues as more a matter of ideological debate:

■ that the rapprochement between capital and labour, when capital drew in sufficient profits for it to be tactically worthwhile to buy off labour unrest with welfare benefits (called the welfare state), has, with the decline of such profits, come to a close;
■ that the welfare state has led citizens down a road to serfdom, in which a 'big brother' bureaucracy has made them dependent and subservient;
■ that the welfare state actually hindered the development of a fully socialist state;
■ that welfare states have existed by being underpinned by inequalities of sex or of race and class.

(See, for instance, Pierson, 1998)

There was then a strong consensus that welfare states were in major difficulties. There was also general agreement that, because the political running and legislative impetus came from the political right, the problem was largely one caused by an inefficient and unresponsive public sector dominated by self-serving professionals. This was translated by Thatcherite governments in Britain into an education system underpinned by league tables for consumer comparison, by formula funding to allocate finance to schools on the basis of their success or failure in this market and by an expanded parental choice to support such moves. While this was happening, public sector agendas concerned with questions of inequality were downplayed or even dropped. A concern to push through these reforms at the institutional level, as a desire to counter the power of 'Dionysian' self-serving professionals (Handy, 1978), led to the creation of a more dominant, strategic and directive breed of manager/head teacher/principal, one who was to assert the primacy of the corporate over the individual perspective. This became the educational version of the 'New Public Management' (Hood, 1991).

Finally, while in the Reagan/Thatcher heyday it might have seemed as if governments were intent on devolving not only implementation, but also, through marketization, dissolving policy and strategy, it has become clear that subsequent New Modernist governments have actually tightened their control of policy. This has increasingly been through a greater use of evaluative strategies, and by governmental use of 'fewer but more precise policy levers' (Neave, 1988, p. 11) for the specification of desired outputs, all of which have meant the increased importance of a directive and supervisory managerialism, underpinned by a particular definition of 'quality'.

Seven Versions of Quality

It is important to note the use of the term 'quality' has always been extremely varied. This chapter will argue for seven different conceptions of the term, which are:

a Traditional quality;
b Expert quality;
c Bureaucratic quality;
d 'Cold' management quality;
e 'Hot' management quality;
f Consumer quality;
g Civic quality.

It will be important to examine not only these versions of quality, but who recommends which versions.

Traditional quality

While this chapter is concerned with the uses of quality in public sector education, and with the infiltration of private sector uses, it is nevertheless important to recognize that the concept of quality has long had an existence and meaning, which lies beyond either of these two sectors. 'Quality' has always existed in a loose 'traditional' sense which conveys notions of high standards, high prices, high status and exclusivity, and this is probably how most members of the general public would describe 'quality' if so asked. Private sector schools certainly use this meaning, trading on notions of status, exclusivity and high standards. In the public sector, the elitist aspects of traditional quality have understandably never been really espoused for welfare state institutions, with an underlying principle of free to all who need their services. Rather the status has been attached more to the service provided, and in this sense professionals could claim that they have given the best to their clients, irrespective of cost. Indeed, cost was originally not seen as a professional problem – though of course, cost was a dominant theme of concern from the welfare state's inception. In the first, traditional sense, then, 'quality' was the kind of service that professionals aspired to provide.

Expert quality

Added to this concept, though, was another, which might be called the 'expert' sense of quality. Professionals would argue that, historically, expert quality in the public sector has been driven by a set of professional ethics which those within a particular profession should not only work to but also internalize. This set of ethics then justified the assertion that professionals should be able to lay down standards of acceptability, which are monitored by these same experts. Indeed, Pollitt (1990, p. 435) described professionalism as in part characterized by the 'self-control of quality'. Professional standards are therefore, at their best, located internally, and in theory at least, there seems much to commend such an approach.

This, however, is not the whole picture, for while it might be called the 'expert' approach, such expert opinion may not be very well supported evidentially. The practice and judgements of welfare state professionals – and teachers in particular – have not always been fully supported by research, measurement and evidence, but instead based upon personal opinion, inductive experience, professional culture and unevaluated past practice. In addition, even where such expert opinion is 'scientific', it is not necessarily incontestable. What evidence is found may depend upon what evidence is looked for, and where it is sought. Finally, an 'expert' approach to quality can too easily assume that there is only one voice worth hearing, yet parents, pupils and business may have equally valid claims. An important point, therefore, is that any notion of quality needs to take into account a variety of perspectives.

Bureaucratic quality

It would be wrong to describe the disillusion with welfare states as solely to do with professional practice. An equal degree of disillusionment has been vented at its traditional practice. Hogett (1991) described traditional welfare state practice as 'bureau-professionalism', and the bureaucratic aspect should not be understressed. Yet bureaucracy has merits which qualify it as both a 'quality' procedure, and as an important tool in the quest for equality. Bureaucratic quality is seen in the clarity of decision-making through the predictability generated; it also makes clear lines of communication and responsibility, and therefore has the potential to provide a more effective service. Finally, it can facilitate equity because decisions are made which are open to scrutiny and challenge.

It can, however, produce a 'ritualism' towards rules (Merton, 1952) which leads to a loss of personal initiative, and to treating people in a routinized and dehumanized manner. In an environment which is rapidly changing, the strengths of bureaucratic predictability may become major weaknesses. Bureaucratic quality, then, is a very strong example of quality with an external locus, having no value base other than a restricted organizational rationality.

While reactions to 'bureau-professionalism' have resulted in both more 'liberated' and aggressive management approaches being imported from the private sector, nevertheless the bureaucratic paradigm is still much in evidence. Indeed, some would argue (e.g. Ritzer, 1993) that with the uncertainties of political, cultural and economic globalization, it is gaining a renascent attraction for many, for its predictability gives a sense of security in an increasingly insecure and unpredictable world. In the UK, the imposition of a National Curriculum on schools could be seen as an example of this kind of response. Yet it is also clear that governments around the world have been, for both economic and ideological reasons, disaffected with the running of welfare states based upon 'bureau-professional' delivery. In response to such criticisms, new forms of quality, which might be encompassed under the umbrella terms 'cold' and 'hot' managerial quality, came to the fore in the early 1980s.

'Cold' managerial quality

Managerial quality is generally predicated upon the belief in the centrality of management in organizational functioning, and, as Pollitt (1992) argues, is governed by the overriding, conviction that

> management . . . [is] the guardian of the overall purposes of the organization, and therefore it is wrong that another group of staff should be able to work to a different set of priorities. (p. 131)

It is sometimes necessary to remind oneself that this is not a natural or given of organizational functioning, so unquestioned is this value, and its attendant practices, at the present time. This is particularly true for the USA, where the modern heroes are the leaders of industry and commerce, and from where there is a plethora of literature which proclaims the undisputed need for their advice and their leadership, and not just with respect to the running of large corporations. In such a climate, the translation of such beliefs into the public sector may be accomplished almost effortlessly. One therefore has to be careful, for just as bureau-professionalism is made up of a number of different concepts and practices, so is the concept of management. For the purposes of this chapter, it is divided into two different kinds. Cold management is the kind of organizational practice which aims at compliance, at the capture and utilization of the time, the motion and the body of the individual. It is not too bothered about employees' enthusiasm and is essentially externally located.

The attempt to locate this kind of managerial quality internally is to be seen in hot management. This kind of organizational approach argues that in the long run it is more efficient and effective to capture the mind, the motivation and the commitment of the individual, for from these will follow the time, the motion and the body. However, while it expends considerable effort in convincing employees to locate quality internally, it is necessarily driven by a managerialist value-base.

Figure 5.1 demonstrates that management approaches can be located along a spectrum, from the obviously 'cold' approaches of targets, outcomes and performance indicators, to the transparently 'hot' cultural and TQM (Total Quality Management) approaches.

```
┌─────────────────────────────────────────┐
│                                           │
│       FROM 'COLD' MANAGEMENT              │
│                                           │
│   • QUALITY ASSURANCE                     │
│   • TARGETS                               │
│   • OUTCOMES                              │
│   • PERFORMANCE INDICATORS                │
│   • MERIT PAY                             │
│   • PERFORMANCE MANAGEMENT                │
│   • THE MARKET                            │
│   • MANAGERIAL FREEDOM                    │
│   • SMALLER ORGANIZATIONAL UNITS          │
│   • CULTURAL MANAGEMENT                    │
│   • TOTAL QUALITY MANAGEMENT              │
│                                           │
│       TO 'HOT' MANAGEMENT                 │
│                                           │
└─────────────────────────────────────────┘
```

Figure 5.1 *A spectrum of managerial approaches*

There is good evidence to suggest that, at least in part, values follow practice (Bottery, 1998). If things have to be done a certain way, in the end the values underpinning those practices become those through which the work, and then wider practice and thought, are internalized. Yet as this process is not deterministic, and there remains room for reflection and disagreement, winning the minds as well as the bodies is an important task for management.

'Hot' managerial quality

This 'cold' managerial quality, then, largely because of its external locus, its failure to engage the commitment of staff, was increasingly supplanted in the UK in the late 1980s by 'hot' managerial quality, which sought to capture the motivation of the individual. It is largely composed of a combination of two different elements intent on generating a greater internal locus for quality: 'culture' approaches to management and Total Quality Management.

The 'cultural' approach to the management of organizations assumes that not only is there

> a pattern of basic assumptions – invented, discovered or developed by a given group as it learns to cope with its problems of external adaptation and internal integration ....
> (Schein, 1985)

but that it is possible for desirable cultures to be created by determined and charismatic managements. Peter and Waterman (1982) suggest that not only is it possible to define the attributes which characterize excellent American commercial companies, but that it is possible to change an employee's values to contribute to the kind of (managerially defined) organizational culture necessary for the cultivation of such attributes. Governments continue to see visionary leadership as the key to excellence in schools, the provision of visionary meaning by such a leader to his or her followers being the means to employees' self-regulation. This attempt at internal location, then, is one of the key characteristics of 'hot' quality, as the attempt is made to move the employee from compliance to commitment.

Total Quality Management (TQM) principles have moved from a hard industrial base into recommendations for the service industries. TQM has many variations, but major characteristics include:

- the responsibility and commitment of all within the organization continually to generate the highest quality;
- the search for, and implementation of, better methods of achieving this;
- the recognition that anyone with whom one has dealings, whether within or without the organization, is a customer, and should be treated with the same service quality;
- the development of things such as quality improvement teams, quality circles, methods of statistical process control and the cost of non-conformance.

TQM appears to provide individuals with more motivation, more involvement, more control over their work. Furthermore, the concept of the internal customer indicates that internal hierarchies should, where necessary, be turned upside down in order to empower front-line individuals, or at the very least to permit them to work out the best way of serving their 'customers'. Certainly, the notion of quality circles is predicated upon the absence of hierarchy and the empowerment of those closest to the location of the problem.

There is much to applaud in TQM, in terms of its insistence on the high standard of any service, and in the increased enjoyment felt by many individuals in their work. Furthermore, there is potential within TQM for greater individuation of approach within schools, through teachers' increased participation in satisfying their 'customers'. Of course, to any government which does not trust its teachers, TQM and other 'hot' management approaches could look very unappealing, and may well be why, in the UK at least, one has heard so little of it in official publications in the last few years.

TQM's mission is to get the employee to identify with the organization's mission of producing better quality. TQM, then, might be interpreted as a strategy to gain organizational commitment which had little to do with individual welfare. Tuckman (1995) develops this critical point when he argues that TQM is in reality a brilliant late-capitalist strategy conceived to:

- institute the relations, the thinking and the values of the market into every relationship (hence the use of the concept of 'internal customers');
- to control individuals through winning their minds, controlling their subjectivities and thence their hearts;
- to reinterpret the meaning of liberationist words like 'empowerment' and 'participation', to mean no more than the right of the individual to participate and be empowered in the delivery of managerially defined agendas;
- to prevent the vocalisation or even realisation of the possibility of other approaches;
- to induct the individual into working harder, in line with managerial policies, to create and regulate an internal order – internal not only to the organization but to the individual.

TQM, then, despite its focus on internal quality location, was conceived, and continues to act, as an aspect of management quality: it attempts to 'capture the discourse', to interpret quality in managerialist terms.

Consumer quality

If much of managerialist quality is underpinned by quality assurance principles of value for money and specified standards, the 'consumer' form of quality is underpinned by the perception that service culture has to be altered from top and bottom. On this account, consumers as well as government and management need a greater voice in the running of services.

Yet while TQM is dictated by a managerialist vision of the use of quality, consumer quality is dictated by consumers' preferences. It could of course be argued that both are concerned with the provision of good service, but their complementarity is highly debatable, for there is room for conflict between customers' desires and managerialist agendas. While top-down policies are concerned with making professionals more responsive and customer-oriented, they have in practice been as concerned with the three 'es' of economy, efficiency and effectiveness, and the first two of these have normally had priority. Customers/parents, on the other hand, usually want the best service for themselves or their loved ones, regardless of cost. Expert quality may then in many cases be more in keeping with consumer quality, for both tend to think of economy and efficiency as secondary to questions of high standards and effectiveness. Where managerial quality is tied to an agenda of cost-cutting, or at best of no-cost-increase, managerial quality may strongly conflict with consumer quality.

TQM implies that quality comes, not from conformance to external standards, but from conformance to *requirements*, the requirements of the customer. Those who are at the point of delivery – the teachers – are those who will understand these needs best, and therefore should have considerably more latitude, be given greater empowerment, in 'product delivery' and quality determination. Such empowerment does not cohere with current 'cold' managerial objectives of control and cost-cutting

If there are problems with consumer quality from a managerial point of view, there are other problems which also must be noted. In managerial and political eyes, the need for consumer quality has been driven by a lack of professional responsiveness to educational 'consumers'. Yet it does not follow that the function of the professional is simply to respond to, and to fulfil, a consumer's preferences. For while it is problematical just who in education is the consumer (student? parent? local community? business? government?), it can also very plausibly be argued that one of the purposes of education is precisely *not* to satisfy the consumer's preferences but to encourage and guide a change in them. There is also a real danger that government and policy-makers will define themselves as the consumers, or spokespeople for consumers. In doing this, they begin to claim that they are both consumer *and* expert. Indeed they may actually wrap into one definition three very different forms of quality and claim hegemony over all three – consumers, experts and management. In so doing, they obliterate important distinctions between the terms, eliminate some of the values behind these versions and in effect 'capture' the entire discourse.

Moreover, governmental and managerial espousal of consumer quality over the last decade has been predicated upon the notion of a consumerism which is private sector and free market in origin and orientation. On this scenario, educational 'consumers'' principal power is that of exit, and governments in the UK in particular have attempted to facilitate the use of this power by setting up internal markets and enhancing parental choice by facilitating movement from one 'product' supplier to another. Pupils and their parents are then encouraged to be active in a market sense, but there are problems here. It is not always possible to move between schools: mobility tends to favour those who have the finance and time to do so, and hence has produced considerable inequities of access. Further, while competition in the educational sector has allowed 'producers' to market and differentiate their products to some extent, they have in many cases been hamstrung by tightening government guidelines on content and practice, which has depressed the ability of suppliers to respond to 'consumers'. Finally, these 'consumers', precisely because a free-market model is being employed, have not been given a major voice in the determination of a public service product or its quality, any more than they are in the design of the goods they buy in their local supermarket. This has not introduced a more active and participative role for such citizens/consumers: they remain consumers of 'wares' designed, accredited, and quality controlled by government agencies. A simple test of this is seen in government quality inspections of schools, the 'Ofsted' inspection: if the parents of a school strongly supported the school and its practices, yet Ofsted gave it a negative report, there is no doubt as to which advice the school would have to follow.

Citizenship, communal good and participation are public sector concepts which are essential for the creation and sustenance of a healthy political community. So while efficiency, effectiveness and economy are certainly values which need to be shared with the private sector, there are other values, such as justice, care, equity and democracy, which need to be added to the kind of list which a healthy public sector should pursue, and which should be central to the mission of the education system. The conflation of the missions of the private and public sectors at present, then, prioritizes the values of the private sector, and downgrades those public and democratic values without which society, schools and the individual citizen may be profoundly damaged.

Civic quality

This then leads to the suggestion that there is a seventh and final definition of quality, unique to the public sector, which needs to be core to the citizen's internal value system: that of civic quality. As Pfeffer and Coote (1991, p. 23) suggest:

> the key to a just and flourishing society is that everyone should have an equal chance in life. From this perspective, welfare services become a common project, shared by all, devoted to the well-being of all; their purpose is to ensure that as far as possible, everyone has an equal chance to participate in society, to enjoy its fruits, and to realise their own potential.

A vibrant citizenry is one which feels empowered by an internal value system, rather than one that is grateful for handouts. Quality based upon privileges granted by professionals and politicians is then no basis for a just and flourishing society. Secondly, research strongly suggests that in the UK at least the customers who are most likely and able to make demands upon a public service are those who probably need it the least – the articulate middle class (Le Grand and Robinson, 1992). Precisely those who are in greatest need, on a definition of civic quality, are likely to be those least served by the criterion of consumer quality. An undue emphasis on 'consumer quality' inevitably leads to inequality. Finally, where in cold managerial quality, economy and efficiency are the key criteria, it is again precisely the under-privileged, the marginalized and the inarticulate who are the ones who will find it hardest to secure their share of the decreasing communal cake. Where in hot managerial quality, consumer responsiveness conflicts with manage-rial and cold quality agendas, it will be redefined to become part of a cold management definition. Without the additional criterion of equity central to a concept of quality, current forms of the term – and those who practise these forms – create an increasingly divided society.

In the era of Thatcher and Reagan, when managerial and consumer forms of quality began their dominance of current agendas, disparities between rich and poor increased dramatically (Pierson, 1998), and as Wilkinson (1996) has shown, this has implications for both rich and poor in a society, as increased inequalities in a society lead to depressed life expectancies for both rich and poor.

Civic qality does not dispense with the other forms of quality. but takes the best from other systems to build a set of values which leads to an empow-ered citizenry. If traditional quality implies high standards and exclusivity, civic quality implies high standards, but as a standard for all. If expert quality is underpinned by the authority of the expert, civic quality embraces the need for research-based evidence, but looks for this beyond the providers of the service. If cold managerial quality implies economy, efficiency and effec-tiveness, civic quality similarly requires evidence of effectiveness (for a lack of effectiveness means a waste of precious resources), and also accepts the need for regard to economy and efficiency, but does not see these as necessar-ily the primary values by which a service or product is evaluated, for other values such as equity and justice have to be incorporated as well. Finally, if both hot managerial quality and consumer quality imply consumer respon-siveness, civic quality accepts the need for this, but adds three caveats. First, public service provision must be informed by the recognition that those who are the most demanding of clients are not necessarily those most in need. Second, the right and need in a democracy for more participation by its citi-zenry means that decisions between different demands need to lie less at the point of delivery and more in the policy-making process. Third, civic quality sees the self-interested consumerism of the market as needing to be supple-mented and on occasions transcended by a vision of the interest of the community. Civic quality, then, reasserts the importance of public sector values. From such a resurgence is created within each individual a richer, civic orientation from which this quality may be generated.

■ Conclusions – the Triumph of Systemic Privatization?

This chapter has suggested that there has been a glossing over of the differences between the public and private sectors, and through the pursuit of almost exclusively private sector agendas, managerialist and consumer uses of quality have produced a reduced professional autonomy, increased political and managerial control over the workings of the education system and the strengthening of an 'evaluative' state. Crucially, they lead to the loss of personal visions concerning what a public good might mean, and of how education might contribute to the development of an internal locus for a concept of quality, based upon the notion of a civic culture.

Judging from the way in which debate about the importance of public sector values has been downgraded in education, or has simply ceased to make it onto policy agendas in recent times, it would seem that the approach of New Labour in the UK is good evidence for the triumph of those Thatcherite policies orientated to a more marketized society, in which private sector concerns have so infiltrated current educational policies that public sector issues are seen as no more than a subset of the private. Systemic privatization has blurred the policy vision.

There is therefore great need for a continued critique by those in education and the public sector in general, which highlights the effects of the loss or prevention of an internal locus of public sector values. Areas to concentrate upon in the development of such value orientation would be

- damage to notions of equality, as market mechanisms widen income difference, and exacerbate inequalities generally;
- the effects upon notions of community, as the model of the self-interested individual weakens communal ties and responsibilities;
- the implications of the blurring of the public and private upon conceptions of democracy, as private sector thinking transforms the citizen with the power of voice into a consumer with the power of exit.

This debate will be enhanced by a continued distinction between concepts of quality, an awareness of 'discourse capture', a sustained critique of the effects of private sector concepts in the public sector and by the need to promote an internal concept of civic quality.

References

Bottery, M. (1998) *Professionals and Policy*. London: Cassell.

DfEE (1999) *Teachers: Meeting the Challenge of Change*. London: Department for Education and Employment.

Feigenbaum, H., Henig, J. and Hamnett, C. (1999) *Shrinking the State*. Cambridge: Cambridge University Press.

Handy, C. (1978) *Gods of Management*. London: Pan.

Hoggett, P. (1991) A new managerialism in the public sector?, *Policy and Politics*, 19(4), 243–56.

Hood, C. (1991) A public management for all seasons?, *Public Administration*, 69(Spring), 3–19.

Le Grand, J. and Robinson, R. (1992) *The Economics of Social Problems* (3rd edn). Basingstoke: Macmillan.

McRae, H. (1994) *The World in 2020*. London: HarperCollins.

Merton, R. (1952) Bureaucratic structure and personality, in R. Merton, A. Grey, B. Hockey and H. Selvin (eds) *Reader in Bureaucracy*. Glencoe, IL: The Free Press.

Neave, G. (1988) On the cultivation of quality, efficiency and enterprise: an overview of recent trends in higher education in Western Europe, 1986–88, *European Journal of Education*. 23(1), 7–23.

Peters, T. and Waterman, R. (1982) *In Search of Excellence*. London: Harper and Row.

Pfeffer, N. and Coote, A. (1991) *Is Quality Good for You?* London: Institute for Public Policy Research.

Pierson, C. (1998) *Beyond the Welfare State*. Cambridge: Polity Press.

Pollitt, C. (1990) Doing business in the temple? Managers and quality assurance in the public services, *Public Administration*, 68(Winter), 435–52.

Pollitt, C. (1992) *Managerialism and the Public Services* (2nd edn). Oxford: Basil Blackwell.

Ritzer, G. (1993) *The McDonaldization of Society*. London: Sage.

Schein, E. (1985) *Organizational Culture and Leadership*. San Francisco: Jossey-Bass.

Tuckmann, A. (1995) Ideology, quality and TQM, in A. Wilkinson and H. Wilmott (eds) *Making Quality Critical*. London: Routledge pp. 54–82.

Wilkinson, R. (1996) *Unhealthy Societies: The Afflictions of Inequality*. London: Routledge.

Part 2

Societal and Organisational Cultures

6

Developing Comparative and International Educational Leadership and Management: A Cross-cultural Model

Clive Dimmock and Allan Walker

Introduction

Educators and politicians in Taiwan, Hong Kong, Japan and Korea expound the necessity for their East Asian school systems to become more like those in the West. They complain that there is too much rote learning, uniformity and standardisation and too little emphasis on creativity, diversity and problem-solving. Meanwhile, their counterparts in the USA and Britain look in the reverse direction to these same East Asian countries and wonder what they can learn from the superior academic results of East Asian students on International Achievement Tests in mathematics and science (Atkin & Black 1997).

This relatively new phenomenon, a reciprocal interest of 'East' and 'West' in each other's school systems, characterised much of the 1990s. Other factors, besides those mentioned, fuelled the tendency to look beyond national boundaries for answers to educational problems.

In this chapter, we affirm that internationalism as an educational phenomenon is desirable, especially in the new millennium of global trade, multi-cultural societies, the Internet and air travel. However, such comparisons can be fatuous and misleading without thorough understanding of the contexts, histories and cultures within which they have developed. This chapter begins with the justification for developing an international and comparative branch of the field. It then goes on to explain the appropriateness of culture as a core concept in developing comparative educational management. A model is then proposed as a useful conceptual framework for drawing valid international comparisons in school leadership and management. Finally, we allude to some challenges and limitations of the approach.

Source: School Leadership & Management, Vol. 20, no. 2, 2000, pp. 143–60. Edited version.

Justification for Comparative and International Educational Leadership and Management

Growing awareness of and interest in the phenomenon of globalisation of educational policy and practice is creating the need for the development of a comparative and international branch of educational leadership and management (Dimmock & Walker 1998a, 1998b). Interest in, if not willingness to adopt, imported policies and practices without due consideration of cultural and contextual appropriateness is justification for developing a more robust conceptual, methodological and analytical approach to comparative and international educational management. Indeed, educational management shows every tendency to continue its narrow ethnocentric focus, despite the internationalising of perspectives taken by policy-makers and others to which we have already alluded.

Globalisation of policy and practice in education is in part a response to common problems faced by many of the world's societies and education systems. Economic growth and development are increasingly seen within the context of a global market place. Economic competitiveness is seen to be dependent on education systems supplying sufficient flexible, skilled 'knowledge workers'. This phenomenon, however, emphasises the need to understand the similarities and differences between societies and their education systems. No two societies are exactly alike demographically, economically, socially or politically.

Anglo-American scholars continue to exert a disproportionate influence on theory, policy, and practice. Thus, a relatively small number of scholars and policy-makers representing less than 8% of the world's population purport to speak for the rest. Educational management has a vulnerable knowledge base. Theory is generally tentative and needs to be heavily qualified and much that is written in the field is prescriptive, being reliant on personal judgement and subjective opinion. Empirical studies are rarely cumulative, making it difficult to build systematic bodies of knowledge. Yet despite these serious limitations, rarely do scholars explicitly bound their findings within geo-cultural limits. Claims to knowledge are made on the basis of limited samples as though they have universal application. A convincing case can be mounted for developing middle range theory applying to and differentiating between different geo-cultural areas or regions. There is a need to develop contextually bounded school leadership and management theories.

A further concern leading to the need for a distinctive branch of comparative educational management is the need for more precise and discriminating use of language. Many writers, for example, glibly use terms such as 'Western', 'Eastern' or 'Asian' in drawing comparisons, when there is likely to be as much variation within each of them as between them.

Why Cultural and Cross-cultural Analysis as the Basis of Comparison?

We turn to the notion of culture, and societal culture in particular. An increasing recognition of the importance of societal culture and its role in understanding life in schools is very recent. 'Culture' is defined as the enduring sets of beliefs, values and ideologies underpinning structures, processes and practices which distinguishes one group of people from another. The group of people may be at school level (organisational culture) or at national level (societal culture). Both Cheng (1995) and Hallinger and Leithwood (1996) have argued for greater cognisance to be taken of societal culture in studies of educational leadership and educational administration.

The suitability of culture

Culture at the organisational level is now a well-recognised and increasingly studied concept in school leadership and management (Bolman & Deal 1992; Duke 1996). Culture at the societal level, however, has not received similar attention. Since culture is reflected in all aspects of school life, and people, organisations and societies share differences and similarities in terms of their cultures, it appears a particularly useful concept with universal application.

Since culture exists at multiple levels (school and sub-school, local, regional and societal) it provides researchers with rich opportunities for exploring their interrelationships, such as between schools and their micro- and macro-environments. It also helps identify characteristics across organisations that have surface similarity but are quite different in *modus operandi*.

Most cross-national studies of educational leadership have ignored the analytical properties of culture. Such neglect has been challenged by researchers such as Cheng (1995), who asserts that, 'the cultural element is not only necessary, but essential in the study of educational administration' (p.99). Specifically, Cheng bemoans the fact that much research in educational administration ignores culture and makes no reference to larger macro- societal, or national cultural configurations.

Limitations of existing comparative approaches

A second argument for a cross-cultural approach to comparative educational leadership and management is that existing comparative education frameworks tend to focus on single levels and to assume structural-functionalist approaches. Single-level frameworks ignore the relationships and interplay between different levels of culture, from school to societal, thereby failing to account sufficiently for context. For example, within-school studies tend to neglect the external school context.

In unravelling the dynamic, informal processes of schools and the leadership practices embedded within them, theoretical tools which stretch beyond structural-functionalist perspectives should be considered. Although structural-functionalist models are useful for fracturing education systems into their constituent elements (structures), their explanatory potential is limited as to how processes, or why various elements, interact. As a result, their analytic power is diminished through adopting static rather than dynamic views of schools.

Cultural borrowing of educational policies and practices

Our third justification for adopting a cross-cultural approach to comparative educational management relates to the globalisation of policy and practice (Hallinger & Leithwood 1996; Dimmock 1998). Policy-makers and practitioners are increasingly adopting policy blueprints, management structures, leadership practices and professional development programmes fashioned in different cultural settings while giving little consideration to their cultural fit.

The dominance of Anglo-American theory, policy and practice denies or understates the influence that culture, and societal culture in particular, may have on the successful implementation of policy. A comparative approach to educational leadership and management can expose the value of theory and practice from different cultural perspectives which may then, in turn, inform and influence existing dominant Western paradigms.

■ A Model for Cross-cultural Comparison in Educational Leadership and Management

An overview of our cross-cultural comparative model is provided in Figure 6.1. The model comprises two interrelated parts:

- a description of the four elements constituting schooling and school-based management (see Figure 6.2 for a breakdown), and
- a set of six cultural dimensions at each of the societal and organisational levels which provide common scales for comparison (see Table 6.1).

Figure 6.1 illustrates the four elements of schools and the two sets of cultural dimensions – societal and organisational. Comparative analysis is aimed at the relationship between the two levels of culture and the four elements constituting the school. In Figure 6.1, organisational culture is conceptualised as internal to the school but bounding the four elements. National or societal culture, however, is depicted as circumscribing the school, but at the same time, spanning the school boundary to interact with organisational culture and to affect the four elements of the school.

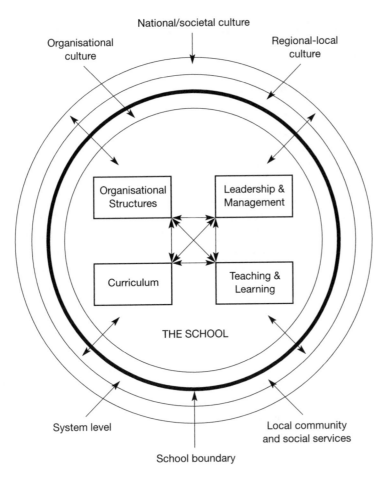

Figure 6.1 *A cross-cultural school-focused model for comparative educational leadership and management*

The school is taken as the unit of analysis for comparison in our framework and is assumed to comprise four elements: organisational structures; leadership and managerial processes; the curriculum; and teaching and learning (Figure 6.1). These four elements provide a convenient way of encapsulating the main structures and processes which constitute schooling and school-based management. Two of the four comprise the managerial and organisational aspects of school life, while the remaining two elements form the core technology of the school concerned with curriculum, teaching and learning.

The Four Elements of Schooling and School-based Management

Organisational structures

'Organisational structures' refer to the more or less enduring configurations by which human, physical and financial resources are established and deployed in schools. Structures represent the fabric or framework of the organisation and are thus closely associated with resources and their embodiment in organisational forms. They also provide policy contexts within which schools have greater or lesser discretion. Thus, schools in strongly centralised systems experience more explicit and rigid policy 'structures' imposed from system levels, whereas schools in more decentralised systems may have more school-based decision-making structures, but fewer policy structures imposed from outside the school. A comparison between the structures of schools is based on the eight aspects outlined below.

1 schools have a physical fabric, consisting of buildings of various sizes and layouts. For convenience, technology might also be included in the school's physical resources.
2 schools possess financial resources which structure possibilities and set constraints as to what they can and cannot do. The extent to which schools can raise revenue themselves and control the distribution of financial resources provides a rich point of comparison.
3 schools in different systems vary according to the extent of curriculum prescription, and over which parts of the curriculum they may have some control.
4 the organisation of the school year, term, week, and day impose nested layers of time structures on most schools. The timetable is a means of structuring the delivery of the curriculum and indicates the relative importance attached to each subject by virtue of the time afforded it.
5 human resources and their configuration constitute a further structure. Students may be selected for entry to schools on the basis of their ability, gender or parents' wealth and are grouped into classes for learning. Classes are structured on the basis of age, ability, gender or a combination thereof.
6 teachers likewise are subject to organisational structures, especially in their teaching.
7 schools vary according to whether and how their structures reflect guidance and counselling functions, and the extent to which these are separated from, or integrated with, the academic structures.
8 schools are characterised by decision-making structures which normally include senior management teams, a host of other school committees or task groups, and a school council or governing body comprising professional and lay members which is responsible for overseeing school policy.

Leadership, management and decision processes

At the core of school administration lie a number of human resource management processes (Figure 6.2). As with structures, the manifestation and importance of these processes in schools reflect cultural characteristics and the relationship with other levels of the system, particularly the degree of centralisation–decentralisation. However, the processes vary even in schools in the same system. This is clearly evidenced by the nature of principalship, and the position, role and power of the principal, which differ between schools and between systems. In some countries, the principal is all-powerful, and is seen as a chief executive of an autonomous unit, while in others, the principal is no more than a line manager or agent acting on behalf of the system. A second and related point of comparison concerns the principal's leadership, style and orientation, reflected, for example, in the degree of authoritarianism–democracy displayed by the principal and the relative emphasis placed on instruction and/or administration. A third group of processes concerns the extent to which there is collaboration and participation of school personnel in the management of the school and the operation of the curriculum. A fourth set of management processes relates to motivation and the extent to which staffs are motivated and how such motivation is achieved.

A fifth group of processes concerns planning; both planning procedures and resultant plans appear to vary considerably between schools. A sixth set is concerned with decision making, the criteria and the methods by which decisions are made. A seventh set of processes relates to interpersonal communication and the way schools vary in their use of written and oral modes of communication and in the extent to which they rely on computer technology for communication inside and outside the school. An eighth group of management processes concerns conflict resolution, the ways in which disputes between school members are handled and resolved. The expectation that schools conduct evaluation, performance management and appraisal activities has added a ninth set of processes, where comparisons are instructive in terms of the extent to which each of these activities exists and the characteristic forms they take. Finally, a tenth group of processes relates to staff development where comparisons between schools in this regard would illustrate the importance attached to staff development and its characteristics.

Curriculum

At the heart of schools is the core technology of curriculum, teaching and learning. The curriculum is an organisational structure, since it represents the form in which knowledge, skills and attitudes are configured for delivery to the students. However, as a structure concerned with core technology, it deserves separate recognition as an organisational structure in its own right. The curricula of schools can be compared according to the characteristics outlined below (see Figure 6.2).

◄────► influence/interaction

Organisational Structures

Degree of
centralisation–decentralisation
influences:

- Physical and technological
  resources
- Financial resources
- Curriculum frameworks
- Time
- Students
- Staff
- Guidance and counselling
- Decision-making structures

Leadership, Management and Decision Process

Degree of
centralisation–decentralisation
influences:

- Position, role and power of
  the principal
- Leadership style and orientation
- Collaboration and participation
- Motivation
- Planning
- Decision-making processes
- Interpersonal communication
- Conflict resolution
- Staff appraisal

Curriculum

- Goals and purpose
- Breadth
- Depth
- Integration
- Differentiation
- Relevance

Teaching & Learning

- Nature of knowledge
- Teacher/student relations
- Teacher/home relations
- Generalist vs. subject specialist
- Learning outcomes
- Guidance and counselling

Figure 6.2 *The four elements of schooling and school-based management*

The first characteristic concerns the goals and purposes of school curricula, which may vary in line with differences in how curriculum developers conceive the nature of knowledge and with how the purpose of the curriculum is defined. The curriculum may be seen, for example, as having primarily instrumental functions related to future employment, or it may be seen as having more intrinsic cognitive priorities. The relative emphasis placed on knowledge, skill and attitude goals and on cognitive, affective, expressive, aesthetic and psychomotor goals, may differ, as might the balance between academic and pastoral development. A second characteristic on which comparisons can be made is curriculum breadth, or the range or spread of subjects and disciplines offered to students. A third characteristic relates to curriculum depth, or the levels, standards or grades at which the curriculum is offered. A fourth concept for curricular comparison is integration, which may vary vertically from one grade level to another, and horizontally between different subject areas at the same grade level. A fifth criterion is curriculum differentiation, which is the degree to which the curriculum caters for students of different abilities. The sixth aspect is relevance. Although elusive, this concept can apply to present and future education, employment, adult citizenship, social stability and social change.

Teaching and learning

Teaching and learning activities, as part of the core technology of schools, are processes which warrant separate identification from managerial processes. Differences in the ways in which schools conduct teaching and learning activities can be compared according to the characteristics outlined below (see Figure 6.2).

An important characteristic concerns the ways in which teachers and students bring definition to teaching and learning. Asian and Western societies, for example, tend to adopt different understandings of what it is to teach and learn. This stems from a fundamentally different conception of the nature of knowledge and important differences in the relationship between the teacher and the student. A third concept for comparison is the teacher–parent relationship. In some cultures, parental involvement in their children's education is encouraged and seen as essential; in others, parents view teaching and learning as exclusively school activities and thus the responsibility of teachers.

A fourth criterion for comparison relates to teaching methods and approaches. While an array of different teaching methods and approaches exist, there are stark contrasts to be made between schools where teaching is predominantly teacher-centred, expository, and didactic and those where it is student-centred. A further characteristic is the role expectation placed on the teacher. In some schools the teacher is expected to be a subject specialist, while in others the teacher is more of a generalist, expected to teach a broader range of subjects. A fifth criterion relates to the importance placed on, and the nature of, specific learning outcomes as goals to guide, and benchmarks for assessing, student learning. Finally, comparisons may be made according to the emphasis placed in teaching on the guidance and counselling of students.

Recognition of common characteristics inherent in all cultures is necessary to facilitate cross-cultural comparison. This approach obviates the need to choose a particular culture as a baseline for comparison. Hence the first component of our model is the definition of a set of cultural dimensions commonly present in all cultures but to different degrees.

Six Dimensions of Societal Culture

Culture is a difficult phenomenon to measure, gauge or even describe. The identification of cultural dimensions, which we define as core axes around which significant sets of values, beliefs and practices cluster, not only facilitates their description and measurement, but promotes comparison between cultures. Dimensions provide common benchmarks against which cultural characteristics at the societal level can be described, gauged and compared (Dimmock & Walker 1998b). Despite their usefulness, however, we agree with Hofstede's (1994) cautionary remarks that: 'They are also constructs that should not be reified. They do not "exist"; they are tools for analysis which may or may not clarify a situation' (p.40).

Our research led to our fashioning the following six-dimensional model (Table 6.1).

Table 6.1 *A cross-cultural school-focused model for comparative educational leadership and management*

National/societal cultures	Organisational culture
Power concentrated/power dispersed	Process–outcome oriented
Group oriented/self-oriented	Person–task oriented
Aggression/consideration	Professional–parochial
Fatalistic/proactive	Open–closed
Generative/replicative	Control and linkage
Limited relationship /holistic relationship	formal–informal
	tight–loose
	direct–indirect
	Pragmatic–normative

Power-concentrated/power-dispersed

The first dimension is modelled on Hofstede's (1991) power–distance construct. We relabelled the dimension as power-concentrated/power-dispersed because this more accurately captures the essence of power relationships in various cultures. Power is either distributed more equally among the various levels of a culture or is concentrated among relatively few. In societies where power is widely distributed, inequity is treated as undesirable and every effort is made to reduce it where possible. In societies where power is commonly concentrated in the hands of the few, inequities are often accepted and legitimised.

Group-oriented/self-oriented

Schemata that describe whether people within a given culture tend to focus on *self* or on their place within a *group* are labelled 'group/self-orientated'. In *self-oriented* cultures, relationships are fairly loose and relational ties tend to be based on self-interest with people regarding themselves as individuals first, and members of a group, second. In *group-oriented* cultures, ties between people are tight, relationships are firmly structured and individual needs are subservient to collective needs. Status is traditionally defined by factors such as age, sex, kinship, educational standing, or formal organisational position, whereas in *self-orientated* cultures, people are judged and status ascribed according to individual performance.

Consideration/aggression

In what we have called *aggression* cultures, achievement is stressed, competition dominates and conflicts are resolved through the exercise of power and assertiveness. In such cultures, school norms are set by the best students, the system rewards academic achievement and failure at school is seen as serious. By contrast, in *consideration* societies, emphasis is on relationship, solidarity and resolution of conflicts by compromise and negotiation. At school, norms tend to be set by the average students, system rewards reflect students' social adaptation and failure at school is taken as unfortunate.

Proactivism/fatalism

This dimension was labelled to reflect the proactive or 'we can change things around here' attitude in some cultures, and the willingness to accept things as they are – a fatalistic perspective, in others. The dimension addresses how different societies and cultures react to and manage uncertainty and change in social situations. In proactive societies, people tend to believe that they have at least some control over situations and over change. They are tolerant of different opinions and are not excessively threatened by unpredictability. In fatalistic cultures, on the other hand, people believe 'what is meant to be, will be'. Uncertainty is often viewed as psychologically uncomfortable and disruptive, and people seek to reduce uncertainty and limit risks by hanging on to tradition.

Generative/replicative

This dimension was so labelled to reflect the fact that some cultures appear more predisposed towards innovation, or the generation of new ideas and methods (generative), whereas other cultures appear more inclined to replicate or to adopt ideas and approaches from elsewhere (replicative). In *generative* cultures people tend to value the generation of knowledge, new ideas and ways of working and they seek to create solutions to problems, to develop policies and ways of operating which are original. In *replicative* cultures, people are more likely to adopt innovations, ideas and inventions developed elsewhere. Whereas these sometimes undergo partial adaptation, they are often replicated *in toto*, with little consideration of alignment to the indigenous cultural context.

Limited relationship/holistic relationship

In *limited relationship* cultures, interactions and relationships tend to be determined by rules that are applied equally to everyone. For example, in deciding a promotion, objective criteria are applied regardless of who are the possible candidates. In *holistic* cultures on the other hand, greater attention is given to relationship obligations (for example, kinship, patronage and friendship) than to impartially applied rules (Dimmock 2000). Dealings in formal and structured situations in *holistic* cultures are driven more by complex, personal considerations.

■ Six Dimensions of Organisational Culture

Qualitative differences between organisational and societal culture stem from the fact that national cultures differ mostly at the level of basic values, while organisational cultures differ mostly at the level of more superficial practices, as reflected in the recognition of particular symbols, heroes, and rituals (Hofstede 1991). This allows organisational cultures to be managed and changed, whereas national cultures are more enduring and change only gradually over long time periods, if at all.

Research studies on the organisational cultures of companies found large differences in their practices (symbols, heroes, rituals), but only minor differences in their values (Hofstede 1995). Most of the variation in practices could be accounted for by six dimensions which provide a useful baseline for organisational culture in our framework. While Hofstede presents the dimensions as either/or choices along six axes, it is possible that some of them might be multi-dimensional rather than uni-dimensional.

Process and/or outcomes-oriented

Some cultures are predisposed towards technical and bureaucratic routines, while others emphasise outcomes. Evidence suggests that in outcomes-oriented cultures people perceive greater homogeneity in practices, whereas people in process-oriented cultures perceive greater differences in their practices. In education, some schools are process orientated, emphasising the processes and the skills of decision-making, teaching and learning, while others are results oriented, stressing learning achievements such as exam results.

Task and/or person-oriented

In task-oriented organisational cultures, emphasis is placed on job performance and maximising productivity, while human considerations, such as staff welfare, take second place and may even be neglected. Conversely, person-oriented cultures accentuate the care, consideration and welfare of employees. It is conceivable that some schools might score high (or low) on both task and person orientations.

Professional and/or parochial

In professional cultures, qualified personnel identify primarily with their profession, whose standards are usually defined at national or international level. In parochial cultures, members identify most readily with the organisation for which they work.

Open and/or closed

This dimension refers to the ease with which resources, such as, people, money, and ideas are exchanged between the organisation and its environment. The greater the transfer and exchange of resources between the environment and the organisation, the more open the culture.

Control and linkage

An important part of organisational culture concerns the way in which authority and control are exerted and communicated between members. In this respect, Hofstede's dimension identifies only one aspect, namely, tightly–loosely controlled cultures. We have added two more aspects, namely, formal–informal and direct–indirect which, taken together, provide a more detailed account of this dimension in schools.

1   *Formal–informal.* Organisations vary in the extent to which their practices are guided by rules, regulations and 'correct procedures' on the one hand, and the extent to which they reflect a more relaxed, spontaneous and intuitive approach on the other.
2   *Tight–loose.* An organisation which has strong homogeneity and commitment in respect of its members' values and practices is tightly controlled (whether control is externally imposed by superordinates or self-imposed by employees). Conversely, a loosely controlled culture is one with only weak commitment to, or acceptance of, shared beliefs, values and practices, and little or no control is exerted to achieve homogeneity either by superordinates or by members themselves.
3   *Direct–indirect.* This aspect captures the linkages and patterns of communication through which power, authority and decisions are communicated. In some organisations, managers assume direct personal

responsibility to perform certain tasks and to communicate directly with their staff, often leapfrogging intermediate levels in the vertical hierarchy or chain of command. In other organisations, managers exert control indirectly by delegating to staff the tasks they would otherwise do themselves.

Pragmatic and/or normative

This dimension defines the way an organisation serves its clients, customers or patrons. Some display a flexible, pragmatic policy aimed at meeting the diversity of customer needs. Others, however, exhibit more rigid or normative approaches in responding bureaucratically, failing to meet individual needs. This dimension measures the degree of client orientation. In the educational context, some schools consciously try to meet individual student needs by offering a more diversified curriculum with flexible timetables and alternative teaching strategies.

Operationalising the Model

Having identified key elements of schooling, school-based management and cultural dimensions, the model needs operationalising. This is achieved by applying the cultural dimensions to the elements of schooling and school-based management. For example, if the researcher is interested in comparing leadership styles and positions in two or more schools in different societal cultures, data would need to be gathered through applying our power concentrated/power distributed cultural dimension to leadership (see Figure 6.2). Other dimensions, such as consideration/aggression, might also be relevant. If the same interest in leadership style and position were examined at the organisational culture level, data would need to be generated by applying relevant organisational culture dimensions to leadership; in this case, person-task and control and linkage (see Table 6.1). In facilitating the data collection process, a number of instruments – both quantitative (survey questionnaires) and/or qualitative (interviews and case studies) – are needed to apply the cultural dimensions to the various elements of the school and school-based management. Depending on the research purpose, a selection of the relevant elements and dimensions may be sufficient.

Conclusion – Challenges and Limitations of the Approach

In pioneering new approaches there are bound to be imperfections, unresolved issues and challenges. We are aware of many pitfalls and difficulties. The concept of culture itself has generated multiple definitions and ambiguities. Alone, it does not have the explanatory power to account for all the differences between schools in different societies. Economic, political and demographic factors, for example, may play a key role. Cultures may not equate with national boundaries. Moreover, there are difficulties in operationalising models such as the one espoused in this chapter.

We contend that a focus on culture as an analytical concept promises robust comparisons between school administration and policy across different geo-cultural areas. Such cross-cultural comparisons can embrace a wider rather than narrower perspective, incorporating school leadership, organisational structures, management, curriculum and teaching and learning, in order to present holistic and contextualised accounts. An international and comparative approach to educational leadership and management would bring greater refinement to the field. Few would dispute the need for such a development in the new millennium.

References

Atkin, J.M. and Black, P. (1997) Policy perils of international comparisons: the TIMMS case, *Phi Delta Kappan*, 79(1), 22–28.

Blake R.R. and Mouton J.S. (1964) *The Managerial Grid*, Houston, TX: Gulf Publishing.

Bolman, L. and Deal, T. (1992) Leading and managing: effects of context, culture, and gender, *Educational Administration Quarterly*, 28(3), 314–29.

Bray, M. and Thomas, R.M. (1995) Levels of comparison in educational studies: different insights from different literatures and the value of multilevel analysis, *Harvard Educational Review*, 65(3), 472–89.

Cheng, K.M. (1995) The neglected dimension: cultural comparison in educational administration, in Wong, K.C. and Cheng, K.M. (eds) *Educational Leadership and Change: An International Perspective*, 87–102, Hong Kong: Hong Kong University Press.

Dimmock, C. (1998) School restructuring and the principalship: the applicability of Western theories, policies and practices to East and south-East Asian cultures, *Educational Management and Administration*, 26(4), 363–78.

Dimmock, C. (2000) *Designing the Learning-Centred School: A Cross-Cultural Perspective*, London: Falmer Press.

Dimmock, C. and Walker, A. (1998a) Towards comparative educational administration: the case for a cross-cultural, school-based approach, *Journal of Educational Administration*, 36(4), 379–401.

Dimmock, C. and Walker, A. (1998b) Comparative educational administration: developing a cross-cultural conceptual framework, *Educational Administration Quarterly*, 34(4), 558–95.

Dimmock, C. and Wildy, H. (1995) Conceptualising curriculum management in an effective secondary school, *The Curriculum Journal*, 6(3), 297–323.

Duke, D. (1996) A normative perspective on organisational leadership. Paper presented at the *Toronto Conference on Values and Educational Leadership*, Toronto, Canada, 4 October.

Gouldner, A. (1957) Cosmopolitans and locals: toward an analysis of latent social roles – 1, *Administrative Science Quarterly*, 2, 291–306.

Hallinger, P. and Leithwood, K. (1996) Culture and educational administration: a case of finding out what you don't know you don't know, *Journal of Educational Administration*, 34(5), 98–116.

Hofstede, G.H. (1991) *Cultures and Organisations: Software of the MInd*, London: McGraw Hill.

Hofstede, G.H. (1994) Cultural constraints in management theories, *International Review of Strategic Management*, 5, 27–48.

Hofstede, G.H. (1995) Managerial values: the business of international business is culture, in Jackson, T. (ed.) *Cross-cultural Management*, 150–165, Oxford: Butterworth-Heinemann.

7

School Culture and Improvement

Louise Stoll

Take five scenarios. The first two involve improvement attempts from outside of schools; the other three, from inside. First, the external efforts. In the attempt to drive up educational standards, a national or state government mandates that all schools will use a 'tried and tested' approach to teaching writing. This will be introduced through professional development and monitoring practices found to be effective when introducing changes elsewhere. A local education authority or district sets up a voluntary school improvement project for its schools in partnership with a university that offers considerable experience in such projects, drawing on an extensive knowledge base on the conditions that support school improvement. In both cases, the 'pill' works in some of the participating schools, but not in others.

Now for the three internal improvement attempts. In the first, a headteacher, newly arrived to her second primary headship, sets up a scheme where staff will observe each other in classrooms and give each other feedback, on the basis that it was both popular and highly effective in her previous school. She receives a distinctly cool response. Elsewhere, an information technology (ICT) teacher goes on an exciting course where he learns about the benefits of and strategies for promoting literacy across the curriculum through ICT. Enthused, he returns and tries to persuade colleagues in other departments to 'get involved', but there is little interest and take up. In the third school, a new headteacher at a middle school observes that staff are not seen to be very involved in decision-making, forward planning is not systematic, and there is little emphasis on teaching and learning. Less than three years later the place is 'buzzing'. Anyone who works in or closely with schools can remember exciting new initiatives that have started with enthusiasm, commitment, and energy, at least on the part of some staff members. Two years later they have disappeared never to be seen again.

Source: Prosser, J. (ed.) (1999) *School Culture*, London: Paul Chapman Publishing. Edited version.

This chapter is concerned with the significance of school culture within school improvement and, in particular, why the cultures in some schools are black holes, in which school improvement efforts disappear, never to see the light of day, and others provide warmth and sustenance for school growth and development.

What is School Improvement?

Until recently, a widely accepted definition of school improvement emanated from the International School Improvement Project (ISIP). Participants concluded that school improvement was:

> a systematic, sustained effort aimed at change in learning conditions and other related internal conditions in one or more schools, with the ultimate aim of accomplishing educational goals more effectively.

> (van Velzen *et al.*, 1985, p. 48)

Assumptions underlying this definition were that school improvement needs to be carefully planned, managed and implemented, even through periods of inevitable turbulence, until changes are 'embedded or built into the structure', where they are part of the school's natural behaviour (Huberman and Miles, 1984). Additionally, throughout the change process, those involved must recognise the need for change, be committed to the focus and feel they have ownership of it, for the change to have any 'meaning' (Fullan, 1991). While real improvement focuses on teaching, learning, the curriculum and conditions that support learning, successful school improvement also extends to other related internal conditions; supporting roles, relationships and structures needing to be directly addressed. Furthermore, while improvement takes place in the school, schools are also located within an educational system where benefits can be reaped by collaborating and co-operating with other schools and being supported by external partners and agencies.

In the mid–late 1990s, in Britain and many other countries schools' external context was very different, with decision-making decentralised to schools within a centralised accountability framework. Recognising this shift, Hopkins *et al.*'s (1994) definition of school improvement has particularly emphasised pupil outcomes, rather than broad educational goals. They succinctly define school improvement as ' . . . a distinct approach to educational change that enhances student outcomes as well as strengthening the school's capacity for managing change' (p. 3), adding:

In this sense school improvement is about raising student achievement through focusing on the teaching–learning process and the conditions which support it. It is about strategies for improving the school's capacity for providing quality education in times of change, rather than blindly accepting the edicts of centralised policies, and striving to implement these directives uncritically. (p. 3)

Based on our work in Canada, Britain and elsewhere, Dean Fink and I offer a view of school improvement as:

a series of concurrent and recurring processes in which a school:

■ enhances pupil outcomes;
■ focuses on teaching and learning;
■ builds the capacity to take charge of change regardless of its source;
■ defines its own direction;
■ assesses its current culture and works to develop positive cultural norms;
■ has strategies to achieve its goals;
■ addresses the internal conditions that enhance change;
■ maintains momentum during periods of turbulence; and
■ monitors and evaluates its process, progress, achievement and development.

(Stoll and Fink, 1996, p. 43)

Understandably, there are several commonalities between the three definitions. All draw out the intricate relationship between school improvement and change. The need to understand the complexity of change when engaged in school improvement is all too often downplayed. Hopkins and colleagues' definition and that of Stoll and Fink also overtly highlight the issue of capacity. Changing practice is notoriously difficult, requiring time and effort to develop new skills, as well as the will to change (Miles, 1987). Determining a school's capacity and readiness for change, therefore, is vitally important for internal and external school change agents (Fullan, 1991). Capacity is vital to school improvement but harder to achieve in some schools than others.

There are, however, two distinctive differences about our own definition. The first is in our use of the words 'to take charge of change', which implies more than just managing change. Even within an externally determined framework, more successful schools are in the driving seat, setting their own direction, adapting mandates to fit their vision, 'colonising' external educational reforms (National Commission on Education, 1995). Successful school improvement is based on an ownership mentality, where schools define their own direction, irrespective of external demands.

Secondly, we explicitly maintain that an essential part of school improvement is that the school 'assesses its current culture and works to develop positive cultural norms'. In the remainder of this chapter, I will examine school culture, and how it can either hinder or support school improvement attempts.

What is School Culture?

School culture is one of the most complex and important concepts in education. In relation to school improvement, it has also been one of the most
neglected. Schein (1985) notes various interpretations of culture: observed
behavioural regularities, including language and rituals; norms that evolve in
working groups; dominant values espoused by an organisation; philosophy
that guides an organisation's policy; rules of the game for getting along in the
organisation; and the feeling or climate conveyed in an organisation. Whilst
agreeing that these meanings reflect the organisation's culture, Schein does not
believe that they are its basic essence. This he considers to be, 'the deeper level
of *basic assumptions* and *beliefs* that are shared by members of an organisation,
that operate unconsciously, and that define in a basic "taken-for-granted" fashion an organisation's view of itself and its environment' (p. 6).

Culture describes how things are and acts as a screen or lens through which
the world is viewed. In essence, it defines reality for those within a social
organisation (Hargreaves D., 1995), gives them support and identity and
'forms a framework for occupational learning' (Hargreaves A., 1994, p. 165).
Each school has a different reality or mindset of school life, often captured in
the simple phrase 'the way we do things around here' (Deal and Kennedy,
1983). It also has its own mindset in relation to what occurs in its external
environment. Culture is, thus, 'situationally unique' (Beare *et al.*, 1989).

A school's culture is shaped by its history, context and the people in it. The
age of the organisation can impact on cultural change. Schein (1985) identifies
three significant developmental periods. In the early years of a new school
dominant values emanate from its 'founders' and the school makes its culture
explicit. It clarifies its values, finds and articulates a unique identity and shares
these with newcomers, whether teachers, pupils or parents. Culture is the 'glue'
that holds everyone together. As time passes, the culture moves into a succes-
sion phase. In 'midlife', the school is well established but needs to continue on
a path of growth and renewal. Changes may have occurred to its external and
internal contexts, altering strengths and weaknesses. Culture is increasingly
implicit. Subcultures have also sprung up. Change becomes much more difficult because of less consciousness of the culture; it is harder to articulate and
understand. 'Maturity and/or stagnation and decline' is most problematical
from the cultural change perspective. This stage is reached if the school has
ceased to grow and respond to its environment. Dysfunctional elements have
surfaced, but challenge of old assumptions is resisted (Fink, 1997).

School culture is also influenced by a school's external context. Locally, a
school's community, including the pupils' parents, may have their own conceptions of what a 'real school' is (Metz, 1991). The Local Educational
Authority (LEA) or school district can also help create an improvement mindset (Stoll and Fink, 1996). Political and economic forces or changes in
national or local educational policies are also influences.

School culture is also very much influenced by the pupils in the school and their social class background. Thrupp (1997) argues that the social mix of the school plays a major role in how it functions, in large part because of the cumulative effect of the reference group processes of the pupils. This takes on added significance when they reach adolescence. At this time of development and maturation, their identities and values are shifting as they establish themselves. The potential for clashes of values between the adults and pupils in a school is considerable!

Changes in society pose challenges to a school's culture, whether they be related to learning, the pupil population, organisational management, rapid technological developments or the changing role of women (Dalin and Rolff, 1993). Such societal changes often demand rapid responses from a school, and yet while culture changes as participants change, it can also be a stabilising force, particularly for those who have been part of the culture for a longer period. It can therefore appear problematic for those in search of quick fix changes because it often seems as if it is an unmovable force. While it presents, therefore, the paradox of being both static and dynamic (Rossman *et al*, 1988), in reality it is constantly evolving (Hopkins *et al.*, 1994) and being reconstructed (Angus, 1996).

What does School Culture Look Like? What can you See and Hear?

From an anthropological standpoint, school culture manifests itself in customs, rituals, symbols, stories, and language (Deal and Kennedy, 1983; Nias *et al.*, 1989; Hargreaves D., 1995) – the 'artefacts' of culture (Schein, 1985). Thus, whether religion or spirituality, pupils' learning, sporting achievements, or discipline are emphasised in assemblies provides a lens on one facet of school culture. Viewed more practically, MacGilchrist *et al.* (1995) argue that school culture is expressed through the ways people relate to and work together; the management of the schools' structures, systems and physical environment; and the extent to which there is a learning focus for both pupils and adults.

Culture can take different forms. As well as pupil culture there can also be a teacher culture, leadership culture, support staff culture, and parent culture. Teacher culture has received most attention in relation to school improvement. Andy Hargreaves (1994) highlights four existing teaching cultures:

■ *Individualism* – these are bounded in metaphors of classrooms as castles, where autonomy, isolation and insulation prevail, and blame and support are avoided.

■ *Collaboration* – teachers choose, spontaneously and voluntarily, to work together, without an external control agenda.

■ *Contrived collegiality* – where teachers' collaborative working relationships are compulsorily imposed, with fixed times and places set for collaboration.

■ *Balkanisation* – where teachers are neither isolated nor work as a whole school. Smaller collaborative groups form, for example, within secondary school departments.

What Can't you See?

Norms are the unspoken rules for what is regarded as customary or acceptable behaviour and action within the school. Morgan (1997) explains, 'Life within a given culture flows smoothly only insofar as one's behaviour conforms with unwritten codes. Disrupt these norms and the ordered reality of life inevitably breaks down' (p. 139). Norms also shape reactions to internally or externally proposed or imposed improvements. It is, therefore, important for those working in schools and those supporting them from outside to understand their norms because the acceptance of improvement projects by a school depends on the fit between the norms embedded in the changes and those within the school's own culture (Sarason, 1996). Some norms are more sacred than others (Rossman *et al.*, 1988).

---

1. Shared goals – 'we know where we're going'
2. Responsibility for success – 'we must succeed'
3. Collegiality – 'we're working on this together'
4. Continuous improvement – 'we can get better'
5. Lifelong learning – 'learning is for everyone'
6. Risk taking – 'we learn by trying somthing new'
7. Support – 'there's always someone there to help'
8. Mutual respect – 'everyone has somthing to offer'
9. Openness – 'we can discuss our differences'
10. Celebration and humour – 'we feel good about ourselves'

Stoll and Fink (1996)

Figure 7.1 *Norms of improving schools*

Cultural norms that influence school improvement are summarised in Figure 7.1. These norms are interconnected and feed off each other. Many are basic to human rights of equity and respect. They focus on fundamental issues of how people relate to and value each other.

One norm, 'collegiality', merits further discussion because it is a much used but complex concept involving mutual sharing and assistance (Fullan *et al.*, 1990), an orientation towards the school as a whole (Nias *et al.*, 1989), and is spontaneous, voluntary, development-oriented, unscheduled, and unpredictable (Hargreaves A., 1994). Judith Warren Little (1990) identified 'joint work' as being most likely to lead to improvement. Examples of joint work include team teaching, mentoring, action research, peer coaching, planning and mutual observation and feedback. These derive their strength from the creation of greater interdependence, collective commitment, shared responsibility, and, perhaps most important, 'greater readiness to participate in the difficult business of review and critique' (Fullan and Hargreaves, 1991).

■ Do Schools have Different Cultures?

Given the different contextual influences described earlier, it is not surprising that schools' cultures vary. What is particularly interesting, however, is that schools with similar contextual characteristics have different mindsets. Over recent years, typologies that describe and label different 'idealised' types of school culture have been created. David Hargreaves (1995) offers one such model based on two dimensions: the instrumental domain, representing social control and orientation to task; and the expressive domain, reflecting social cohesion through maintaining positive relationships. Four types of school cultures sit in different and extreme places on the two dimensions:

- Traditional   low social cohesion, high social control – custodial, formal, unapproachable;
- Welfarist   low social control, high social cohesion – relaxed, caring, cosy;
- Hothouse   high social control, high social cohesion – claustrophobic, pressured, controlled;
- Anomic   low social cohesion, low social control – insecure, alienated, isolated, 'at risk'.

A fifth culture is also proposed, that of an effective school, demonstrating optimal social cohesion and optimal social control, with fairly high expectations and support for achieving standards. Hargreaves emphasises these are 'ideal cultures' because real schools 'move around' and, indeed, departments within schools may fall within different parts of this model.

Rosenholtz's (1989) 'moving and stuck' schools model, although simplistic, is powerful because it conveys stark contrasts. You can visualise two schools next door to each other, with similar intakes, in the same school system, facing the same external government mandates, and yet their mindsets are different. The moving school feels 'freedom to' focus on its priorities; the stuck school seeks 'freedom from' outside demands. Rosenholtz's dimensions have been expanded by Hopkins and colleagues (1994) into 'four expressions of school culture', sitting on two continuums; one of effectiveness and ineffectiveness in terms of outcomes, and the other representing the degree of dynamism of the improvement process, from dynamic to static.

Our model (Stoll and Fink, 1996) focuses on the current effectiveness of the school, and whether it is improving or declining, because the rapidly accelerating pace of change makes standing still impossible, so schools are either getting better or they are getting worse. These two concepts allow us to look at school cultures on two dimensions, effectiveness–ineffectiveness, and improving–declining (see Figure 7.2).

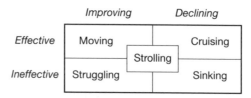

Figure 7.2 *A typology of schools*

'Moving schools' are not only effective in 'value added' terms and for a broad range of pupil learning outcomes but people within them are also actively working together to respond to their changing context and to keep developing. They know where they are going and have systems and the 'will and the skill' (Louis and Miles, 1990) to get there. There are some schools that are clearly 'high performing' as well as adding value. Others, in more deprived inner city or isolated rural areas, are making tremendous strides in extremely difficult circumstances. All, however, are underpinned by the norms of improving schools.

'Cruising schools' are often perceived as effective by teachers, school community and outside inspectors because they appear to possess many qualities of an effective school. Their pupils achieve in spite of teaching quality. League tables and other rankings based on absolute achievement rather than 'value added' can give the appearance of effectiveness. Cruising schools are smugly marking time and not seeking to prepare their pupils for the changing world into which they are going. They possess powerful underpinning norms of contentment, avoidance of commitment, goal diffusion, being reactive, perpetuating total top-down leadership, conformity, nostalgia, blame, congeniality, and denial (Stoll and Fink, 1998). In such schools, if school improvement initiatives are to take hold, it will be essential to challenge and change these norms.

'Strolling schools' are neither particularly effective nor ineffective. Moving towards some kind of school improvement at an inadequate rate to cope with the pace of change, it therefore threatens to overrun their efforts. They have ill-defined and sometimes conflicting aims which inhibit improvement efforts. They may not show up on league tables or other similar indicators as 'disasters' but nonetheless they seem to be meandering into the future to the detriment of their pupils.

'Struggling schools' are ineffective and they know it. They expend considerable energy to improve. While there may be considerable unproductive thrashing about as they determine the what and how of the change process, there is a willingness to try anything that may make a difference. Ultimately they will succeed because they have the will, despite lacking the skill.

'Sinking schools' are failing schools. They are not only ineffective; the staff, either out of apathy or ignorance, are not prepared or able to change. Isolation, self-reliance, blame and loss of faith are dominating norms, and powerfully inhibit improvement.

■ How are Culture and Structure Related?

There is a close link between culture and structure: indeed, they are interdependent. Most school improvement efforts focus on changes to structures:

■ time – an example would be rearranging the school year into four or five periods with shorter breaks between;
■ space – for example, moving the science and mathematics departments of a secondary school onto the same corridor to promote collaboration;
■ roles and responsibilities – creating a post for a 'school improvement co-ordinator' or, indeed, a 'super teacher'.

This is because structures are relatively easy to manipulate and are visible, but for these structures to effect change, it is also necessary to attend to the underlying culture. Structures can also influence culture. Collaborative cultures can be fragile (Fink, 1997). If greater collegiality between teachers in schools is desirable, but the timetable does not allow teachers to meet during the day, this will act as a barrier.

How can Culture Become a Black Hole for School Improvement?

Many school improvement initiatives, particularly those introduced by national and other policy-makers, tend to emphasise what are described as empirical-rational change strategies (Chin and Benne, 1970). These are based on the fundamental assumption that schools are rational places and that the people within them will adopt proposed changes if it has been shown that these will benefit them:

> it was believed that research for new knowledge and the proper technologising and dissemination of that knowledge could solve technical, societal, indeed, *any* problems that might be encountered. It was primarily a matter of attention, application, and money – of engineering.

> (House, 1974, p. 225)

Such ideas emanate from Clark and Guba's (1965) linear analysis of four aspects of educational change (see Figure 7.3). The National Literacy Strategy in Britain (DfEE, 1997) is an example of such a rational model. Drawing on a range of research on effective literacy strategies and some aspects of the educational change and improvement literature, the model, while not compulsory, was intended to be implemented in every primary school in the country.

Research – to advance knowledge to serve as a basis for development
Development – to invent and build a solution to an operating problem
Diffusion – to introduce the innovation to practitioners
Adoption – to incorporate the innovation into schools
Based on House (1974)

Figure 7.3 *Clark and Guba's model of the stages of educational change*

The failure of 'top-down' approaches and disappointing results of subsequent 'bottom-up' practitioner approaches which often did not lead to improvement in pupils' performance (Reynolds *et al.*, 1993) meant that by the 1990s, scholars were suggesting that change occurred best with a 'top-down, bottom-up' approach in which the larger system provided guidance and support while the actual change process was left to schools.

House (1974, p. 235) explains that behaviour is determined more by the 'complex nature of the school as a social system', than staff development opportunities where teachers learn about and are shown new teaching strategies. But how do we make sense of those 'situational constraints'? Morgan (1997) recommends using metaphors because they 'lead us to see, understand and manage organisations in distinctive yet partial ways' (p. 4). One of the metaphors Morgan applies is the cultural metaphor: 'It focuses attention on a human side that other metaphors ignore or gloss over . . . it shows how organisation ultimately rests in shared systems of meaning . . .' (p. 147). It is an important metaphor, but it is important to remember that it is not the only one and that culture can interact with other metaphors.

One metaphor, however, that has been offered to draw together rational, structural and human aspects is that of an iceberg. It has been used to convey the difference between surface aspects and those below the surface when considering the management of change (Plant, 1987; Garrett, 1997). As all improvement is change, anyone who is trying to bring about improvement needs to understand how what goes on below the surface is likely to influence surface aspects of improvement. So, for example, the organisation, structures, roles and responsibilities, and necessary professional development opportunities for externally mandated literacy hours and school-selected technology projects are surface aspects. What is going on below the surface, however, is the real essence of school culture – people's beliefs, values and the norms that will influence how they react to these initiatives – as well as micro-political issues and the emotions people bring to their work (Hargreaves, 1997; Fink, personal communication).

School Culture and Micro-Politics

Most observers of micro-politics in schools tend to view it as the underlying frame with which to view how schools change or stay the same. Pollard (1985) is one who appears to see the link between two powerful undercurrents of school improvement. While he does not discuss school culture, per se, he chooses to describe the 'rather intangible "feel" of schools as organisations' (p. 115) as 'institutional bias'. In considering understandings of reality and normative behaviour which evolve between teachers, pupils, parents and others, he rejects terms such as 'ethos' or 'climate' 'because of the unquestionable impression of cohesion which they sometimes tend to convey and because of their weak treatment of the issues of power and influence in a school' (p. 115).

Micro-politics particularly come into play in relation to the issue of sub-cultures within schools. Indeed, it could be argued that the concept of one holistic culture is too simplistic, particularly in a large secondary school. Any school may be composed of different and competing value systems, based on gender, race, language, ethnicity, religion, socio-economic status, friendship, and professional affiliation, all of which have the power to create 'a mosaic of organisational realities' (Morgan, 1997, p. 137). If role differences are added to these – between teachers, pupils, senior managers, support staff and parents – groups with their own common interests potentially could pull a school in several directions.

If we focus on teachers, closer 'webs' are often formed by subsets of colleagues with different beliefs, attitudes, norms and social relationships (Siskin, 1994). Departmental divisions can prove powerful barriers to whole-school communication and collegiality. While Hargreaves (1994) argues that small group collaboration, itself, is not a problem, balkanised cultures are characterised by insulation of subgroups from each other; little movement between them; strong identification, for example, seeing oneself as a primary teacher or chemistry teacher, and with views of learning associated with that subgroup; and micro-political issues of status, promotion, and power dynamics.

Essentially, 'Where two or more cultures coexist and interact, there will be conflicts of values in the day-to-day interaction' (Marshall, 1991, p.142). What this means it that even if one group of teachers believes that it is important to make a particular change to their teaching practice, for example adopting a new literacy approach or introducing Information Technology (ICT) across the curriculum, another group may have very different beliefs about the way to teach literacy or the importance of ICT.

Resolving these inter-group issues is often viewed as essential to the development of shared values, a necessary prerequisite of school improvement.

How can Culture Become a Fertile Garden for School Improvement?

Good seeds grow in strong cultures (Saphier and King, 1985). Understanding the school's culture, therefore, is an essential prerequisite for any internal or external change agent. In my work with teachers, headteachers and others involved in the improvement process, I frequently ask them to locate their school and parts of their school on the typology of schools (Figure 7.2 p. 100 above), and to explain why they have picked the specific location. I also encourage them to consider which three norms (Figure 7.1 p.98) it is most necessary for them to address in their own schools. Practitioners seem to find such typologies and norms help them understand the cultural processes and issues of their workplace.

There are three steps those in leadership roles can take. First, get to know their culture, by asking all involved participants what the school really stands for; noting how people spend their time; finding out which people play key roles in the cultural networking, and reflecting on the values they represent. Second, consider how the school culture encourages or inhibits pupil progress, development and achievement, and accomplishment of school goals. To what extent is balkanisation evident? Third, arrange opportunities where people can discuss and re-examine their values.

The role of leadership in relation to school culture is central. Leaders have been described as the culture founders (Schein, 1985; Nias *et al.*, 1989), their contribution or responsibility being the change of school culture by installation of new values and beliefs. Schein (1985) argues the possibility that the 'only thing of real importance that leaders do is to create and manage culture' (p. 2).

A Word of Caution

Strong cultures are viewed by some as promoting dominant interests through managerial manipulation (Bates, 1987; Jeffcutt, 1993); culture becomes problematic when treated as 'a variable – as something "the organisation has" which has to be manipulated and controlled' rather than 'something "the organisation is" – as the product of negotiated and shared symbols and meanings' (Angus, 1996, p. 974, drawing on Meek, 1988). For example, within schools, senior managers may re-arrange the timetable to enable teachers to work together. Such a managerial arrangement can be seen as an example of contrived collegiality (Hargreaves, 1990).

Morgan (1997) helpfully distinguishes between the need to create networks of shared meaning, linking people around positive visions, values and norms, and the use of culture as a manipulative management tool – 'values engineering'. He suggests that leaders and managers should ask themselves, 'What impact am I having on the social construction of reality in my organisation?' and 'What can I do to have a different and more positive impact?' (p. 148).

Reculturing

Reculturing is the process of developing new values, beliefs and norms. This is no task for the faint-hearted. Indeed, Morgan (1997) maintains it is:

> a challenge of transforming mind-sets, visions, paradigms, images, metaphors, beliefs, and shared meanings that sustain existing . . . realities and of creating a detailed language and code of behaviour through which the desired new reality can be lived on a daily basis . . . It is about inventing what amounts to a new way of life. (p. 143)

For such change to occur, 'normative–re-educative' strategies are necessary (Chin and Benne, 1970). These emphasise the pivotal importance of clarifying and reconstructing values: 'These approaches centre on the notion that people technology is just as necessary as thing technology in working out desirable changes in human affairs' (p. 45). Most significantly, they focus on the need to improve problem-solving capacities of those within organisations, a key capacity for school improvement.

Returning to the link between culture and structure, Fullan (1993) proposes:

> the interesting hypothesis that reculturing leads to restructuring more effectively than the reverse. In most restructuring reforms new structures are expected to result in new behaviours and cultures, but mostly fail to do so . . . It is much more powerful when teachers and administrators begin working in new ways only to discover that school structures are ill-fitted to the new orientations and must be altered (p.68).

If schools are to become professional communities (Louis, Kruse *et al.*, 1995) and to continue to be effective in the future, they will need to build structures which promote interrelationships and interconnections, and simultaneously develop cultures that promote collegiality and individuality (Hargreaves, 1994). Although it sounds paradoxical, not only must the school's culture promote group learning but it must honour individuals, 'mavericks', because creativity and novelty will be required to deal with an unknowable future and prevent 'groupthink' (Janis, 1972). In effect, cultures and counter-cultures will need to interact to find innovative solutions to complex and unpredictable circumstances (Fink and Stoll, 1998).

Reculturing, however, needs to go beyond redefining teacher cultures; it must include pupil and community cultures as well. Pupils can be a conservative force when teachers attempt to change their practice (Rudduck, 1991; McLaughlin and Talbert, 1993). Similarly, as noted earlier, communities are often resistant to change (Fink, 1997). Change agents must therefore attend to both.

■ Conclusion

Real improvement cannot come from anywhere other than within schools themselves, and 'within' is a complex web of values and beliefs, norms, social and power relationships and emotions. Changing schools is not just about changing curricula, teaching and learning strategies, assessment, structures, and roles and responsibilities. It requires an understanding of and respect for the different meanings and interpretations people bring to educational initiatives, and the nurturing of the garden within which new ideas can bloom.

References

Angus, M. (1996) Devolution of school governance in an Australian state school system: third time lucky?, in O.S.G. Carter and M.H. O'Neill (eds) *Case Studies in Educational Change: An International Perspective*, London: Falmer Press.

Bates, R. (1987) Corporate culture, schooling and educational administration, *Educational Administration Quarterly*, Vol. 23, No. 4, pp. 79–155.

Beare, H., Caldwell, B.J. and Millikan, R.H. (1989) *Creating an Excellent School: Some New Management Techniques*, London: Routledge.

Chin, R. and Benne, K.D. (1970) General strategies of effecting change in human systems, in W.G. Bennis, K.D. Benne and R. Chin (eds) *The Planning of Change* (second edition), London: Holt, Rinehart and Winston.

Clark, D.L. and Guba, E. (1965) *An Examination of Potential Change Roles in Education*, paper presented on Innovation in Planning the School Curriculum, University of London.

Dalin, P. and Rolff, H. (1993) *Changing the School Culture*, London: Cassell.

Deal, T.E. and Kennedy, A. (1983) Culture and school performance, *Educational Leadership*, Vol. 40, No. 5, pp. 140–41.

DfEE (1997) *The Implementation of the National Literacy Strategy – Literacy Task Force*, London: HMSO.

Fink, D. (1997) *The Attrition of Change*, unpublished doctoral thesis, Milton Keynes: The Open University.

Fink, D. and Stoll, L. (1998) Educational change: easier said than done, in A. Hargreaves, M. Fullan, A. Lieberman and D. Hopkins (eds) *International Handbook of Educational Change*, Leuven: Kluwer.

Fullan, M. (1993) *Change Forces: Probing the Depths of Educational Reform*, London: Falmer Press.

Fullan, M., Bennett, B. and Rolheiser Bennett, C. (1990) Linking classroom and school improvement, *Educational Leadership*, Vol. 47, No 8, pp. 13–19.

Fullan, M. and Hargreaves, A. (1991) *What's worth Fighting For? Working together for your School*, Toronto: Ontario Public School Teachers' Federation. Published as *What's worth Fighting for in your School* (1992), Buckingham: Open University Press.

Garrett, V. (1997) Managing change, in B. Davies and L. Ellison (eds) *School Leadership for the 21st Century: A Competency and Knowledge Approach*, London: Routledge.

Hargreaves, A. (1994) *Changing Teachers, Changing Times: Teachers' Work and Culture in the Postmodern Age*, London: Cassell.

Hargreaves, A. (1995) Cultures of teaching: a focus for change, in A. Hargreaves and M.G. Fullan, (eds) *Understanding Teacher Development*, Cassell/Teachers' College Press,

Hargreaves, A. (1997) Rethinking educational change: going deeper and wider in the quest for success, in A. Hargreaves (ed.) *Rethinking Educational Change with Heart and Mind*, ASCD Yearbook: Alexandria, VA: Association for Supervision and Curriculum Development.

Hargreaves, D.H. (1994) *The Mosaic of Learning: Schools and Teachers for the Next Century*, London: Demos.

Hopkins, D., Ainscow, M. and West, M. (1994) *School Improvement in an Era of Change*, London: Cassell.

House, E.R. (1974) *The Politics of Educational Innovation*, Berkeley, CA: McCutchan.

Huberman, M. and Miles, M.B. (1984) *Innovation Up Close*, New York: Plenum.

Janis, I. (1972) *Victims of Groupthink*, Boston, MA: Houghton Mifflin.

Jeffcutt, P. (1993) From interpretation to representation, in J. Hassard and M. Parker (eds) *Postmodernism and Organizations*, London: Sage.

Little, J.W. (1990) The persistence of privacy: autonomy and initiative in teachers' professional relations, *Teachers College Record*, Vol. 91, No. 4, pp. 509–36.

Louis, K.S., Kruse, S.D. and associates (1995) *Professionalism and Community: Perspectives on Reforming Urban Schools*, New York: Corwin Press.

Louis, K.S. and Miles, M.B. (1990) *Improving the Urban High School: What Works and Why*, New York: Teachers College Press.

MacGilchrist, B., Mortimore, P., Savage, J. and Beresford, C. (1995) *Planning Matters: The Impact of Development Planning in Primary Schools*, London: Paul Chapman Publishing.

McLaughlin, M.W. and Talbert, J.E. (1993) *Contexts that Matter for Teaching and Learning*, Palo Alto: Center for Research on the Context of Secondary School Teaching.

Meek, V.L. (1988) Organizational culture: origins and weaknesses. *Organization Studies*, Vol. 9, No. 4, pp. 453–73.

Metz, M.H. (1991) Real school: a universal drama amid disparate experience, in D.E. Mitchell and M.E. Metz (eds) *Education Politics for the New Century: The Twentieth Anniversary Yearbook of the Politics of Education Association*, London: Falmer Press.

Miles, M.B. (1987) Practical guidelines for administrators: how to get there, paper presented at the Annual Meeting of the American Educational Research Association.

Morgan, G. (1997) *Images of Organization*, Thousand Oaks: Sage.

National Commission on Education (1995) *Success against the Odds: Effective Schools in Disadvantaged Areas*, London: Routledge.

Nias, J. (1989) *Primary Teachers Talking: A Study of Teaching as Work*, London: Routledge.

Nias, J., Southworth, G. and Yeomans, R. (1989) *Staff Relationships in the Primary School: A Study of Organizational Cultures*, London: Cassell.

Plant, R. (1987) *Managing Change and Making it Stick*, London: Fontana.

Pollard, A. (1985) *The Social World of the Primary School*, London: Holt, Reinhart and Winston.

Reynolds, D., Hopkins, D. and Stoll, L. (1993) Linking school effectiveness knowledge and school improvement practice: towards a synergy, *School Effectiveness and School Improvement*, Vol. 4, No. 1, pp. 37–58.

Rosenholtz, S.J. (1989) *Teachers' Workplace: The Social Organization of Schools*, New York: Longman.

Rosenholtz, S.J. (1989) Workplace conditions that affect teacher quality and commitment: implications for teacher induction programs, *The Elementary School Journal*, Vol. 89, No. 4, pp. 421–39.

Rossman, G.B., Corbett, H.D. and Firestone, W.A. (1988) *Change and Effectiveness in Schools: A Cultural Perspective*, New York: SUNY Press.

Rudduck, J. (1991) *Innovation and Change*, Buckingham: Open University Press.

Saphier, J. and King, M. (1985) Good seeds grow in strong cultures, *Educational Leadership*, Vol. 42, No. 6, pp. 67–74.

Sarason, S.B. (1996) *Revisiting 'The Culture of the School and the Problem of Change'*, New York: Teachers College Press.

Schein, E.H. (1985) *Organizational Culture and Leadership*, San Francisco, CA: Jossey-Bass.

Siskin, L.S. (1994) *Realms of Knowledge: Academic Departments in Secondary Schools*, Washington and London: Falmer.

Stoll, L. and Fink, D. (1996) *Changing our Schools: Linking School Effectiveness and School Improvement*, Buckingham: Open University Press.

Stoll, L. and Fink, D. (1998) The cruising school: the unidentified ineffective school, in L. Stoll and K. Myers (eds) *No Quick Fixes: Perspectives on Schools in Difficulty*, London: Falmer Press.

Thrupp, M. (1997) The school mix effect; how the social class composition of school intakes shapes school processes and student achievement, paper presented to the Annual Meeting of the American Educational Research Association, Chicago.

van Velzen, W., Miles, M., Eckholm, M., Hameyer, U. and Robin, D. (1985) *Making School Improvement Work*, Leuven: ACCO.

8

Helping Practitioners Explore
their School's Culture

David Hargreaves

Introduction

It is assumed in this chapter that the motive for exploring one's own school culture is to enhance effectiveness or as an element of a programme of school improvement. I assume also that you, the practitioner, are a headteacher or a senior member of staff engaged in such an endeavour.

As a school leader, you have in this regard three major tasks in relation to school culture – diagnostic, directional and managerial. The *diagnostic* task is that of finding a method or technique of diagnosing the present character of your school's culture. The *directional* task is that of deciding in what ways you want the school's culture to change. The *managerial* task is that of devising and implementing a strategy for moving the school's culture in the chosen direction. The three are, of course, inter-linked. To take the most obvious example, all the methods suggested below of diagnosing your school's culture are heavily value-loaded and your preference for one or other diagnostic tool will influence the way in which you solve the subsequent directional and managerial tasks. So observe how your own values shape your preferences and prejudices at the diagnostic stage.

Diagnosing your School's Culture

The initial questions you face are these.
Who is to be involved in making the diagnosis? You alone? The head and senior management? The whole staff? Governors? Students? Parents? Outsiders/

Source: Prosser, J. (ed.) (1999) *School Culture*. London: Paul Chapman Publishing. Edited version.

critical friends, such as inspectors, advisers and consultants? The main arguments for involving as many people as possible are that you may uncover very different perceptions of aspects of the school's culture and this will affect subsequent action; and the involvement of people in the diagnosis may motivate them to engage in a later development of, or change in, the school's culture.

How much time and energy are you prepared to give to the diagnostic task? Simple diagnostic devices don't take much time, but they naturally lack depth. Indeed, simple devices often use the concept of school culture in simplistic fashion, whereas there may in reality be a staff culture (with its own subcultures) and a very different student culture (again with sub-cultures) as well as conflicting perceptions of both by governors and parents and outsiders. How much time can you afford for what degree of depth?

Is your method of diagnosis direct or indirect? I discuss direct methods below, but it's worth remembering that there are indirect methods, such as your school's internal review, the views of students and parents, an Ofsted report, and all such evidence that comes to you anyway as feedback on the character or ethos of the school, though the word culture may not be used. Such evidence is important, since it can be used to check on the validity of the perceptions of the school's culture emerging from the use of a more direct method.

Perhaps the simplest direct method is to draw on one of the 'two-by-two' typologies and ask those involved to say which type the school is closest to and then engage in the discussion that arises from attempts to classify the school in this way. For instance, by getting the participants to judge whether the school is broadly effective or ineffective, and improving or deteriorating, you can place the school's culture in one of the five cells in Stoll and Fink's (1996) ingenious typology. In my experience, participants find this difficult (except in extreme cases) since they judge the school is effective in some ways and not in others, and the same for the improving-declining dimension. Moreover, in a period of massive change in schools, few teachers feel the label 'strolling' to be appropriate to them. However, the basic concepts are easy to understand and could, with a brief explanation, also be handled by parents and many pupils.

A rather different four element typology of schools is suggested by Handy and Aitken (1986, pp. 83ff).

- *The club culture* (a spider's web) – the school as an informal club of like-minded people whose task is to achieve the mission of the head who is at the centre of things.
- *The role culture* (a pyramid) – the school as a set of job-boxes co-ordinated to execute the work of the organization, which the head manages through a formal system and procedures of a bureaucratic kind.

- *The task culture* (a grid) – the school as a friendly matrix of variably composed groups and teams which achieve a range of planned tasks to solve organizational problems.
- *Person culture* (a cluster) – the school as a minimally organized resource for the development of its members' talents and exercise of their skills.

Another four-element typology of teacher (not school) cultures is that offered by Andy Hargreaves (1994) – individualism, collaboration, contrived collegiality and balkanization.

Both these typologies could be turned into a diagnostic instrument in which teachers are presented with cameos of each culture type and use these to make a diagnosis of their own school culture. In practice, participants will rarely identify the school with a single type and will be influenced by the labels. Larger schools and almost all secondary schools, for example, inevitably display a degree of balkanization, and collaboration and individualism may characterize different parts of the school or different aspects of life in school. A collaborative culture sounds desirable, but the other three cultures are clearly objectionable. Although there is much insightful detail into teachers within the four types, they may strike some as rigid (can't a school be a mix of types?) and static (doesn't a school vary its mix of types over time or between situations?). Though to teachers a 'person culture' will probably have more favourable connotations than a 'role culture', the labels are more neutral in the typology devised by Handy and Aitken, who emphasize that a real school will rarely be of a single type. 'Successful schools, they say, get 'the right mix at the right time', an appropriately dynamic model of how school cultures work, but difficult to capture in a written diagnostic instrument.

At the other extreme are schemes and devices that are conceptually more complex but also much more time-consuming to use. Take, for example, two typologies I devised (Hargreaves D., 1995). The first assumes that all schools, like all social collectivities, face two fundamental tasks: one is to achieve the goals for which they exist, and the other is to maintain harmonious relationships. These two tasks are often in tension, in that pressure to achieve a key goal (e.g. student achievement) may be at a cost in relationships (e.g. making students work hard). Schools require *social controls* over teachers and students so that they work together in orderly ways, concentrate on teaching and learning and avoid the ubiquitous possibilities of distraction and delay. At the same time, schools have to try to maintain *social cohesion*, social relationships that are satisfying, supportive and sociable. This I easily turned into another two-by-two typology, in which there are four extreme types in the corners, according to whether the social control and social cohesion dimensions are high or low, as follows (see Figure 8.1).

The 'formal' school culture (high social control, low social cohesion) puts pressure on students to achieve learning goals, including curriculum targets and exam or test performance, but with weak social cohesion between staff and students. School life is orderly, scheduled, disciplined with a strong work ethic. Academic expectations are high, with a low toleration for those who don't live up to them. To students, staff are relatively strict, though institutional loyalty is valued. The school is often 'a tight ship' fostering 'traditional values'.

The 'welfarist' school culture (high social cohesion, low social control) has a relaxed, friendly and cosy atmosphere. The focus is on individual student development within a nurturing environment and child-centred educational philosophy. Work pressure is low; so academic goals get a lower priority than, or even become displaced by, social cohesion goals of social adjustment and life skills. The 'caring' inner-city school with a strong pastoral system exemplifies this friendly climate of contentment.

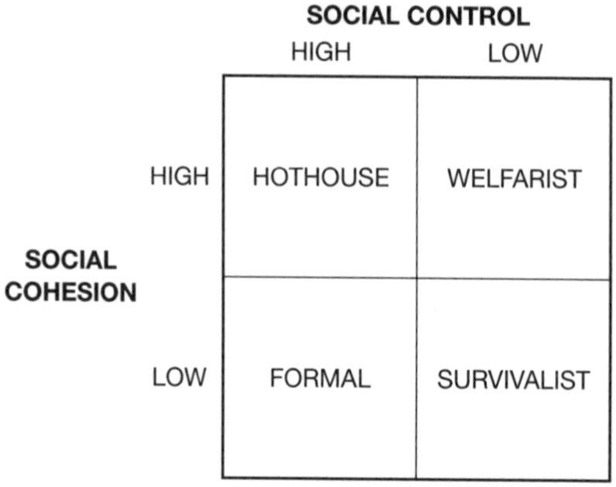

Figure 8.1

The 'hothouse' school culture (high social cohesion, high social control) is rather frenetic. All are under pressure to participate actively in the full range of school life. The motto is *join in, enjoy yourself, and be a success.* Expectations of work, personal development and team spirit are high. Teachers are enthusiastic and committed and want pupils to be the same. It is a culture that is not overtly coercive or tyrannical, but teachers and students easily become anxious that they are not pulling their weight or doing as well as they should.

The `survivalist' school culture* (low social cohesion, low social control), in its most extreme form, veers towards the 'school in difficulty' or 'failing school' – social relations are poor, teachers striving to maintain basic control and allowing pupils to avoid academic work in exchange for not engaging in misconduct. Lessons move at a leisurely pace; students under-achieve. Teachers feel unsupported by senior colleagues and enjoy little professional satisfaction. Life is lived a day at a time. Many students feel alienated from their work which bores them. The ethos is often one of insecurity and low morale.

When this typology is turned into diagnostic devices (Ainscow *et al.*, 1995), it is one in which all the staff of a school participate as an activity on a professional training day. Staff sit at tables in groups of four. On the table before them is the square of the typology, but it is divided into an 8-by-8 games board as for chess. At each corner is a different coloured marker, to indicate the four types clearly but without the use of names that might introduce bias. 'Players' are then given a set of four cards, each of a colour to match that on a corner, and on each of which is a description of one type of school. For example, the cameo of the 'formal' school (secondary version) reads:

> We regard ourselves as a well-disciplined sort of school, one that sets store on traditional values. The head runs the place as something of a 'tight ship' with high expectations of us teachers. There's a strong emphasis on student learning and we're expected to get good exam results and everybody's very proud when we do. We also like to do well in games and athletics, which is another important aspect of achievement. We expect students to be independent and to stand on their own feet whatever their background. We're clear what the school stands for and what we're about. We're naturally rather suspicious of new ideas and put more trust in what's been shown to work best through past experience.

Players are asked to think about their own school in relation to the four cameos by reading through the cards privately and without discussion. They then place their own school, *as it now is*, in one of the 64 squares and record this on a personal grid supplied to each player. This usually requires some hard thinking, as only rarely does a player locate the school exactly in a corner. Usually players see the school being pulled in different directions, so finding the extent of the 'mix', and thus the appropriate square on the grid, demands reflection. They are then asked to say in which square they would *ideally* like the school to be, and record that also on the grid. Each group then shares their private records. They are encouraged to try to reach consensus on the 'actual' and 'ideal' location of their school. This group discussion is in itself a contributor to staff development.

The technique has been tried in some 150 schools – primary, secondary and special – in different areas of the UK and has never failed to be a professional development and/or research activity that staff enjoy. The culture of their school, as it is and as they would like it to be, is rarely discussed quite so explicitly in the everyday life of the school, but it's a topic on which staff have definite views. While staff take a coffee break, the individual records (*not* the group ones) are collated and transferred to two transparencies, one for 'actual' and one for 'ideal'. These are then revealed to the staff.

In some schools, there is considerable consensus as to the school's actual and ideal climate. In others, there is more agreement on the one than on the other. Figure 8.2 gives the results of the activity in a secondary school with 38 staff. The dots represent the actual school culture, and the stars the ideal. You can make sense of the patterns in various ways, of which the simplest is to divide the square into the quadrants closest to each corner. Only one teacher (a newcomer?) places the actual school culture in the survivalist quadrant, and it is no-one's ideal. Evidently most staff (25) locate the school in the formal culture quadrant, but only one teacher places the ideal here. A clear majority (31) locate their ideal in the hothouse quadrant, and most of the rest are not far distant. Indeed, ten teachers think the school is already in this quadrant. Here is a case where there is greater agreement on where the school culture should be than where it is – a positive state of affairs on which to build.

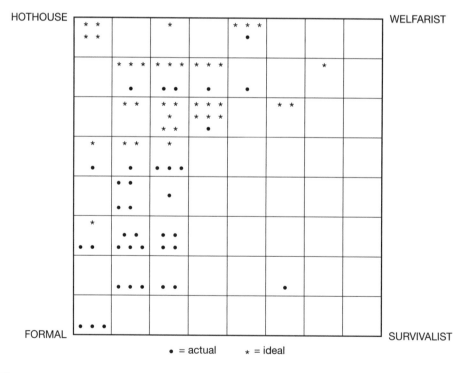

Figure 8.2

Results sometimes come as a surprise, especially to the head and senior management teams, because they underestimate the extent to which staff may deviate from the management values and perceptions. As Alvesson (1993, p. 29) notes, 'Organizational culture and managerial culture are not the same', a fact of which staff are always conscious but about which management develops a convenient amnesia. Indeed, it is worth asking the SMT to sit on a separate table, since this both helps other players to be open in what they say and provides an independent record of SMT perceptions, which are sometimes out of line with the rest of the staff. 'Maps' of the school's actual and ideal cultures are worthwhile, but bear in mind their limitations. Remember the Handy and Aitken point that actual (and ideal) cultures are dynamic, being a mix of types that at the best will vary over time and by situation. This is occluded by the static maps, but the conversations of the teachers, both while completing the task in groups and while discussing the maps in the feedback session, are much more informative about how the culture of the school is understood and experienced by staff.

There is no space here to report on the fascinating variety of outcomes of this activity; different patterns of cultures require different approaches to the follow-up. Where the staff are more agreed on their ideal culture than on the actual, the discussion can focus positively on what is inhibiting them from moving towards the ideal. In the few cases where there is low agreement on both actual and ideal, the follow-up needs to handled with great sensitivity.

For these reasons, it is probably best if the technique is led by an outsider, such as a consultant or an LEA adviser. Do *not* be tempted to lead it yourself: this will provoke suspicion and discourage honest responses and open discussion. NQTs and teachers who are new to the school should not have their views recorded on the collective version, for it has been shown that they tend to be 'deviant' and so reduce consensus: it evidently takes a year or two for teachers to be able to judge a school's culture with any accuracy. There is a student version of the technique, which works well with both upper primary and secondary students. This can be illuminating for a brave staff, not least because students tend to take a harsh view of the actual culture and see a greater gap than do staff between actual and ideal.

This diagnostic device has considerable potential. You can use the cameos developed in Cambridge manual (Ainscow *et al.*, 1994) or invent your own. Indeed, you can change the character of the basic concepts to suit your own purposes. For example, you could take the dimensions from the Stoll and Fink typology, write up four new cameos (effective + improving; effective + declining; ineffective + improving; ineffective + declining) for the corners but still use the grid and the approach with players working on the actual and ideal.

If you think this technique is too complex and time-consuming, but are unhappy with the very simple diagnostic methods, then there are devices that fall between the two. For instance, you can take any bi-polar set of concepts or practices relating to school culture, choosing whatever seems to fit your circumstances or preferences, and set them out on a scale of eight steps as follows:

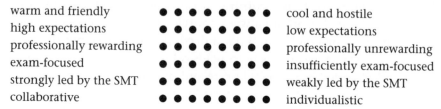

warm and friendly	● ● ● ● ● ● ● ●	cool and hostile
high expectations	● ● ● ● ● ● ● ●	low expectations
professionally rewarding	● ● ● ● ● ● ● ●	professionally unrewarding
exam-focused	● ● ● ● ● ● ● ●	insufficiently exam-focused
strongly led by the SMT	● ● ● ● ● ● ● ●	weakly led by the SMT
collaborative	● ● ● ● ● ● ● ●	individualistic

The staff simply mark the dot closest to their own view of where the school's culture now is, and where they would like it to be. The overall range and average scores, which are readily calculated, are then reported back for discussion and action planning.

A similar technique has been used by MacBeath (1998) in his adaptation of Stoll and Fink's teacher questionnaire as a tool for examining school climate and organizational health. The 54-item questionnaire is laid out as shown in Table 8.1.

Table 8.1

The school now
1 = strongly agree
2 = agree
3 = uncertain
4 = disagree
5 = strongly disagree

The effective school
1 = crucial
2 = very important
3 = quite important
4 = not very important
5 = not at all important

1 2 3 4 5		1 2 3 4 5
1 2 3 4 5	Pupils respect teachers in this school	1 2 3 4 5
1 2 3 4 5	Teachers believe that all children in this school can be successful	1 2 3 4 5
1 2 3 4 5	Teachers regularly discuss ways of improving pupils' learning	1 2 3 4 5
1 2 3 4 5	Teachers regularly observe each other in the classroom and give feedback	1 2 3 4 5
1 2 3 4 5	Standards set for pupils are consistently upheld across the school	1 2 3 4 5
1 2 3 4 5	Teachers share similar beliefs and attitudes about effective teaching and learning	1 2 3 4 5

The collated responses can be used to provide a diagnosis of the school's current culture and to generate a staff discussion of future directions and appropriate action plans.

One of my own models (Hargreaves D., 1995) adopted a similar method, as part of an attempt to develop a more systematic and sophisticated approach to school culture by assuming that it is more than a set of teacher attitudes or perceptions, but at the same time is not reducible to the two dimensions used in many typologies. Five dimensions or underlying structures are proposed – political, micropolitical, maintenance, development, and service. The **political structure** refers to the character and formal distribution of power, authority and status among the staff. The **micropolitical structure** is the informal network of individuals and groups who plot, plan and act together to advance their interests. The political and micropolitical structures interlock, often as a contest between the official functioning of the school and the unofficial manoeuvring of the staff groupings with distinctive subcultures. Maintenance and development (Hargreaves and Hopkins, 1991) are structures that arise from the school's dual needs for stability and change. **Maintenance structures**, such as standing committees and procedures, are often hardly noticed because of their sheer familiarity, but they are powerful in their impact. At the same time, the management of change requires **development structures** or temporary systems for specific, short-term development tasks. Maintenance and development structures, like political and micropolitical structures, are often in tension. The **service structure** forges the social relations, including rights and duties between the staff and the school's clients – students, parents and governing bodies.

This typology organizes the possible variations in these five dimensions around two types of school, labelled as *traditional* and *collegial*. Staff are presented not with single words or phrases but short cameos. For example, the political structure reads:

The real decisions in this school are made by the head and senior staff though there is consultation sometimes   ● ● ● ● ● ● ● ●   Before major policy decisions are taken there's full and free discussion by the whole staff and attempts are made to get full agreement

and the development structure reads:

This is a supportive place if teachers want to try out new ideas. There's often somebody to try them out with. Staff are encouraged by management who make time for teachers to do new things   ● ● ● ● ● ● ● ●   There are some good ideas around, but they usually come from management, not classroom teachers, so it's a bit of a top-down school. If you do something new, do it on your own in private

As you will perhaps imagine, staff tended to locate the school's present culture (very much) more to the left than the SMT in the political dimension and more to the right on the development dimension. Indeed, the evident gap, sometimes considerable, between the staff's perceptions and those of head and SMT is in my view one of the more useful outcomes of these activities.

Again, you could use the Cambridge cameos or invent your own. Cameos are more interesting and thought-provoking for teachers, but you cannot be sure which elements within the cameo are being responded to. Using single words or phrases avoids this problem, but they are less interesting and, because one side is easily seen as the 'right' response i.e. the one favoured by management, they are less likely to elicit honest reactions. Whichever format you use, the activity is best presented as staff development led by an outside friend of the school rather than by you.

■ Choosing the Direction for your School's Culture

My advice is that whilst you are diagnosing the school's actual culture you also tap staff (and perhaps student) conceptions of the school culture they would like, but this assumes you trust them to choose a new cultural direction. If all or most staff can agree on a future direction at the time that they diagnose the present culture, there is a motivational spur to close the gap and to work out the positive strategies for so doing. Where the gap between ideal and actual is relatively small, there is a boost to morale; where the gap is relatively large, then means for devising strategies for change should be discussed immediately to prevent demoralization.

If you think staff would not make a prudent choice and/or you have your own strong views on what the future culture should be, you will prefer a diagnostic technique that does not entail stating a preference for an ideal culture. Your own view of the future direction of the school and the associated change in culture will normally be sufficiently loose to allow all the staff to believe that their ideas have much to contribute and that it is through discussion and debate that some of the shape and much of the detail will be determined. In other words, whilst you do not specify very precisely the culture you want, you may wish to enhance your understanding of culture in order to enrich your preference for the *kind* of organization and/or community you want the school to be.

School leaders tend, for understandable reasons, to want a culture that is clear, consistent and consensual. All the staff are pulling in the same shared direction, the argument goes, so we are more likely to achieve our goals. Indeed, this is the implicit line of much writing on school cultures, which in recent years have emphasized collaboration as a key to school effectiveness and improvement. In striving for such an ideal, school leaders risk blinding themselves to lack of consensus that characterizes organizations in real life and to exaggerating the negative effects of a lack of consensus. Of course, a school at war with itself is unlikely to be happy or successful or effective, but the alterntive is not necessarily conflict-free consensus and collaboration.

Homogeneity is not always a sign of strength. Elements of dissent and ambiguity within a culture are potentially healthy, particularly when (as is generally true today) schools need to be highly adaptable if they are to prosper in a turbulent environment. Whilst ineffective schools resemble unhappy families in some respects, the 'happy family' model of school culture may not be as desirable as it appears at first sight. The most effective school leader may be a skilful *manager* of ambiguity and conflict rather than their *destroyer*. Where teachers feel they have to suppress their differences and dissent, especially from school leaders, there is a risk of creating the mere appearance of a happy family that masks a deeper discord. The cleverest heads learn how to channel dissent along positive paths that indirectly contribute to the school's goals – or at least into the harmless side-roads where most of us like or need to dawdle sometimes. In other words, their model of the school cultures is less one of *sub-cultural division of an organization* and more one of *multi-cultural diversity within a pluralistic community*. We can learn to apply the concept 'multi-cultural' positively more widely than to the school's ethnic composition (cf Hofstede, 1991, and Cray and Mallory, 1998). Wise leaders know which slightly deviant minorities to cultivate: one can never be sure when they might be needed.

School effectiveness arguably depends most of all on the classroom effectiveness of each teacher. For school leaders to provide conditions in which each classroom teacher is maximally effective in the art and science of teaching for student learning, a 'thin' school culture, or one that has a bare content requiring staff assent may be all that is required. The current fashion is for a 'thick' school culture – lots of it, requiring consensus to themes and close collaboration in its enactment. There is something to be said for a 'thin' culture that focuses on supporting high quality, somewhat individualistic, classroom practitioners, not least because such a culture may be more easily achieved by school leaders than the 'thick' cultures of many textbooks!

If you find these tensions as fascinatingly provocative as I do, you will enjoy Joanne Martin's *Cultures in Organizations* (1992), which outlines three perspectives on organizations – integration, differentiation and fragmentation – from which any particular organization, such as your school, may be interpreted and understood. Because she emphasizes that any organization can be looked at with profit from each perspective, you will come away not with simple recipes, but with an enriched understanding of how your school culture needs to be examined from these different perspectives if you are to understand and shape it.

Managing the Change to the New Culture

This, it almost goes without saying, is the most difficult of the three tasks, but is easier to accomplish if you have a clear diagnosis of the current culture and a sharp picture of the culture towards which the school is striving. School leaders don't always meet these basic criteria before setting about cultural change. I've known heads who have tried to change their school culture without taking steps to verify the nature of the school's actual culture and with only the vaguest of visions for the future culture.

As with the diagnostic task, there are direct and indirect methods of cultural, change. In the direct method, there is a 'full frontal' attempt to change the staff's shared beliefs, attitudes and values at the core of an institutional culture. This approach seems to be encouraged in parts of the literature, as in Schein's (1985, p. 2) much-quoted contention that 'the only thing of real importance that leaders do is to create and manage culture'. This often leads to the assumption that the staff will be persuaded, on some kind of rational basis, to shed older beliefs, attitudes and values under the spell of the new ones offered by the leader's stated vision. In reality most people's beliefs, attitudes and values are far more resistant to change than leaders typically allow, and direct attempts to change them may stimulate increased resistance. Schools, especially secondary ones, function in part as sophisticated bureaucracies. That is good, insofar as bureaucracies entail rational decision making, orderliness and fairness – try feudalism as an alternative! Remember Max Weber's warning that:

> Once it is fully established, bureaucracy is among those social structures which are the hardest to destroy, . . . And where bureaucracy of administration has been completely carried through, a form of power relation is established that is practically unshatterable (Gerth and Mills, 1948, p. 228).

It is prudent, then, to assume that only under rather unusual circumstances will staff beliefs, attitudes and values or operating systems be open to rapid change. Such circumstances include the following.

■ *The school faces an obvious crisis.* It is not enough for the leader(s) to recognize the crisis or simply to announce to a sceptical audience that, as the saying goes, the *status quo* is not an option. The crisis must be evident to all. Examples include a highly critical Ofsted report or a rapidly falling roll which puts staff jobs or even the viability of the school in jeopardy. Acknowledging the need for change to resolve the crisis motivates staff to listen to potentially persuasive arguments about future directions and the steps that need to be taken. The lack of a crisis is the enemy of cultural change. Remember John Harvey Jones's (1988, p. 127) dictum that:

the engine of change is dissatisfaction with the present . . . It is much more difficult to change things when everything is apparently going well.

■ *You are a charismatic leader/headteacher.* If you have real charisma, cultural change can be more radical and achieved faster, but most school leaders are not particularly charismatic and do not command instant trust, loyalty and followership. Unless you have powerful evidence to the contrary, assume charisma is not your strongest card. If you are entering your second headship, don't assume that any charisma attributed to you by the staff of your first school automatically carries over into a second. Charisma is more context-bound and situation-specific than some people imagine. Remember, too, that staff talk themselves *into* new beliefs, attitudes and values more readily than they let you talk them *out* of old values and attitudes.

■ *You are the successor to a very poor leader/headteacher.* This can be almost as valuable as an obvious crisis. Staff will be looking for a change that is strongly led, either because the previous direction was mistaken or (more likely) the school simply lacked direction. For a few months at least staff will be unusually open to new ideas and arguments. If, on the other hand, you are following someone who was regarded as a very good leader/head, then it will be very difficult, if not impossible, to change the cultural direction in any speedy or direct way.

If none of these special conditions applies, assume that cultural change will be rather slow and will involve indirect methods.

The nature and process of the culture of the school as a learning organization are yet to be adequately explored, analysed and reported. It is usually said that such a school has a capacity for managing change and that indicators of this are features such as staff development or a focus on professional inquiry and reflection. Underlying such features as well as the culture of the effective school are, I suspect, three capabilities that lie at the organizational core. These are:

■ **a monitoring capability**, or scanning the school's internal and external environment for pressures and problems, for opportunities and for partnerships. This capability provides the school with the skill of linking internal self-evaluation to external potentialities.
■ **a proactive capability**, or having a can-do philosophy, relishing challenge, and so looking ahead positively, taking into account the long-term as well as the short-term view. This capability generates optimism and confidence.
■ **a resource deployment capability**, auditing the full range of the, school's resources (human and intellectual as well as material and

financial) and directing them to the key purposes of schooling. This capability breeds goal achievement.

If these deep capabilities – which reflect, respectively, the spatial, temporal and resource dimensions of organizational life – are visible through the school's culture, then the school is probably well placed to enjoy continuing effectiveness in an unstable and changing environment. The art is finding ways of checking whether they do indeed lie below the surface of the school's overt culture, which can be frustratingly opaque to those who seek to understand and influence it.

References

Ainscow, M., Hargreaves, D.H., Hopkins, D.M. and Black-Hawkins, K. (1994) *Mapping Change in Schools: the Cambridge Manual of Research Techniques*, obtainable from Barbara Shannon, School of Education, University of Cambridge, Shaftesbury Road. Cambridge CB2 2BX.

Ainscow, M., Hargreaves, D.H. and Hopkins, D. (1995) Mapping the process of change in schools, *Evaluation Research in Education*, Vol. 9, No. 2, pp. 75–90.

Alvesson, M. (1993) *Cultural Perspectives on Organizations*, Cambridge: Cambridge University Press.

Cray, D. and Mallory, G.R. (1998) *Making Sense of Managing Culture*, International Thomson Business Press.

Gerth, H.H. and Mills, C.W. (1948) *From Max Weber: Essays in Sociology*, London: Routledge and Kegan Paul.

Handy, C. and Aitken,R. (1986) *Understanding Schools as Organizations*, London: Penguin Books.

Hargreaves. A. (1994) *Changing Teachers, Changing Times: Teachers' Work and Culture in the Postmodern Age*, London: Cassell.

Hargreaves. D.H. (1995) School culture, school effectiveness and school improvement, *School Effectiveness and School Improvement*, Vol. 6, No. 1, pp. 23–46.

Hargreaves. D.H and Hopkins, D. (1991) *The Empowered School*, London: Cassell.

Harvey Jones, J. (1988) *Making It Happen: Reflections on Leadership*, London: Fontana/Collins.

Hofstede, G. (1991) *Cultures and Organizations,* London: HarperCollins.

MacBeath, J. (1998) The coming of age of school effectiveness, Keynote address, International Congress of School Effectiveness and Improvement, Manchester.

Martin, J. (1992) *Cultures in Organizations*, Oxford: Oxford University Press.

Stoll, L. and Fink, D. (1996) *Changing our Schools: Linking School Effectiveness and School Improvement*, Buckingham: Open University Press.

Part 3

Strategic Leadership and Managing Change

9

Strategy, External Relations and Marketing

Nick Foskett

Schools and colleges have always interacted with their external environments in both pro-active and reactive ways. Until the 1990s, however, educational institutions were emphatically 'domesticated' environments (Carlson, 1975) protected from the impact of market forces, funding was guaranteed, catchment areas were delimited and protected, and their quality of education/training was not linked to funding in any explicit way. Building an external relations component into institutional planning or strategy was simply a matter for professional judgement, and its presence or absence depended on the management's view of what the proper relationship was with external stakeholders. Political and social change, however, embedded in a commitment to the ideology of the market and of consumer choice in pursuit of the three 'Es' of economy, efficiency and effectiveness (Farnham, 1993), has been steadily absorbed into the educational culture and given statutory authority through legislation. Schools and colleges have moved into a 'wild' environment (Carlson, 1975), characterised by market accountability, financial responsibility, and a key focus on explicit demonstrations of quality that enable consumer comparison of institutions.

Marketisation has characterised the public sector in many western countries in parallel to the processes in the UK, shifting schools and colleges to focus on marketing and external relations management – but to varying degrees. In some states for example, the USA and Denmark – the tradition of school engagement with the comunity has always supported the notion of partnership with a wide range of external stakeholders (OECD, 1997). In Spain, Sweden and France some elements of competition between state schools and colleges have been enhanced, and the need to take stronger

---

Source: Lumby, J. and Foskett, N. (eds.) (1999) *Managing External Relations in Schools and Colleges*. London: Paul Chapman Publishing. Edited version.

account of public perceptions of school quality has become established in schools (Agudo, 1995; Van Zanten, 1995). In contrast, in Australia and New Zealand, as in the UK, the implanting of models of parental choice into the school system has pushed schools strongly towards adopting competitive stances in external relations management (e.g. Waslander and Thrupp, 1997).

The challenge of managing the external relations of schools and colleges has clearly been increased by marketisation. This chapter examines the nature of external relations management and marketing, its interpretation and development by schools and colleges, and its place in institutional strategic planning.

External Relations and Marketing – Deconstructing Alien Concepts

The concept of marketing is for most educationists an imported, even alien, concept. Foskett (1996) has shown how there is a wide range of interpretations of marketing amongst managers in secondary schools and confusion about its relationship to public relations, promotion, advertising and external relations management – an idea confirmed in the FE sector by Pieda (1996), Smith, Scott and Lynch (1995) and Foskett and Hesketh (1997).

Many definitions of marketing have emerged from within the discipline of 'management' (e.g. Christopher, McDonald and Wills, 1980), but it is possible to identify two specific perspectives – marketing as an overall philosophy for an organisation, and marketing as a functional area of management. As a functional area marketing involves the application of strategies to effect the sale of a product or service. As an overall philosophy, however, marketing is central to the operation of an organisation and 'is not a specialised activity at all (but) encompasses the entire business – it is the whole business' (Drucker, 1954, p. 56).

Three types of organisational orientation may be identified from this analysis. Product-oriented organisations are concerned primarily with the product, be it a 'good' or a 'service', that they have the expertise in producing. Sales-oriented organisations recognise that selling is central to their survival, and an emphasis is placed on promotion of their 'products' through advertising and sales techniques. Foskett suggests that:

Such a sales-oriented culture is often the marketing stereotype . . . The first response of an educational institution moved from the market-protected positions of monopoly power (e.g. impermeable school catchments or LEA allocation of particular courses to particular FE colleges), or of great excess demand over supply (e.g. applications to higher education in the 1970s) is to seek to sell what it already offers very vigorously.

(1998, p. 49)

A market-oriented organisation, in contrast, is one in which the customer is central to its operation, and its emphasis is on satisfying customer requirements by providing goods and services that customers want. Such an orientation has implications for the organisation and its management, for each element of the organisation's operation, from strategic planning to 'front-of-house' activities, will be dictated by the customer-focus.

Marketing in education, however, is complicated by two important issues. Firstly, service industries, even in the private sector, have not traditionally taken a strong marketing perspective. Cowell (1984) explains this in a number of ways:

- Service products are inherently intangible which makes their promotion difficult, particularly where the 'product' is long term in its rewards (e.g. education).
- Services in the professional sector may see marketing as unethical, compromising the objectivity of their relationship with their 'client'.
- Some service sectors experienced demand far in excess of their ability to provide it (e.g. higher education), so promotion was unnecessary.
- Most educational organisations have enjoyed monopoly power (e.g. over a specified type of provision or a tightly demarcated catchment area), and so have perceived no need for marketing.
- Little professional guidance or training on adopting a marketing perspective has been available.

Secondly, traditional concepts of professionalism and public service in education do not sit easily with the notion of marketing. The view of the professional as 'expert' and the monitor of quality may be interpreted to mean that responsiveness to the market is unnecessary. Indeed, in education the customer may be seen not as the pupil or parent, but in terms of professionally defined notions of either an academic discipline or the needs of society as a whole. As Gray has suggested:

The purposes for which public sector institutions such as schools were established go far beyond mere customer satisfaction. (They) have public service duties and responsibilities . . . (to) tackle real needs which may not be appreciated by those customers.

(1991, p. 25)

Educational institutions, therefore, have many different external links which go beyond transactional or exchange relationships. While such relationships do exist – for example, in the recruitment of students/pupils they are only a small component of the totality of external relations which must be sustained. These are illustrated in Figure 9.1.

(a) Transactional-based external relations

■ As an education/training provider in the education/training market – for example, in 'selling' FE courses, or selling a 'primary education' to parents for their childeren.
■ As professional client – for example, in purchasing advisory services from the LEA.
■ As commercial customer – for example, in the purchase of supplies.
■ As a competitor – for example, in bidding for commercial contracts or for a share of earmarked funding from local, national or EU sources.

(b) Relationship-based external relations

■ As partners with 'customers' – for example, the relationship with parents in supporting pupils' development.
■ As professional partner – for example, relationships with service providers such as educational psychologists.
■ As community partner – for example, relationships with community organisations such as the church or the police.
■ As professional player – for example, in responding to consultations on educational initiatives.
■ As professional adviser – for example, in providing advice to parents on special needs support.

(c) Public accountability external relations

■ As political servant – for example. in receiving delegated funds through local or national funding, or in implementing government literacy initiatives.
■ As accountable public body – for example, in being subject to local or national inspection, or generating public examination results that appear in league tables.

Figure 9.1 *External relationships of schools and colleges*

These functions are not, of course, distinct and the overlap and feedback between them is very important. For example, a school's role as community partner, if effective, will contribute to its recruitment of pupils, as will its performance in the quality assurance processes operated by Ofsted. The importance of this is emphasised by Foskett and Hesketh (1997) who identify the significance of 'word of mouth' in parents' and students' choice of school or college, which, although a secondary product of the school's activities, may account for two-thirds of the influence on parental choice of school (Foskett, 1995; Carroll and Walford, 1997).

While managing these external relationships is of great importance to the institution, each is embedded in its internal processes. Worcester's Law (Worcester, 1985) asserts that 'no organisation can sustain a good reputation that it does not deserve'. A perception that marketing is simply about choosing the message the institution wants to convey and then communicating that by public relations and promotional activity ignores the importance of underpinning the image with effective quality assurance. This, in turn, suggests three important issues for managers:

1. External relations management cannot be the domain of only a small group. It is neither something that only senior managers do nor can it simply be delegated to junior colleagues. While in a large institution specific functions (e.g. media relations) may be undertaken by specialists, and the whole process will need co-ordination from senior management, each member of the organisation has an important role.
2. Effective external relations will probably require significant 'internal marketing' (Robinson and Long, 1985) to support it. This is the process of sharing vision amongst the whole organisation and generating strategies for actioning the vision from internal consultation.
3. Staff are key players within this process, since their activities define the quality of the organisation, and they represent a key stakeholder group with whom 'management' must manage relationships with great care. This link between staff support, quality and external relations is recognised in much of the quality management research in education (Murgatroyd and Morgan, 1993; West-Burnham, 1997), and is exemplified by the Investors in People movement.

So what is the relationship between external relations management and marketing? External relations management relates to:

> Those aspects of an organisation's activities that in any way cause it to relate to an audience beyond its own boundaries. This includes both processes with an overtly external connection and those processes which, while largely internal to the organisation, have a direct impact on some external (stakeholder).

> (Foskett, 1992, p. 6)

Such processes need management whether or not an organisation is market-focused. Putting up a sign which says 'Parents must not proceed beyond this point' at the school gate is managing external relations, but is probably not very effective marketing! Where an institution is market-focused, however, all external relations management has a marketing component, since it is designed to support the notion that all of the organisation's activities are focused on customers and clients, that marketing is an holistic philosophy for the school or college. Such a perspective means that the harsh equation of 'marketing = selling' can be replaced by a perspective which is much more in tune with educational philosophies.

Figure 9.2 is a model of marketing that includes both traditional educational values and the discipline of the market. Marketing is represented as a 'field', with an individual's or organisation's precise conceptual location representing a balance between recruitment, quality and community responsiveness. Such a location will depend on the 'micro-market' conditions the organisation finds itself in, and will change over time. A college under threat from declining student numbers may focus its marketing perspective on the bottom left of the model, while a neighbouring institution in a more secure market position might be located more centrally or towards one of the other corners. In all cases, however, there is a component of each of the three elements in the marketing perspective that a school or college must adopt – quality and community relationships can never be ignored in favour of 'pure' recruitment activity. This emphasis on links with stakeholders in non-transactional relationships emerges strongly from an analysis of marketisation in a number of European countries (OECD, 1997), and Cardno (1998) emphasises the centrality of the community links in the context of government guidance on strategic planning in New Zealand schools.

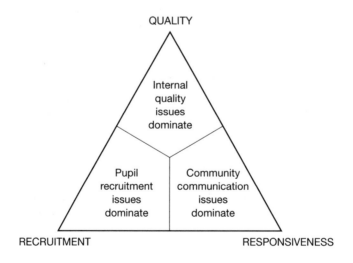

Figure 9.2 *The marketing triad model*

This model links to an important concept that has emerged in the marketing of small businesses (Payne *et al*, 1995; Grönroos, 1997) – relationship marketing. This recognises that small organisations (and all schools and most colleges are small organisations) sell not just a product or service but a relationship which is based on partnership, mutual trust and confidence (Stokes, 1996). A number of ideas emerge from this:

■ Such an approach reflects what has traditionally been regarded as good 'educational' practice in most schools and colleges, and sits more comfortably with educationally driven philosophies.
■ It emphasises the importance of managing all external relations in support of effective long-term relationships with external client groups.
■ It confirms Drucker's (1973, p.4) perspective that effective marketing almost removes the need for 'selling', for 'the aim of marketing is to know and understand the customer so well that the product or service fits him and sells itself'.
■ Most schools and colleges have extensive experience in developing these relationships, so that 'even while claiming an innocence of marketing, or more vehemently, an antipathy towards it, (schools and colleges) are actually rather good at it' (O'Sullivan and O'Sullivan, 1995).

Strategy, Management and External Relationships

Accountability and autonomy have made a commitment to strategy a core requirement for educational institutions, both statutorily and pragmatically. Strategic management is, in essence, taking proactive responsibility for the future and long-term development and direction of the whole institution. Middlewood (1998), drawing on the work of Mintzberg (1995). Fidler (1996) and Weindling (1997), distinguishes clearly between strategic thinking and operational management. Strategic thinking is long-term, reflective, conceptual and creative, emphasising the identification of opportunities in response to a continuous scanning of the environment, and is concerned with achieving the institution's vision. Operational management is short-term and immediate, leading to action in a small time frame, and concentrates on concrete, often routine, functions focusing on the internal context of the institution. Strategic thinking and operational management are clearly not separate, indeed they must not be so for each must inform the other, but they represent opposite ends of a management activity spectrum.

Strategic management is intimately involved with the institution's external environment. Hanson and Henry (1992) emphasise the importance of 'strategic marketing' to educational institutions, where most of the organisation's planning is intimately linked to its awareness of the environment in which it operates. This they distinguish from 'project marketing' (the most-practised form of marketing', ibid, p. 258), which is short-term and is the management of specific market needs.

Johnson and Scholes (1993) indicate that the whole concept of strategic management comprises three components, within each of which we can identify external relations components:

■ strategic analysis
■ strategic choice
■ strategic implementation.

Strategic analysis

Strategic analysis is about ensuring that strategy is linked to the market. The organisation's environment provides the parameters within which it may operate, and comprises the market environment and the socio-political environment. Every organisation is constrained by external economic circumstances, and the political environment in which policy decisions are made. While the opportunities for actively influencing these are limited, no organisation needs to be entirely the victim of external circumstances. A key aspect of strategic analysis is collecting sufficient 'intelligence' and data to be able to make reasoned judgements about future trends, scenarios and patterns. Sensing this component of the external environment is often highly subjective and requires astute political judgement, but the view from the crow's nest this provides means that careful adjustments of the tiller can avoid the ship foundering on the rocks (Foskett, 1997).

Sensing the market environment is also subjective, but much less so. Market analysis seeks to describe the organisation's present and future markets in terms of:

■ market characteristics – size, constraints, character, patterns of change and future development
■ competition – the nature and behaviour of competitors
■ buyer behaviour – the decision-making processes of customers.

Such market intelligence can be obtained formally through a marketing research programme (Davies and Scribbins, 1985) or informally through gathering information from inside or outside the organisation (Martin, 1995).

While strategy must be informed by market considerations, many other factors are also of importance, for schools and colleges have a broad social remit in addition to the market imperatives. The FEFC (1997) has identified a number of factors which impact on college strategy, including:

- the overall direction of the institution
- needs and market analysis
- staff skills
- finance and estate management issues
- the local labour market.

Planning and marketing are tightly linked, therefore, but are not the same thing. It is the role of management to make judgements about the importance of the market in their planning decisions and strategic choices. Gray (1991) sees strategic planning as deriving from strategic analysis, however, with all strands of institutional plans building from marketing analysis techniques. The product of this process has three components:

1 An institutional plan
2 Thematic plans for each component of the institutional plan (e.g. curriculum, estates, finance)
3 A marketing plan, which identifies both future marketing activity (e.g. promotion, public relations) and future marketing research and evaluation activities.

Strategic choice

Strategic choice is, in essence, choosing the broad approaches that the organisation will take to achieve its aims. Kotler and Fox (1995) identify three elements of marketing strategy formulation, which are intended to ensure that the institution 'plays' in the market in the most effective way.

1 *Target market strategy*. This involves identifying which segments of the market the institution wishes to operate in – a college may choose to focus, for example, on 16–19-year-old academic-track students rather than vocational courses. Schools, while constrained because of statutory curriculum requirements, may still focus on particular market segments (e.g. as a technology school).
2 *Competitive positioning strategy*. This involves identifying the distinguishable features on the institution that make it distinctive from competitors in the same market segments – for example, a small school may emphasise its friendly, community ethos, while a large school may emphasise its range of facilities.
3 *Marketing mix strategy*. This involves identifying the specific combination of elements that the organisation will present to promote itself, and is often characterised by the idea of the five Ps (Product, Place, Price, Promotion and People).

Strategic implementation

The final stage in Johnson and Scholes' (1993) model is strategic implementation, which involves turning the strategy into practice. This includes
establishing appropriate systems, acquiring and applying the relevant
resources, operating the systems, and evaluating/measuring their effect.
Within this process, two important management issues can be identified.
Firstly, the establishment of effective internal quality assurance systems
should ensure that the service or product meets customer expectations.
Secondly, it is important to develop mechanisms for collecting external data
on how programmes and activities are perceived.

■ Case Studies in the Management of Marketing and External Relations

How far do these principles operate in the 'real world' of educational institutions, though? Few detailed research-based case studies exist either in the
school sector or in FE. From the research of Foskett (1995), Gewirtz, Ball and
Bowe (1995), James and Phillips (1995), Glatter, Woods and Bagley (1996)
and Woods, Bagley and Glatter (1998), the following features of external relations management in schools emerge:

- A steady cultural shift towards accepting the need to operate actively in a
  market environment.
- A very varied interpretation of marketing, but with a strong 'product-centred'
  perspective in schools.
- A reactive, ad hoc approach to marketing, with the dominance of short-
  term promotional activities.
- An emphasis on short-term 'crisis management' approaches, dealing with
  recruitment issues.
- A failure to recognise the dynamic nature of markets and the presence of
  market threats even to institutions in currently strong positions. Schools
  successful with their image and recruitment are frequently complacent
  and do not seek to scan the market.
- The absence of any coherent form of marketing research.
- The adoption of undifferentiated marketing strategies by schools, most
  seeking to be 'all things' to all potential pupils. Glatter, Woods and Bagley
  (1996, p. 22) suggest that popular schools 'have no incentive to differentiate
  further' and less popular schools seek 'not to sharpen but to blunt any
  difference and thereby share the mutual benefits from being similar'.

In primary schools, practice is similar to that of secondary schools, but is even more 'conservative' in approach (Stokes, 1996; Minter, 1997). As Foskett (1998, p. 54) indicates:

> A strong commitment to educational values drives them, together with the establishment of strong relationships with the community. The role of word-of-mouth is so important that a 'selling' orientation is of little assistance, so many primary schools have, by default, and without reference to the 'canons' of marketing, adopted a strategy that is 'relationship marketing'.

Although marketing has become a major preoccupation for FE institutions and a substantial marketing function has been developed in larger colleges with significant specialist marketing teams, many smaller colleges still place marketing as a peripheral activity in the job portfolios of middle and senior managers. Research into FE marketing by Smith et al. (1995), Hemsley-Brown (1996), Pieda (1996) and Foskett and Hesketh (1997) suggests that:

■ There is considerable diversity in the organisation and systems adopted to deal with marketing.
■ As with schools, the emphasis is on short-term 'project' marketing rather than strategic marketing integrated into long-term institutional planning.
■ Considerable expertise has been developed in the use of promotional strategies traditionally associated with large commercial organisations.

The three case studies below are presented to provide a more detailed perspective on these developments, although it is important to recognise the unique character of the market places within which each of the instititions operates. They are not presented here as being 'typical', but serve to illustrate some of the pressures and responses schools and colleges have experienced in the market place.

Case study 1 – Grove Primary School

Grove Primary School is a 7–11 junior school in a small village in a rural part of central southern England. It takes most of its pupils from the village infant school, and in 1996 had 75 pupils on roll. This represented a steady decline from 95 three years earlier, indicating a growing disenchantment in the village with the school. In 1996 the headteacher left and the new head was appointed by the governors with a brief to reverse the decline in numbers. The strategy employed by the head was not based *explicitly* on any marketing principles (the head denies any knowledge of marketing!), but on a clear five-element approach:

1. recognition that word-of-mouth is the most important promotional tool for any school, especially in a strong community like the village
2. personal relationships between all the staff and all external stakeholders (parents, neighbours, suppliers, LEA) must be positive, optimistic, welcoming and indicative of the pursuit of quality
3. quality is identified by good achievement in school performance league tables
4. the head must take the lead in spending as much time as possible with parents of potential pupils, and respond to all invitations for the school to participate in local activities
5. the head scans the external environment for opportunities to enhance the school's relationships with stakeholders, and to identify potential threats as they arise.

The school has no formal marketing plan, and marketing is not mentioned in the School Development Plan. While the governors monitor the results of marketing, they take no active part in the process, and the head is clear that 'I am the school's marketing'. Such a pattern of activity is clearly based on relationship marketing rather than transactional marketing, but indicates a school which is, in reality, highly responsive to its market environment. In this school, the success is:

■ a roll for 1998/9 of 105
■ a number of pupils now admitted from infant schools at some distance from the school
■ a number of affluent parents in the village opting to use the school rather than preparatory schools
■ the appointment of an additional member of staff.

A number of key principles emerge from this example. The importance of seeing marketing in the primary school as relationship marketing is under-lined, which in turn emphasises the need to be concerned with all external relations processes and not just recruitment. Linked to this is the centrality of quality assurance and the pursuit of measurable success in underpinning external perceptions, which in itself requires the engagement of all staff with responding to the external environment. Thirdly, the importance of moni-toring the environment is clear, as is the identification of a clear set of strategies and priorities.

Case study 2 – Greenstreet Community School

Greenstreet Community School is an 11–16 mixed comprehensive school serv-ing, principally, a large local authority housing estate in a city in southern England. While its performance in public examinations has improved in recent years, and it performs well in relation to its intake of pupils, it is still amongst the poorest performers in the LEA. It has never recruited up to its maximum intake number, and has substantial competition from other local schools, including a similar school at the other end of the estate. Important threats are the school's reputation for bullying and boys' underperformance, and new buildings at its major competitor school. Significant strengths include a strong community education programme, a highly regarded staff, a strong sports tradition and an attractive campus. A new head was appointed in 1997.

The school has never had an explicit marketing plan and external relations management had always been a (poorly developed) responsibility of the headteacher, who had never spent much time promoting strong links with external organisations. The new head, on appointment, established a primary aim of filling all the places in the next year's intake and establishing Greenstreet as the first choice school in the locality through:

- short-term promotional developments to address current under-recruitment through, for example, establishing good links with the education reporter of the local newspaper, and feeding regular stories in relation to pupil achievement
- focusing in the medium term on improving examination results through establishing teaching and learning issues as the key focus for all staff, addressing in particular boys' under-achievement and the linked issue of behaviour; innovative developments included a cross-curricular literacy programme and the introduction of vocational programmes for 14–16-year-olds
- identifying the characteristics that might make Greenstreet distinctive within the local schools market; this included, for example, emphasising and developing the community character of the school with internal appointments of staff to develop strong literacy and music outreach programmes
- establishing mechanisms for sensing the external environment – for example, commissioning a survey of feeder school pupils and parents to gain their perceptions of the school and its competitors
- developing appropriate political links through the generation of good relationships with the LEA, community groups and the local post-16 institutions.

Despite these developments no explicit marketing plan was created. Each approach was either a feature of a short-term component of the development plan or else a strategy developed in the head's own practice. The strategy, though, demonstrates clearly the recognition of both short-term and long-term marketing needs, the link between long-term aims and issues of broad external relations management, the focus on partnership as much as 'exchange' relationships, and the importance of quality assurance and teaching and learning as guarantors of future success in the market.

Case study 3 – Lowlands College

Lowlands College is an urban further education college in north-west England. At the time of incorporation in 1992 it emphasised strongly traditional vocational and craft-based programmes, with a small 'academic-track' sector and some self-funding business training programmes. Its strengths were its industrial links and its reputation for quality vocational training. Its weaknesses were its traditional 'dirty hands' image, and its location in a declining inner city area. Prior to incorporation, the local authority had channelled 'academic' work to two sixth form colleges in the city. Marketing was the responsibility of a Vice Principal and the Head of Business Studies, but no explicit marketing plan or strategy existed. Following incorporation the college was faced with a declining Average Level of Funding and a highly competitive market with expansion targets of 25 per cent over four years.

Lowlands reorganised its marketing organisation and operations. A Marketing Officer and Assistant were appointed, line managed by the Vice Principal (Planning), with a responsibility for promoting the college's programmes. A separate Community and Enterprise Office (CEO) was established, led by a middle management appointee, reporting to the Vice Principal (Curriculum), with a brief to review the needs of the college's client groups, to identify new markets and to generate new sources of income. The CEO was also charged with establishing a marketing database and undertaking appropriate marketing research. The integration of these activities fell to the Senior Management Team with the responsibility for the college's strategic plan. The Strategic Plan contains a section on 'Marketing' which focuses on promotional activities. Other sections in the plan include a theme within 'Curriculum' on 'New developments and potential', and a further section on 'Managing relationships with external partners'.

Key decisions on strategy included the choice not to expand substantially 'academic-track' provision, but to focus on vocational and business-funded training programmes. The college chose, despite the decline in engineering employment, to establish a high quality IT-based engineering provision for training, and to develop a training and conference suite for the regional business community. A franchise Year 1 engineerng programme was established with a local university. In the period 1992–95 the college expanded its market share of engineering and business programmes in the region, but overall expansion meant that targets were not met. By 1998 the college's financial position had deteriorated, and a merger with one of the local sixth form colleges was being negotiated.

Lowlands demonstrates the challenges of managing external relations in a highly competitive post-compulsory environment. The college adopted a strong sales-oriented approach which, in turn, led to the planning of external relations and marketing being diluted within the college's strategy. The decision to focus on existing areas of expertise was not based on external scanning, although this choice recognised the need to be distinctive in the market. The college was handicapped by its own inexperience with marketing as it moved from a 'domesticated' to a 'wild' environment, and the inclusion of marketing into the strategic planning process for the college was a bolt-on to existing planning. A college of similar history nearby used its market analysis to re-focus the college's programmes towards business education, with an aggressive pursuit of the academic-track market of local school sixth forms. Its future is much more secure than that of Lowlands.

▌ Conclusion

Managing external relations and managing marketing are tightly linked processes for all institutions. At a strategic planning level, the strategy needs to be driven by the institution's interaction with its external environments, including its markets. In turn the strategy drives the way the institution operates directly in the market, and shapes the character of the wide spectrum of relationships that influence external perceptions of the 'quality' of the institution. The education system is characterised by considerable diversity in marketing and external relations practice. The 'sales-oriented' perspective still dominates, with marketing detached from mainstream institutional planning. However, since most schools and colleges are small businesses, an approach based more strongly on the concept of 'relationship marketing' may link together more firmly an institution's educational mission and its market situation. In conclusion, Smith, Scott and Lynch's perspective on marketing in FE still describes the situation across the educational world:

> Marketing is on the march, (but) . . . institutions are at different stages of
> development in marketing terms, marketing philosophies are often poorly
> articulated, marketing functions have yet to be adequately defined, and the
> organisation of marketing remains inchoate (and occasionally illogical).

> (1995, p. 110)

▌References

Agudo, J. (1995) The education market in Zaragoza. Paper presented to the European Conference on Educational Research, Bath, UK.

Cardno, C. (1998) Working together – managing strategy collaboratively, in D. Middlewood and J. Lumby (eds.) *Strategic Management in Schools and Colleges*, London: Paul Chapman Publishing.

Carlson, R. (1975) Environmental constraints and organisational consequences: the public school and its clients, in J. Baldridge and T. Deal (eds.) *Managing Change in Educational Organisations*, Berkeley, CA: McCutchan.

Carroll, S. and Walford, G. (1997) Parents' response to the school quasi-market, *Research Papers in Education*, Vol. 12, No. 1, pp. 3–26.

Christopher, M., McDonald, M. and Wills, G. (1980) *Introducing Marketing*, London: Pan.

Cowell, D. (1984) *The Marketing of Services*, Oxford: Butterworth.

Davies, P. and Scribbins, K. (1985) *Marketing Further and Higher Education*, Harlow: Longman for FEU.

Drucker, P. (1954) *The Practice of Management*, New York: Harper and Row.

Drucker, P. (1973) *Management Tasks, Responsibilities and Practice*, London: Harper and Row.

Farham, D. (1993) *Managing the New Public Services*, Basingstoke: Macmillan.

Fidler, B. (1996) *Strategic Planning for School Improvement*, London: Pitman.

Foskett, N.H. (1992) An introduction to the management of external relations in schools, in N.H. Foskett (ed.) *Managing External Relations in Schools*, London: Routledge.

Foskett, N.H. (1995) *Marketing, management and schools – a study of a developing market culture in secondary schools*. Unpublished PhD thesis, University of Southampton.

Foskett, N.H. (1996) Conceptualising marketing in secondary schools – deconstructing an alien concept, in *Proceedings of the 'Markets in Education, Policy, Process and Practice' Symposium*, University of Southampton.

Foskett, N.H. (1997) Staring into the black hole, *Management in Education*, Vol. 11, No. 4, pp. 3–6.

Foskett, N.H. (1998) Linking marketing to strategy, in D. Middlewood and J. Lumby (eds.) *Strategic Management in Schools and Colleges*, London: Paul Chapman Publishing.

Foskett, N.H. and Hesketh, A.J. (1997) Constructing choice in contiguous and parallel markets: institutional and school-leavers' responses to the new post-16 market place, *Oxford Review of Education*, Vol. 23, no. 3, pp. 299–320.

Gewirtz, S., Ball, D. and Bowe, R. (1995) *Markets, Choice and Equity in Education*, Buckingham: Open University Press.

Glatter, R., Woods, P. and Bagley, C. (eds.) (1996) *Choice and Diversity in Schooling: Perspectives and Prospects*, London: Routledge.

Gray, L. (1991) *Marketing Education*, Buckingham: Open University Press.

Grönroos, C. (1997) From marketing mix to relationship marketing – towards a paradigm shift in marketing, *Management Decision*, Vol. 35, No. 4, pp. 322–9.

Hanson, E.M. and Henry, W. (1992) Strategic marketing for educational systems, *School Organisation*, Vol. 12, no. 2, pp. 255–67.

Hemsley-Brown, J. (1996) *Marketing post-sixteen colleges; a qualitative and quantitative study of pupils' choice of post-sixteen institutions*. Unpublished PhD thesis, University of Southampton.

James, C, and Phillips, P. (1995) The practice of educational marketing in schools, *Education Management and Administration*, Vol. 23, No. 2, pp. 75–88.

Johnson, G. and Scholes, K. (1993) *Exploring Corporate Strategy*, 3rd edition, Hemel Hempstead: Prentice-Hall.

Kotler, P. and Fox, K. (1995) *Strategic Marketing for Educational Institutions*, 2nd edition, New York: Prentice-Hall.

Martin, Y. (1995) What do parents want? *Management in Education*, Vol. 9, No. 1, pp. 12–14.

Middlewood, D. (1998) Strategic management in education: an overview, in D. Middlewood and J. Lumby, (eds.) *Strategic Management in Schools and Colleges*, London: Paul Chapman Publishing.

Minter, K. (1997) *Marketing in the primary school*. Unpublished MA (ed) Thesis, University of Southampton.

Mintzberg, H. (1995) Strategic thinking as seeing, in B. Garratt (ed.) *Developing Strategic Thought*, London: Harper Collins.

Murgatroyd, S. and Morgan, C. (1993) *Total Quality Management and the School*, Buckingham: Open University Press.

OECD (1997) Parents as Partners in Schooling, Paris: OECD.

O'Sullivan, C. and O'Sullivan, T. (1995) There's beauty in candlelight: relationship marketing in the non-profit sector, in *Proceedings of the Annual Conference of the Marketing Education Group*, Bradford: MEG.

Payne, A., Christopher, M., Clark, M. and Peck, H. (1995) *Relationship Marketing for Competitive Advantage: Winning and Keeping Customers*, Oxford: Butterworth-Heinemann.

Pieda (1996) *Labour Market Information for Further Education Colleges: a Handbook for Practitioners*, Manchester: Pieda.

Robinson, A. and Long, G. (1985) Substance v. trappings in non-advanced FE, *Journal of Further and Higher Education*, Vol. 12, No. 1, pp. 23–40.

Smith, D., Scott, P. and Lynch, J. (1995) *The Role of Marketing in the University and College Sector*, Leeds: Heist Publications.

Stokes, D. (1996) Relationship marketing in primary schools, in *Proceedings of the 'Markets in Education, Policy, Process and Practice' Symposium*, University of Southampton.

Van Zanten, A. (1995) Market forces in French education. Paper presented to the European Conference on Educational Research, Bath, UK.

Waslander, S. and Thrupp, M. (1997) Choice, competition and segregation: an empirical analysis of a New Zealand secondary school market, in A. Halsey, H. Lauder, P. Brown, and A. Wells (eds.) *Education, Culture, Economy and Society*, Oxford: Oxford University Press.

Weindling, D. (1997) Strategic planning in schools: some practical techniques, in M. Preedy, R. Glatter, and R. Levačić (eds.) *Educational Management: Strategy, Quality and Resources*, Buckingham, Open University Press.

West-Burnham, J. (1997) *Managing Quality in Schools*, 2nd edition, London: Paul Chapman Publishing.

Woods, P., Bagley, C. and Glatter, R. (1998) *School Choice and Competition: Markets in the Public Interest?* London: Routledge.

Worcester, R. (1985) Familiarity breeds favourability, *The Times*, 7 November.

10

Understanding Strategy Development

Gerry Johnson and Kevan Scholes

Introduction

This chapter provides explanations of how strategies come about in organisations. There are different explanations of this and these are discussed in terms of three 'lenses' – or ways of seeing things, which employ and build on different organisational theories in order to enable the reader to consider strategy development processes critically.

All three ways of looking at strategy development are useful:

- *Strategy as design*: the view that strategy development can be a logical process in which forces and constraints on the organisation are weighed carefully through analytic and evaluative techniques to establish clear strategic direction and in turn carefully planned in its implementation is perhaps the most commonly held view about how strategy is developed and what managing strategy is about. It is usually associated with the notion that it is top management's responsibility to do this and that top management leads the development of strategy in organisations.
- *Strategy as experience*: here the view is that future strategies of organisations are based on the *adaptation* of past strategies influenced by the experience of managers and others in the organisation, and are taken-for-granted assumptions and ways of doing things embedded in the cultural processes of organisations. In so far as different views and expectations exist, they will be resolved not just through rational analytic processes, but also through processes of bargaining and negotiation. Here, then, the view is that there is a tendency for the strategy of the organisation to build on and be a continuation of what has gone before.

Source: Johnson, G. and Scholes, K. (2002) *Exploring Corporate Strategy*, 6th edition. Harlow: Financial Times/Prentice Hall. Edited version.

■ *Strategy as ideas*: neither of the above lenses is especially helpful in explaining innovation. So how do new ideas come about? This lens emphasises the potential variety and diversity which exist in organisations and which can potentially generate novelty. If we are to understand how innovations and innovative strategies come about, it is necessary to understand how this potential diversity contributes to it. Here strategy is seen not so much as planned from the top but as *emergent* from within and around the organisation as people cope with an uncertain and changing environment in their day-to-day activities. New ideas will emerge, but they are likely to have to battle for survival against the forces for conformity to past strategies that the experience lens explains. Drawing on explanations from evolutionary and complexity theories, the ideas lens provides insights into how this might take place.

It is important to understand these different explanations because all three provide insights into the challenges that are faced in managing the complexity of strategy.

Table 10.1 summarises the three lenses discussed above. In many respects it has to be recognised that the design lens, especially in its emphasis on

Table 10.1 *Three strategy lenses*

	Strategy as: Design	Experience	Ideas
Overview summary	Deliberate positioning through rational, analytic, structured and directive processes	Incremental development as the outcome of individual and collective experience and the taken for granted	Emergence of order and innovation through variety and diversity in and around the organisation
Assumptions about organisations	Mechanistic, hierarchical, logical	Cultures based on history, legitimacy and past success	Complex systems of variety and diversity
Role of top management	Strategic decision makers	Enactors of their experience	'Coaches', creators of context and 'champions' of ideas
Implications for change	Change = implementation of planned strategy	Change incremental with resistance to major change	Change incremental but occasionally sudden
Underpinning theories	Economics; decision sciences	Institutional theory; theories of culture; psychology	Complexity and evolutionary theories

analysis and control, is the orthodox approach to strategy development most commonly written about in books, taught at business schools and verbalised by management when they discuss the strategy of their organisations. However, the other lenses are important because they raise significant challenges in thinking about and managing strategy. The experience lens is rooted in evidence of how strategies develop incrementally based on experience and the historical and cultural legacy of the organisation; and suggests that it is much more difficult to make strategic changes than the design lens might imply. The ideas lens helps an understanding of where innovative strategies come from and how organisations cope with dynamic environments. It also poses questions about whether or not top management really has control over strategic direction to the extent the design lens suggests.

■ Strategy Development Processes in Organisations

The previous section has dealt with different explanations of how strategies develop. These are not mutually exclusive explanations. They are different lenses through which it is possible to understand and explain what goes on in organisations. People who work in, or observe, organisations (for example, consultants or students) are likely to see a variety of processes occurring which contribute to strategy development. These lenses help provide a means of understanding and interpreting the causes and the effects of such processes. The sections which now follow consider some of these observable strategy development processes and use the different lenses to explain them.

Strategic planning systems

Often, strategy development is equated with strategic planning systems. In many respects they are the archetypal manifestation of the design approach to managing strategy. Such processes may take the form of highly systematised, step by step, chronological procedures involving many different parts of the organisation. Organisations which have sophisticated and extensive planning systems may well be populated with managers who believe that strategies can and should be developed in such ways and who may argue that a highly systematic approach is *the* rational approach to strategy formulation. The evidence of the extent to which the formalised pursuit of such a systemised approach results in organisations performing better than others is, however, equivocal – not least because it is difficult to isolate formal planning as the dominant or determining effect on performance. This is not to say that formalised planning does not have its uses.

- It can provide a structured means of *analysis and thinking* about complex strategic problems, at its best requiring managers to *question and challenge* the received wisdom they take for granted.
- It can encourage a *longer-term view* of strategy than might otherwise occur. Planning horizons vary, of course. In a fast-moving consumer goods company, 3–5 year plans may be appropriate. In companies which have to take very long-term views on capital investment, such as those in the oil industry, planning horizons can be as long as 14 years (in Exxon) or 20 years (in Shell).
- It can be used as a means of *control* by regularly reviewing performance and progress against agreed objectives or previously agreed strategic direction.
- It can be a useful means of *coordination*, for example by bringing together the various subunit strategies within an overall organisational strategy, or ensuring that resources within a business are coordinated to put strategy into effect.
- Strategic planning may also help to *communicate* intended strategy.
- It can be used as a way of involving people in strategy development, therefore perhaps helping to create *ownership* of the strategy.
- Planning systems may provide a sense of security and logic for the organisation and, in particular, management who believe they *should* be proactively determining the future strategy and exercising control over the destiny of the organisation.

Whilst, on the face of it, planning is most obviously explained through the design lens, it can also be explained through the other lenses, and these suggest other possible benefits.

- The experience lens suggests that strategy actually develops on the basis of more informal sensing of the environment on the basis of people's experience or through the cultural systems of the organisation. Here, planning is not seen as directing the development of strategy so much as drawing together the threads of a strategy which emerges on the basis of that experience and, perhaps, post-rationalising it. So the strategy comes to look as though it has been planned. Of course, even if the formally stated strategy of an organisation is post-rationalised, it may nonetheless be important to ensure effective communication of it, and this can be aided by a systematic planning system.
- The ideas lens also emphasises the emergence of strategy from within the organisation rather than from the top; so again planning may be seen here as making sense of that emergent strategy. Planning systems also provide a selection mechanism by which new ideas can be evaluated. Plans typically embody the strategy as it is generally accepted, so, in a sense, new ideas and innovations have to compete for their survival, or prove their worth, against such plans and planning processes.

There are, however, dangers in the formalisation of strategic planning, and some of these can be understood by reference to the different lenses.

First, looking through the design lens itself, there are evident problems in the way in which strategic planning systems are put into effect in some organisations.

■ The managers responsible for the implementation of strategies, usually line managers, may be so busy with the day-to-day operations of the business that they cede responsibility for strategic issues to specialists. However, the specialists do not have power in the organisation to make things happen. The result can be that strategic planning becomes an *intellectual exercise* removed from the reality of operation.

■ The process of strategic planning may be so cumbersome that individuals or groups in the firm might contribute to only part of it and *not understand the whole*. This is particularly problematic in very large firms. One executive, on taking over as marketing manager in a large multinational consumer goods firm, was told by his superior: 'We do corporate planning in the first two weeks of April, then we get back to our jobs'.

■ There is a danger that strategy becomes thought of as *the plan*. Managers may see themselves as managing strategy because they are going through the processes of planning. Strategy is, of course, not the same as 'the plan': strategy is the long-term direction that the organisation is following, not a written document on an executive's shelf. This highlights the difference between *intended* and *realised* strategies.

■ Strategic planning can become over-detailed in its approach, concentrating on extensive analysis which, whilst sound in itself, may miss the major strategic issues facing the organisation. For example, it is not unusual to find companies with huge amounts of information on their markets, but with little clarity about the strategic importance of that information. The result can be *information overload* with no clear outcome.

The experience lens also highlights dangers.

■ Planners can *overlook the importance of the experience of those in an organisation* and see centrally planned strategy, as determining what goes on in an organisation. As was explained in discussing the experience lens, the individual and collective experience of an organisation will influence its strategy; and the experience of those responsible for strategy implementation will affect how a strategy is implemented. If formal planning systems are to be useful, those responsible for them need to ensure that they draw on such experience. This may account for why more and more organisations are changing to more inclusive ways of developing strategy, involving different levels of management. However, the sorts of danger highlighted next, remain.

- The strategy resulting from deliberations of a corporate planning department, or a senior management may not be *owned* more widely in the organisation. In one extreme instance, a colleague was discussing a company's strategy with its planning director. He was told that a strategic plan existed, but found it was locked in the drawer of the executive's desk. Only the planner and a few senior executives were permitted to see it!
- Strategies are more or less successfully implemented through people. Their behaviour will not be determined by plans. So the *cultural and political dimensions* of organisations have to be taken into account. Planning processes are not typically designed to do this.

The ideas lens also adds to an understanding of the pitfalls of formal planning.

- Formal systems of planning, especially if linked to very tight mechanisms of control, can result in an inflexible, hierarchical organisation with a resultant *stifling of ideas and dampening of innovative capacity*.
- Planning can become obsessed with the search for a definitively *right strategy*. It is unlikely that a 'right' strategy will naturally fall out of the planning process. It might be more important to establish a more generalised strategic direction within which there is the sort of flexibility that the ideas lens would emphasise. As Mintzberg puts it: 'If you have no vision, but only formal plans, then every unpredicted change in the environment makes you feel your sky is falling in'.[1]

Certainly there has been a decline in the use of formal corporate planning departments. On the other hand, there has been a growth of *strategy workshops* where participants remove themselves from day-to-day responsibilities to tackle strategic issues facing their organisation. Such events may well use the sorts of techniques of analysis and planning described in this chapter. However, rather than just relying on these to throw up strategic solutions, a successful workshop process works through issues in face-to-face debate and discussion, drawing on and surfacing different experiences, assumptions, interests and views. In this respect it is seeking to tackle the design of strategy, whilst facing up to the realities of the cultural and political processes of the organisation. Whilst such events are typically for groups of senior managers, perhaps the board of an organisation, organisations are beginning to see benefits in similar events across other levels of management.

Strategic leadership

Strategy development may also be strongly associated with an individual. A **strategic leader** is an individual upon whom strategy development and change are seen to be dependent. They are individuals personally identified with and central to the strategy of their organisation: their personality or reputation may result in others willingly deferring to such an individual and seeing strategy development as his or her province. In other organisations an individual may be central because he or she is its owner or founder; often the case in small businesses. Or it could be that an individual chief executive has turned round a business in times of difficulty and, as such, personifies the success of the organisation's strategy.

Again the three lenses help explain and raise questions about how such individuals develop their ideas about strategy, and how they influence strategy development.

■ The design lens suggests that individuals have thought this all through analytically. Whilst a plan may not exist as a written document, it exists in terms of analysis and evaluation carried out by that individual. This could be by using the sorts of technique associated with strategic planning and analysis; or it might simply be that the individual has consciously, systematically and on the basis of their own logic, worked through issues their organisation faces and come to their own conclusions.

■ The experience lens suggests that the strategy advanced by the individual is formed on the basis of that individual's experience, perhaps within the organisation or perhaps from some other organisation. The strategy advanced by a long-established chief executive may strongly reflect or be informed by his or her organisation's paradigm; and the strategy advanced by a chief executive new to an organisation may be based on a successful strategy followed in a previous organisation.

■ The strategy of an organisation might also be associated more symbolically with an individual, for example the founder of a business. Such a figure may come to embody the strategic direction of the organisation. In effect the strategy and the individual become embedded in the history and culture of that organisation. This is often the case in family-controlled businesses.

The ideas lens provides additional insights to the role of the strategic leader:

■ Evolutionary theorists emphasise the way in which strategies develop from competing ideas, so tend to diminish the role of so-called strategic leaders. However, the potential importance of all overall vision, mission or intent and the (perhaps few) guiding rules associated with these are recognised as important; and some writers see this as *the* role of the strategic leader. Indeed, it is a role for which successful strategic leaders are often applauded because such a vision can provide sufficient clarity within which the discretion of others in the organisation can be exercised.

■ However, some complexity theorists would argue for the importance of recognising the importance of high intuitive capacity and would accept that strategic vision can be associated with an executive with such a capacity, who sees what others do not see and espouses new ways of working.

■ Others point out that new businesses or business activities are usually created by individual entrepreneurs. They may be correct, but evolution suggests that for every successful entrepreneur there are likely to be many who fail. The few that succeed will, indeed, be applauded as innovatory and creative, but they were the product of a diverse population of ideas most of which did not succeed.

Organisational politics

Managers often suggest that the strategy being followed by the organisation is really the outcome of the bargaining and power politics that go on between important executives. Such executives are continually trying to position themselves such that their views prevail or that they control the resources in the organisation necessary for future success. The **political view** of strategy development is, then, that strategies develop as the outcome of processes of bargaining and negotiation among powerful internal or external interest groups (or stakeholders). This is the world of boardroom battles often portrayed in film and TV dramas. What do the lenses have to say about this?

The design lens suggests that such political activity gets in the way of thorough analysis and rational thinking. On the whole it is seen as an inevitable but negative influence on strategy development. Certainly, the interests of different stakeholders and the protection of those interests can get in the way of strategy development.

It is, however, the experience lens which most helps explain the likelihood of political activity and some of the implications that flow from this.

■ If people in organisations are rooted in their experience, it is not surprising that, in approaching problems – often major problems – from that point of view, they seek to be protective of their views in the face of different views based on different experience. This may be linked to the exercise of power.

■ The outcome of such political processes may well be inertia. So political activity may then be seen as one explanation of incremental, adaptive strategy development. There are at least two reasons for this. First, if different views prevail in the organisation and different parties are exercising their political muscle, compromise may be inevitable. Second, it is quite possible that it is from the pursuit of the current strategy that power has been gained by those wielding it. Indeed it may be very threatening to their power if significant changes in strategy were to occur. In such circumstances it is likely that a search for a compromise solution which accommodates different power bases may well end up with a strategy which is an adaptation of what has gone before.

■ The experience lens also suggests that the analytic processes that go into planning may not be entirely based on objective and neutral facts. Views of the world – of the marketplace, of technological development, of organisational competences and so on – that are stated and regarded as important in a plan will have been espoused and supported by a group of managers. The fact that a view is accepted and is in the plan may be the result of the powerful influence they have and may, in turn, provide them with added power. The objectives which are set may reflect the ambitions of powerful people. Information is not politically neutral, but rather can be a source of power for those who control what is seen to be important; so the withholding of information, or the influence of one manager over another because that manager controls sources of information, can be important. Powerful individuals and groups may also strongly influence the identification of key issues and indeed the strategies eventually selected. Differing views may be pursued, not only on the basis of the extent to which they reflect environmental or competitive pressures, for example, but also because they have implications for the status or influence of different stakeholders. Planning is, in this sense, political, or at least has a political dimension.

■ All of this suggests that political activity has to be taken seriously as an influence on strategy development. Whatever thinking goes into the strategy will need to go hand in hand with activity to address the political processes at work.

The ideas lens also suggests that organisational politics can be seen as a manifestation of the sort of conflict that results from innovation and new ideas. The variety and diversity that exist in organisations takes form in new ideas supported or opposed by different 'champions'. In this sense such battling over what is the best idea or the best way forward is to be expected as an inevitable manifestation of innovatory organisations. Indeed, arguably, if such conflict and tensions did not exist, neither would innovation. However, this lens would warn against the excesses of this. In so far as differences and conflict help spawn new ideas they can be productive; but there comes a point where this is not so, where inertia is the likely outcome.

Logical incrementalism

In a study of major multinational businesses, Quinn[2] concluded that the management process could best be described as *logical incrementalism*. Managers have a view of where they want the organisation to be in years to come and try to move towards this position incrementally. They do this by attempting to ensure the success and development of a strong, secure, but flexible core business, building on the experience gained in that business to inform decisions about the development of the business and perhaps experimenting with 'side bet' ventures. Such experiments cannot be expected to be the sole responsibility of top management – they have to be encouraged to emerge from lower levels, or 'subsystems', in the organisation. Effective managers realise that they cannot do away with the uncertainty of their environment by trying to 'know' about how it will change. Rather, they try to be sensitive to environmental signals through constant scanning and by testing changes in strategy in small scale steps. Commitment to strategic options may therefore be tentative in the early stages of strategy development. There is also a reluctance to specify precise objectives too early, as this might stifle ideas and prevent experimentation. Objectives may therefore be fairly general in nature. Overall, **logical incrementalism** can be thought of as the deliberate development of strategy by 'learning through doing' or the 'crafting' of strategy.

This view of strategy making is similar to the descriptions that managers themselves often give of how strategies come about in their organisations. They see their job as 'strategists' as continually, proactively pursuing a strategic goal, countering competitive moves and adapting to their environment, whilst not 'rocking the boat' too much, so as to maintain efficiency and performance. Quinn himself argues that 'properly managed, it is a conscious, purposeful, pro-active, executive practice'.[3]

Again the strategy lenses help explain and interpret these findings. First the design lens.

- Logical incrementalism does not fit a neat sequential design approach to strategy development. The idea that the implementation of strategy somehow follows a choice, which in turn has followed analysis, does not hold. Rather, strategy is seen to be worked through in action.
- However, whilst strategy is not designed in terms of being pre-planned, it is nonetheless rationally thought through, taking account of the forces in the environment and the competences of the organisation.

The experience and ideas lenses help provide an understanding of how this happens and some of the benefits. Both these lenses emphasise the importance in strategy development of the activities and contribution of people throughout the organisation, in the 'subsystems' of the organisation, rather than just at the top.

- Sensing of environmental changes is done through these subsystems, drawing on the experience and sensing of people at different levels and in different roles in the organisation.
- The variety of these people's experience, emphasised by the ideas lens, is critical because it ensures sufficient diversity in the way the complexities of the environment and organisational capabilities are understood and interpreted. The top management role of providing overarching vision rather than tight control is also in line with the ideas lens.

- It can be argued that if strategies are developed in such a way, it has considerable benefits. Continual testing and gradual strategy implementation provides improved quality of information for decision-making, and enables the better sequencing of the elements of major decisions. Since change will be gradual, the possibility of creating and developing a commitment to change throughout the organisation is increased. Because the different parts, or 'subsystems', of the organisation are in a continual state of interplay, the managers of each can learn from each other about the feasibility of a course of action. Such processes also take account of the political nature of organisational life, since smaller changes are less likely to face the same degree of resistance as major changes. Moreover, the formulation of strategy in this way means that the implications of the strategy are continually being tested out. This continual readjustment makes sense if the environment is considered as a continually changing influence on the organisation.

The learning organisation

The concept of the *learning organisation*, and strategy development as a learning process, became popularised in the 1990s. In many respects it corresponds to the aspects of logical incrementalism described above, especially in so far as it starts with the argument that the uncertainty and complexity of the world of organisations cannot readily be understood purely analytically. The world to which organisations have to adapt appears to be so turbulent and unpredictable that traditional approaches to strategic management are simply not appropriate; there is little to be gained from formalised planning approaches with predetermined fixed objectives and analysis that may take weeks or months to work through. The idea that top managers can formulate strategies implemented by others also becomes redundant because top managers are less in touch with such a complex and turbulent world than others within the organisation.

It is the characteristics of the experience and ideas lenses that more closely match those of the learning organisation.

- There is a need for the continual challenge of that which is taken for granted in the organisation; so there is a need to develop organisations which are *pluralistic*, in which different, even conflicting, ideas and views are welcomed; in which such differences are surfaced and become the basis of debate.
- *Experimentation* is the norm, so ideas are tried out in action and in turn become part of the learning process.
- This is more likely to take place where *informality* of working relationships is found. New ideas emerge more through *networks* of working relationships than through hierarchies; more through dialogue, even storytelling, than through formal analysis. If organisations are seen as *social networks*, the emphasis is not so much on hierarchies as on different interest groups which need to cooperate with each other, negotiate what

should be done and find ways of accommodating different views. For example, a multinational firm working on a global scale is unlikely to be solely reliant on formal structural processes to make things happen. It is likely that it will be dependent on the network of contacts that builds up over time between different parts of the organisation across the world.

■ This is also a political process of *bargaining and negotiation*, so conflict and disagreement will occur; but this is an inevitable outcome of diversity and variety in organisations, and should not necessarily be regarded as negative in the process of strategy development. The dangers are at the extremes; that conflict and disagreement become so pronounced that they get in the way of the benefits of diversity; or that the fear of diversity leads to formalised systems of planning and control that can dampen innovation and learning.

■ Within this view, the job of top management is to create this sort of organisation by building teams and networks that can work in such ways; by allowing enough *organisational slack* that there is time for debate and challenge; and by releasing control rather than holding on to it. This may be done, for example, through the development of different types of organisational structure and through the development of the everyday behaviour and culture of the organisation.

The **learning organisation** is, then, one capable of continual regeneration from the variety of knowledge, experience and skills of individuals within a culture which encourages mutual questioning and challenge around a shared purpose or vision.

Imposed strategy

There may be situations in which managers face what they see as the imposition of strategy by agencies or forces external to the organisation. Government may dictate a particular strategic course – for example, in the public sector, or where it exercises extensive regulation over an industry – or choose to deregulate or privatise an organisation previously in the public sector. This may not be the choice or even the wish of the managers. Businesses in the private sector may also be subject to such imposed strategic direction, or significant constraints on their choices. The multinational corporation seeking to develop businesses in some parts of the world may be subject to governmental requirements to do this in certain ways, perhaps through joint ventures or local alliances. An operating business within a multidivisional organisation may regard the overall corporate strategic direction of its parent as akin to imposed strategy. Increasingly, managers in long-established businesses see themselves as having little choice but to change the way they do business as a result of the development of new forms of e-business and radical changes in the business environment, not least of which are new ways of doing business.

The different lenses also provide useful insights here.

■ Whilst an imposed strategy may not be developed by the managers in the organisation concerned, the strategy has presumably been developed elsewhere and the sorts of explanation of strategy development already given may help explain how that has occurred.
■ It might be argued – indeed governments have argued – that such imposed strategy is a way of overcoming the sort of strategic inertia that had arisen as a result of strategies developing incrementally on the basis of history, experience, existing cultural norms or the compromises that result from bargaining and negotiation of powerful groups in an organisation.
■ The argument may also be put forward that the imposition of a general strategic direction can provide impetus for innovation and creativity. It creates the sort of overall declaration of intent and provides sufficient principles and guidelines for change to create 'adaptive tension' and competition of ideas, whilst avoiding over-prescription and control of behaviours and solutions.

Multiple processes of strategy development

This discussion of different lenses and different strategy development processes raises three further important points:

■ First, it has to be recognised that there is no one right way in which strategies are developed. For example, the way in which strategies develop in a fast-changing environment is not likely to be the same – nor should it be – as in an environment in which there is little change.
■ Second, it is very likely that the way in which strategies are developed will be seen differently by different people. For example, senior executives tend to see strategies more in terms of design whereas middle management tend to see strategies rather more as the result of cultural political processes. Managers who work for government organisations or agents of government tend to see strategy as more imposed than those in the private sector. People who work in family businesses tend to see more evidence of the influence of powerful individuals, who may be the owners of the businesses.
■ Indeed, it is unlikely that any one process described above singularly explains what is occcurring in the development of strategy in any organisation. There will be multiple processes at work. For example, if a planning system exists, it will not be the only process at work in the development of strategy. There will undoubtedly be some level of political activity, and elements of the strategy could well be imposed. Table 10.2 shows how different processes take form in different organisational contexts.

Table 10.2 *Some configurations of strategy development processes*

Dominant dimensions	Characteristics	Rather than	Typical contexts
Planning incrementalism (Logical incrementalism)	Standardised planning procedures Systematic data collection and analyses Constant environmental scanning Ongoing adjustment of strategy Tentative commitment to strategy Step-by-step, small-scale change	Intrusive external environment Dominant individuals Political processes Power groups	Manufacturing and service sector organisations Stable or growing markets Mature markets Benign environments
Incremental Cultural Political	Bargaining, negotiation and compromise amongst conflicting interests of groups Groups with control over critical resources more likely to influence strategy Standardised 'ways of doing things' Routines and procedures embedded in organisational history Gradual adjustments to strategy	Deliberate, intentional process Well-defined procedures Analytical evaluation and planning Deliberate managerial intent	Professional service firms (e.g. consultancy or law firms) Unstable, turbulent environment New and growing markets
Imposed Political	Strategy is imposed by external forces (e.g. legislation, parent organisation) Freedom of choice severely restricted Political activity likely within organisation and between external agencies	Strategy determined within the organisation Planning systems impact on strategy development Influence on strategic direction mainly by managers within the organisation	Public sector organisations, larger manufacturing and financial service subsidiaries Threatening, declining, unstable and hostile environments

The findings above are based on a survey of perceptions of strategy development processes undertaken at Cranfield School of Management In the 1990s.

■ References

From H. Mintzberg, *The Rise and Fall of Strategic Planning*, Englewood Cliffs, NJ:Prentice Hall, 1994.

J.B. Quinn's research involved the examination of strategic change in companies and was published in *Strategies for Change*, Homewood, IL: Irwin, 1980. See also J.B. Quinn, 'Strategic change: logical incrementalism ', in H. Mintzberg, J.B. Quinn and S. Ghoshal (eds), *The Strategy Process* (European edition), London: Prentice Hall, 1995.

See J.B. Quinn, *Strategies for Change, op. cit.*

11

Strategic Analysis: Obtaining the Data and Building a Strategic View

Brent Davies and Linda Ellison

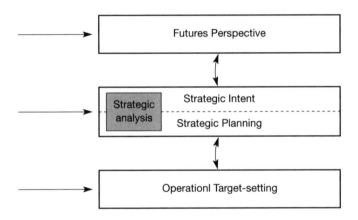

Strategic analysis aims to form a view of the key factors which will influence the school in the medium-term. These factors will affect the strategies which are chosen to achieve the strategic intent and the strategic plan. Strategic analysis can be seen in practical terms to involve two sequential processes: first obtaining strategic data and, second, building an aggregated strategic view of the school through interpreting and integrating that data to turn it into useful information.

Source: Davies, B. and Ellison, L. (1999) *Strategic Direction and Development of the School.* London: Routledge. Edited version.

Obtaining Strategic Data

What sort of area or activities should be part of the strategic analysis? In Table 11.1 we put forward a taxonomy of four areas for analysis and indicate the corresponding information needed and some of the approaches available for collecting the data.

Although the information will usually be assembled by the senior management team, to appreciate fully the strategic position of the school it is necessary to understand how a wide range of stakeholders, such as pupils, staff, employers, governors and the community, view the situation which the school faces and its possible direction. Those responsible for aspects of the analysis need to look beyond their normal sources of information if the work is to have validity.

The sections which follow take the reader through the four areas in Table 11.1.

Table 11.1 *Taxonomy of strategic data collection*

Area for analysis	Data needed	Available approaches
The environment	international trends national trends regional/local trends	PESTLE analysis (political, economic, socio-cultural, technological, legal, educational)
The school's customers or stakeholders	existing and potential customers or clients	market segmentation demographic and survey data
	their values, wants and needs	preference surveys
The school's product and service	areas of strength and weakness, growth and contraction	SWOT analysis, GRIDS
	perceptions of the school	internal evaluation external inspection attitude surveys
The competitors	the products and services offered, their strengths and weaknesses	SWOT analysis, customer survey data
	perceptions of their provision	competitor analysis inspection reports

Analyse the environment

One of the most significant strategic roles for school leadership is 'managing the boundaries', that is seeing beyond the boundaries of the school and understanding the interface between the school and its environment. Those who engage constantly in futures thinking should be very aware of the global trends. We seek to encourage schools to look to international comparisons, particularly within education and, closer to home, to gather data on what is happening or likely to be happening at national and local levels, both in education and more generally.

For the purposes of strategic analysis, the external environment can be sub-divided into international (or global), national (or macro) and regional/local (or micro). This categorisation affects the degree of detail which is available and, sometimes, the degree of its impact over time. There are many analytical frameworks which can be used (such as a PESTLE analysis which examines political, economic, socio-cultural, technological, legal and educational factors) in order to categorise the trends and to check that all areas have been covered. It is important to choose a framework which covers the relevant areas and which can be readily used by those in school without being too much of a drain on people's time.

The international environment

It seems probable that organisations (including schools) which survive and prosper will be those which have flexibility and can respond rapidly to change. The global trends should indicate some significant implications for schools such as:

- the technology of learning will change;
- learners and teachers in various locations will be brought closer together by communication systems;
- a very wide range of information will be quickly and cheaply accessible;
- pupils will need to be prepared for the world after school in which work will be varied, more internationally based and more often of a service rather than a production nature.

An understanding of this international environment will allow schools to offer a range of experiences to pupils and staff and to benchmark themselves against similar schools elsewhere.

The national environment

The PESTLE framework is a useful tool for identifying and classifying the national trends that will impact on schools and the learning process in the future. *Political* developments which can affect schools would include: the role of the public sector in general and in education in particular; policies on appropriate types of school; admissions policies. In the *economic* category, schools need to consider: national trends in employment, in terms of the percentage likely to be in work, the nature of that work, the pay and conditions patterns; the nature of the economy and the impact of European policy; trends in public expenditure; trends in educational funding such as relating it to outputs and mixing sources (private/public; state/parental top-up). *Socio-cultural* trends which might be identified could include the changing gender roles and a more mobile and multi-cultural society, the emphasis on lifelong learning and the involvement of the community in that learning.

Although it is difficult to keep pace with changes in *technology*, the global trends can be identified at the national level. These would include the ability to store, retrieve and transmit large amounts of information very quickly, the availability of technology in the home, the community and in education. In the UK, schools must consider trends in European *legislation* as well as that which might emerge nationally.

The local environment

Schools are increasingly being affected by a variety of factors in the local or regional environment such as:

■ the development of regional government and associated policies and projects;
■ local government policies;
■ industrial or rural regeneration projects;
■ levels of employment/unemployment;
■ housing developments;
■ demographic trends;
■ transport infrastructure;
■ community expectations of local services;
■ competitors in the provision of education;
■ lifelong learning initiatives;
■ the broadening of educational options at all stages.

Often it is not necessary to have precise information but, rather, a grasp of the significant trends. Local and regional bodies can usually supply any details which are required and often have graphs indicating trends. The school must consider whether or not such information is a prediction of the future or merely an extrapolation of the past.

Undertaking the environmental analysis.

All staff need to have an awareness of the trends in the external environment and their likely impact on schools so that they can understand the reasoning behind various proposals at the school level and the need for flexibility and responsiveness. Groups may be formed and individuals named to keep an eye on trends at each level. Such groups could include governors, staff, parents, and pupils and could meet, say, twice a year. The case example shown below demonstrates a possible outcome of this type of analysis.

Case example 11.1: a PESTLE analysis at the national level

Political

- Significantly enhanced levels of consumer choice, reflected in the differentiation between schools and the ability to choose a school.
- Greater international co-operation.

Economic

- Relating value-added educational gains to resource levels, allowing schools to be compared in terms of 'value for money' and forcing them to achieve increased performance with the same resource level.
- Considerable changes in staffing patterns and arrangements, more para-professionals, core and periphery staff, fixed-term performance-led contracts, school-site pay bargaining,
- Greater varieties of finance with blurring between state-only and private-only funding of schools.
- Contracting-out of educational as well as service elements of schooling.

Socio-cultural

- A re-examination of the boundaries between different stages of education and between education and the community.
- A focus on the importance of learning.

Technological factors
- Radical changes in the nature of teaching and learning as the impact of the new teaching and learning technologies gathers pace.

Legal
- The increasing use of short-term contracts for staff.

Educational
- A focus on high achievement.
- The development of centralised curriculum and testing frameworks which provide measures of output and value-added, thus increasing information for parental choice.
- Redefinition of the leadership and management functions in schools.

Analyse the school's customers or stakeholders

Here the purpose is to identify two main sets of strategic information:

■ who are the customers or stakeholders and who might they be in the future? This can be achieved through market segmentation;
■ what do the clients/ customers want from the school? This information can be gathered in a variety of ways, for example through preference surveys.

There are several caveats to offer to those who may consider these approaches. Vast amounts of data may be gathered with considerable time implications. It is better to think carefully about the type of information which the school requires before asking a lot of people a lot of questions. Also, the responses, particularly to attitude surveys, can be very disturbing. There needs to be careful preparation in relation to planning the dissemination of results. It is unwise to gather data and then to take no action on issues that arise.

Market segmentation

Market segmentation is used to divide diverse clients or stakeholders into more homogeneous groups in order to identify particular wants, needs and influencing factors. Appropriate products and services can then be developed and effective means of communication can be devised. A first step could be to divide the clients/customers into those internal and those external to the school. Once the segments have been identified, the school can then move on to examine a range of information such as numbers, gender, educational experience, preferences and attitudes.

When looking at *internal stakeholders*, it is important to consider the various groupings within the school so that any future direction is related to their varied needs. The most obvious categorisation would be into pupils and their parents, members of staff (teaching and support), governors, regular visitors and helpers. Within these categories, there are various sub-divisions, for example of pupils according to age, staff according to experience or function, governors according to areas of interest or influence and visitors according to affiliation and purpose.

There is a need to consider the wider *external stakeholders*, both individuals and groups, within and beyond the education system. These can include former and prospective pupils and their parents, prospective staff, the local community, commerce and industry, the Local Education Authority and other educational institutions. In the wider context there would be national bodies such as the Teacher Training Agency, the General Teaching Council and the Office for Standards in Education (OFSTED).

Preference surveys

In countries which offer parents and pupils a choice of schools, the very survival of the school depends on taking account of their values and-
preferences (or wants). An awareness of preferences allows the school to
develop appropriate activities and then to target those most likely to benefit.
It avoids the school falling into the trap of 'producer capture' in which the
deliverers determine the product without reference to the consumers. It is,
however, important for educational leaders to avoid the reactive approach in
which an over-emphasis is given to a wide spectrum of consumer demands
so that the educational needs of children are not being met.

In its strategic analysis, the school must gather information on the *preferences (or wants)* of the various client groups. It would not be possible or
appropriate to react to all the preferences expressed. If school leaders are fully
informed about clients' preferences, they are then able to adjust provision if
it is inappropriate or to communicate more effectively the existing provision.

When examining parental wants there should be a examination of current
wants and future possible wants or preferences. This can be achieved by:

■ interviews;
■ focus groups
■ questionnaires;
■ secondary data available locally or from national statistics and research
  projects.

Research by West (1992) showed that middle class parents who chose schools
in a different LEA to their home did so because of their perceptions of discipline, good examination results and a pleasant atmosphere. The research by
Glatter, Woods and Bagley (1995) which covered a range of types of school,
socio-economic circumstances and area demonstrated that parents have
common priorities when choosing schools:

■ child's preference for the school;
■ standard of academic education;
■ nearness to home/convenience for travel;
■ child's happiness at the school.

The core business of the school is to meet the *needs* of the pupils so it is
important to identify these clearly. The school must ensure that it has efficient ways of bringing together a wide range of data and information, much
of it from school records.

In order to ensure that the school develops the capability to meet the
pupil needs, there must be an analysis of the developmental requirements
(for knowledge, skills and understanding) of the other internal clients such as
the staff and governors.

Analyse the school's product and service

The product and service of a school needs to be analysed in its broadest sense. While much of the professional focus will be on the curriculum and assessment, those outside the school may make their judgements based on the effectiveness of communications, pupil behaviour and the possession by the pupils of basic and social skills. In planning an analysis of its product and service, all the school's provision should be listed, especially bearing in mind those areas which the clients feel are its significant activities. This would include:

- the formal curriculum;
- learning and teaching strategies used (in terms of range and effectiveness);
- measures of literacy, numeracy and cognitive ability;
- assessment and testing processes;
- ability and attainment levels on entry and exit;
- numbers with special educational needs;
- results from key stages and GCSE/A-level;
- calculations of value-added – over time, by individuals, teachers and pupils, by teams and in proportion to resources;
- extra-curricular activities;
- pupil discipline and appearance;
- relationships;
- resources levels and utilisation of resources – time, materials, hardware;
- staff skills and abilities in terms of learning and teaching skills and experience;
- perceptions of the pupil experience from the customer viewpoint;
- environment;
- ethos.

Various tools and techniques are available to analyse the situation in each area. The suitability of each will depend on a range of factors such as the time available, the people to be involved and the culture of the organisation.

SWOT analysis

This commonly used tool provides an analysis of the strengths and weaknesses of the school, the opportunities which are available and the threats which it faces, as perceived by a range of stakeholders. This is a quick and easy means of gathering information although it must be interpreted with care. The process is more fully developed in our book *Strategic Marketing for Schools* (Davies and Ellison 1997b). We also use the technique later in this chapter as a means of integrating and interpreting data.

Guidelines for Review and Internal Development in Schools (GRIDS)

This process provides a detailed and structured school-based review process which can be used to gain the involvement and commitment of staff (see Abbott *et al.* 1988).

Attitude surveys

These will enable the school to assess the perceptions which the existing and potential customers have of education in general and of the school in particular. If information gathered is to be valid, school leaders must give serious thought to the data collection process and to anonymity. We have been involved in different research projects in this area. In one, a group of schools wanted more information on the drift of pupils to another group of schools (see Davies and Ellison 1993). Another project involved us in working with each school to investigate the perceptions of a large number of pupils, their parents and all the staff (see Davies and Ellison 1997b).

Internal monitoring and evaluation

These processes would take place as part of the school's normal management cycle and would provide an ongoing source of information for the planning process.

External inspection

All maintained schools in England and Wales have now been inspected by OFSTED and, in many cases, by others brought in to give an external perspective. The reports provide a wealth of data which can be built into the planning process. In the case of an OFSTED inspection, the school has to draw up an Action Plan and this will form an integral part of the school's normal planning process.

We feel that it is important to strike a cautionary note about the need to find out what the clients *really* think, rather than to make assumptions about their perceptions of the school's product and service. Also, these perceptions may not reflect the reality in the school but be the result of poor communication. Further investigation may be needed and a range of clients should be considered because different clients and client groups will have a different perception of the same aspect of provision.

Analyse the competitors

The information gathered about competitors and potential competitors can be very significant in determining the appropriate strategic direction of the school. There are considerable issues here because of parental choice, developments in the learning technology and changes in the funding of education and in the continuum of education itself.

There is a tendency to see local schools as the competitors but the traditional product and service of the school can now, and increasingly will in the future, be offered by a range of other 'providers' such as satellite, the World Wide Web, the National Grid for Learning, private agencies, industry and commerce, parents and the community. The conclusion to be drawn here is that any analysis of competitors must go far beyond the usual brief consideration of what 'the school down the road' is doing. Using concepts developed by Porter (1980) and Bowman and Asch (1987), we have developed a framework for analysing a school's competitors (see Figure 11.1). We believe that the existing and potential new providers of education can pose a threat to the school while the various stakeholders exercise power. It is important to analyse the nature of these threats and power relationships in order to be proactive in planning the school's response.

Each of the four areas will now be discussed.

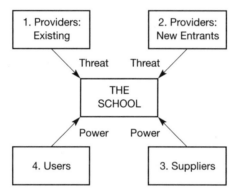

Figure 11.1 *Competitive forces on the school*
Source: Adatpted from Davies and Ellison (1997b, p.59)

Existing providers

It is important to analyse schools that are in the immediate environment as they exert power in the form of rivalry. Many schools need to look beyond the immediate area as rivals such as independent schools and those specialising in the performing arts draw from a wider catchment area.

New entrants

In the rapidly changing environment, schools as learning organisations are increasingly under threat as alternatives emerge from which pupils and their parents may choose. Sometimes these are new schools or developments of existing schools such as the move into a different age range. More often, in times of constrained resources for public expenditure and teacher recruitment problems, the competition comes from alternative forms of education. Home schooling becomes more feasible as information technology becomes more sophisticated and able to provide curriculum programmes, learning resources, links to other organisations and so on. It is useful for senior leaders in the school to consider the position from the new entrant's point of view, asking such questions as 'Why does the new entrant feel that there is a demand for the product or service? Or 'How does the new entrant perceive the existing providers?' Another interesting perspective is that of the pupils and parents: they often have very positive views, seeing a new provider as offering an exciting alternative.

Schools need to consider whether they can turn threats into opportunities by integrating the ideas into their own provision or whether they should compete based on other stregnths. There is a need to think creatively and to look beyond education for trends which can be ascertained from the broader changes in the economy and technology.

Suppliers

Suppliers of goods or labour to the school can exert a powerful force so it is important to bear them in mind during strategic analysis. Analysis of the situation will allow the school to make appropriate plans or develop strategic intent to ensure that cost-effective supplies of goods and labour are available and that it is not driven by such powers.

Users

A school is mainly funded on a *per capita* basis so that an appropriate number of 'users' in the form of pupils or other funded learners is critical to its ability to remain cost-effective and 'in business'. It might be useful to consider here the nature of the power which users hold. If, for example, there are several ways of obtaining a similar type of education, then it is easy for users to change and they are quite powerful. Thus, issues such as a differentiated curriculum and a lack of geographical competitors weaken the power of the user. Conversely, a national curriculum, an effective transport system (or parents to act as 'chauffeurs') or a technology-based alternative strengthen the power of the user.

The users of the output of education, i.e. other schools, the community and employers, exert power on schools. It is important to analyse their requirements in order to inform strategic developments.

Building an aggregated strategic view

Once all the information has been gathered together, it needs to be organised in some useful way in order to inform the choice of direction for the school. There are many ways in which this *integration* of information can be achieved. We describe below the use of five tools or models which we have chosen because they have proved useful to a variety of school leaders with whom we have worked:

1 Boston Consulting Group matrix
2 General Electric Screen
3 Macro SWOT
4 Kawasaki's matrix
5 Little's lifecycle portfolio matrix

Each of the models allows the school to build up a rounded picture which can promote discussion about developments. In order for the pattern built up to be valid, the planning team or senior management team must consider the information from a range of sources and perspectives. If a balanced view does not appear to be available, it will be necessary to return to the data gathering process. It is not intended that this approach is used for on-going maintenance activities but for new areas for expansion, areas for regeneration or for close-down. The models represent different types in that some do little to suggest the way forward but simply piece together information whereas others suggest strategies which might be adopted by the school. The reader can use one or more of these models to build up a strategic picture of the school.

1 Boston Consulting Group matrix

The Boston Consulting Group (BCG) matrix was devised for the analysis of strategic positioning and strategic development in business units within large companies. We believe that the process can usefully be employed to bring together information about strategic positioning and strategic possibilities within a school. The matrix is shown in Figure 11.2 and can be explained as follows:

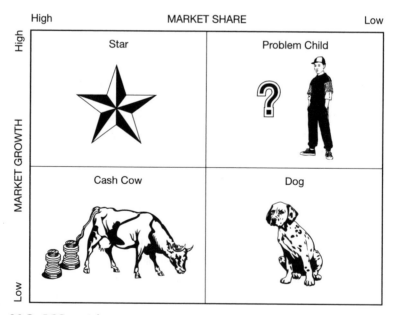

Figure 11.2 *BCG matrix*

- A product can be defined as a *star* if it has a high market share in a growing market. In the case of stars, the product may be supported by considerable investment. This is felt to be worthwhile in order to maintain the lead in the market.
- A product is considered to be a *problem* child (or question mark) if it is positioned in a growing market but there is doubt whether the product will be successful in terms of its competition with other products. Thus, if a large amount of resource is expended and the success of that investment is not yet known then the product may end up as a star (if successful) or a dog (if unsuccessful). At the present time a question mark hangs over that investment. Many new product launches are in this category initially.
- A *cash cow* has a high market share in a mature, low growth market. Little investment is needed in these more stable conditions and, because of the high market share, unit costs should remain below those of the competitors. The products that are cash cows therefore bring in more income than they expend so that they provide the 'cash' to maintain the products in the other segments of the matrix.
- *Dogs* are in the unfortunate position of having a low market share in a stable or declining market. They tend to drain human and financial resources, largely because of diseconomies of scale and, therefore, high unit costs.

A school using this BCG approach would use the strategic data which it has obtained in order to locate its products on the matrix. Although, for convenience, we have placed items in discrete quadrants, in practice a product may be located on the borderline between two or more quadrants. In our case examples for secondary and primary schools, we have identified several school 'products' and located them on the matrix.

Case example 11.2: secondary school BCG

The school has experienced a sustained and significant increase in pupils in the sixth form studying psychology. This could be considered to be a star product as there seems to be a growing market for this subject for a wide variety of careers and, within the range of A levels offered, it is taking an increasing share of option preferences. There are significant indications that more pupils are staying on because this option is available in the school.

The school's problem child is its move to develop a greater focus on independent learning for pupils using various forms of information technology. At the moment it is a growing area with more and more quality software and other applications becoming available. The school is, however, having to invest heavily in this development when it is short of resources. Also, the reluctance of teachers and parents to see this as an alternative to traditional teaching has meant that it takes a very low share of total learning and teaching time. Either the move to develop this area will lead to a significant expansion of both the range and quality of learning opportunities or it will become an expensive bolt-on facility to the traditional learning curriculum.

The cash cows can be considered to be GCSE teaching in English and maths. The school is increasingly being judged on its literacy and numeracy outcomes at 16. Quality provision in these two subjects will ensure continued parental choice of the school and, hence, funding through the pupil unit component of the school budget.

Like many organisations, the school has a few products which might be classified as 'dogs'. Here it is the school meals service. The school is situated near the middle of the town centre and pupils can choose from many alternative food sources at lunchtime. The present meals service is seen as expensive and the choices offered do not meet pupil expectations.

Stars A level Psychology	Problem Children IT based independent learning
Cash Cows GCSE English and Maths teaching Years 10–11	Dogs School meals

Figure 11.3 *BCG matrix: secondary example*

Case example 11.3: primary school BCG

The star, as far as the school is concerned, is its information technology provision. It has invested heavily in turning its library area into a learning resource centre with a significant number of multi-media machines linked to the Internet. It has also organised a deal with a computer supplier for parents to buy a lap-top computer for their children over a three-year period. It is seen by parents as the leading school in the growing area of technology and, as a result is significantly oversubscribed

The problem child for this school is its literacy programme. Decisions are needed about the most effective way to proceed as other schools already have a significant advantage in this area. The school has no option as to whether to develop this area so it must decide where to invest its resources to achieve high levels of literacy, especially for those whose reading age is below their chronological age. It is investigating several approaches. These options have considerable resource implications but should achieve significantly higher literacy scores in the government's target setting process. The key questions to resolve, however, concern which option or combination and at what resource level.

The school's cash cow is basic numeracy. The school has excellent learning schemes and achieves very good results in this area at Key Stage 1. As a result it retains a good impression with parents and secures an excellent intake for the school.

The dog product in this school is peripatetic music. The whole concept of extracting pupils for music tuition is disliked by children but the tutors are not available at any other time. Parents are increasingly disatisfied with the quality of provision and the lack of stability of staffing so they are seeking alternative provision in the community. The school will need to decide whether this area is worthwhile now that the government requires the school to focus on literacy and numeracy.

Stars Information technology	**Problem Children** Reading recovery programmes
Cash Cows Basic numeracy teaching up to Key Stage 1	**Dogs** Peripatetic music

Figure 11.4 *BCG matrix: primary example*

The use of the BCG matrix

In both the primary and secondary examples, the strategic purpose of the activity is threefold. First, it provides a means of integrating the data gathered in the strategic analysis in order to determine the current position of key elements of the school's activities. Second, it focuses attention on action that needs to be undertaken to maintain star positioning, to ensure that problem children move to the left and not down to the dog category, to reinforce the core cash cow activities and, finally, to either damage limit or eliminate items in the dog category. Third, the matrix can be used as a means of articulating what the school believes its products will be in five years' time and which categories they will be in; most significantly it should identify the problem children that require investment and development in the near future.

2 General Electric Screen

The General Electric (GE) Screen or Industry Attractiveness Matrix can be used by a school as a tool for gaining an aggregated strategic view of its position. It allows the school to analyse its provision against two categories of factors:

Factors relating to sector/market attractiveness:	Factors relating to relative business strength:
market size	relative market share
profit margins	management skills
competition	product/service quality
growth rate	reputation
supplier power	location

Case example 11.4: a GE Screen for a primary school

Brentwich Primary School has interpreted the business descriptors into the educational framework shown in Figures 11.5 and 11.6.

Sector/Market Attractiveness	Interpreted Criteria
Market size	The number of pupils starting school over the next 5 years
Profit margins	Results in (i) literacy and numeracy (ii) Key Stage 1 and 2 results
Competition	Other competing primary schools – state and independent
Growth rate	Increase in value-added
Supplier (or client) power	Parental and community attitude to the school

Figure 11.5 *Market attractiveness criteria for Brentwich Primary School*

Relative Business Strength	Interpreted Criteria
Relative market share	Percentage of pupils in the catchment area attending the school
Management skills	Leadership and management skills of senior staff and subject leaders
Product/service quality	Quality of learning and teaching
Reputation	Reputation of the school in the community and media
Location	The attractiveness of the school's situation

Figure 11.6 *Relative business strength criteria for Brentwich Primary School*

As part of the strategic analysis, the school collected data from four groups: the senior management team, classroom teachers, the parents and the governors and asked them to rate the school on a 1–10 scale on each of the criteria. The outcomes were as shown in Figures 11.7 and 11.8.

	Senior Management Team	Teachers	Parents	Governors
Market size	8	8	6	6
Results (profit margins)	7	7	4	5
Competition	6	5	8	5
Growth rate	7	8	6	5
Supplier (or client) power	8	7	6	7

Figure 11.7 *GE Screen analysis for Brentwich Primary School – market attractiveness*

	Senior Management Team	Teachers	Parents	Govenors
Relative market share	5	7	6	5
Management skills	7	7	4	4
Product/service quality	4	7	6	4
Reputation	7	6	7	6
Location	4	3	8	5

Figure 11.8 *GE Screen analysis for Brentwich Primary School – relative business strength*

The school should focus on where there are low scores or, very significantly, where there is a different perception by the different groups. Examples of the differences would be the perception of the results of the school between the senior management and teachers on one side and the parents and governors on the other. This would merit serious attention as would management skills. It can be seen that this tool not only provides a means of bringing together the data and highlighting areas for attention in terms of high and low scores but it shows the different perceptions of the various stakeholder groups.

3 Macro SWOT

Many schools or subject areas have used a SWOT analysis which considers strengths, weaknesses, opportunities and threats. Usually, the strengths and weaknesses are related to internal factors and the opportunities and threats relate to the external environment. The tool can be used as a method for drawing together information from a variety of techniques – a macro approach – as well as in the usual way to focus on a particular product or aspect of provision. A SWOT format can be used to compile a macro picture from all the evidence gained through strategic analysis. This does not simply involve filling in the details from the data, but requires that senior leaders in the school consider the validity of the data gathered so that it provides valuable information. It is thus a more rational approach than the subjective use of the tool simply to gather stakeholders' perceptions.

The SWOT approach is quick and easy and does not require any special skill or equipment in order to carry it out or to analyse it. The tool can be made more sophisticated by introducing sub-categories against which to place the information. This overcomes the criticism that, because of their diversity the results cannot easily be summarised or aggregated. The information is not weighted so care must be taken in interpretation otherwise minor and major issues may be given equal prominence. Unlike Little's Lifecycle Analysis (see p.178), the process does not suggest any strategies – other than the possibility of turning weaknesses into strengths and threats into opportunities.

In our case example, we have used some of the sub-categories which we suggest earlier in this chapter as aspects of the school's provision which should be covered by the data-gathering process.

Internal factors	External factors
■ Curriculum	■ Political, legal and economic factors
■ Learning and teaching	■ Central/local educational changes
■ Assessment and results	■ Demographic and socio-cultural trends
■ Extra-curricular activities	■ Employment trends
■ Discipline and appearance	■ Technology
■ Financial resources	■ Customers
■ Premises	■ Other providers
■ Staffing, staff skills and abilities	
■ Governors	
■ Ethos/culture	

Case example 11.5: a SWOT matrix for Shrewbridge School

At Shrewbridge School, the data gathering exercise has been summarised in the chart shown in Figure 11.9.

	Strengths	**Weaknesses**
Curriculum	Literacy and language	Creative arts Numeracy
Learning and teaching	Variety of approaches and resources available	Differentiation Extension materials for the more able
Assessment and results	Good use of baseline entry data Steadily rising results in English	Targeting of individuals Maths results level over last 3 years
Extra-curricular activities	Sport	Few music or drama activities
Discipline and appearance	Clear behaviour policy	Inconsistent application of rewards and sanctions Unclear uniform policy
Financial resources	Balanced budget over last 2 years PTA income £3000 per year	Lack of partnership with community to attract other funds
Premises	Welcoming entrance and reception area	Toliets need refurbishing
Staffing, staff skills and abilities	Stable staff with a little turnover	Inconsistent application of policies
Governors	Regularly attend meetings and school functions	Staff unhappy about their presence in lessons
Ethos/culture	Happy, willing pupils	Lack of shared vision and values, especially amongst staff
	Opportunities	**Threats**
Political, legal and economic factors	Targeted-funds and support for numeracy	Fewer quality teachers entering or remaining in the profession
Central/local educational changes	Further rationalisation of the core curriculum	Possibility of a new school on the other boundary of the estate Increased focus on achievement of numeracy targets
Demographic and socio-cultural trends	New estate and new industrial complex should increase the local population	Cost of houses may mitigate against the families who might use this school
Employment trends	New developments in the area	Workers may commute because of the cost of housing
Technology	To harness technology to raise standards of numeracy	Cost and lack of staff skills
Customers	Community networks available to improve communication	Pressure to provide a wider range of art, music and drama facilities
Other providers	Dissemination of literacy skills to other providers within the region	Community perceptions and hopes of a new school

Figure 11.9 *Completed SWOT matrix*

4 Kawasaki's matrix

In his book *How to Drive the Competition Crazy*, Guy Kawasaki (1995) draws on a number of his experiences from the corporate world with Apple Computers. We have adapted one of his models to use as a strategic analysis tool. We use it to interpret data into what could be considered a feasible/desirable dimension which can be seen to operate as a matrix where the school's ability to provide (feasible) with the perceived value to the client (desirable) are set against one another as in Figure 11.10.

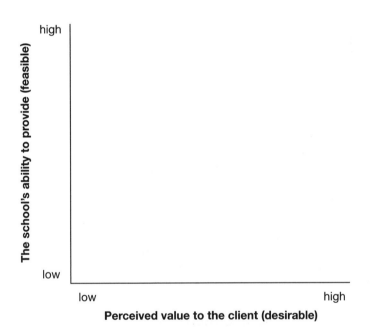

Figure 11.10 *Kawasaki's matrix*
Source: Davies and Ellison, 1997, p. 216; adapted from Kawasaki, 1995, P. 76; itself based on Richey, 1994, pp. 47–51. Excerpted by permission of the original publisher, from *the Marketer's Visual Tool Kit* by Terry Richey. © 1994 Timberline Strategies Inc. Published by AMACOM, a division of American Management Association. All rights reserved.

Case example 11.6: a Kawasaki analysis of Lincoln School's provision

In Lincoln School the ability to provide sufficient high quality information technology facilities is moderate while parental expectations in this area are high.

Similarly, while parents may consider Saturday morning games as very desirable, the ability of the school to persuade staff to work on Saturday mornings is limited. The school can offer after-school music provision to a high standard and parents are happy with this. This situation is summarised in Figure 11.11.

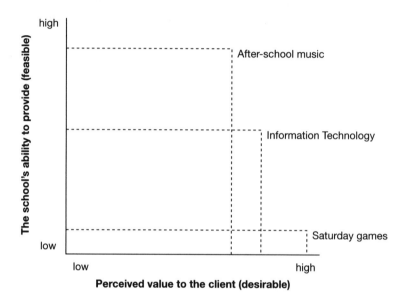

Figure 11.11 *Matching provision and parental expectations*

This type of analysis not only relates the strategic position between provider and receiver but defines the feasibility and suitablity of such an option.

5 Little's Lifecycle Portfolio matrix

The Arthur D. Little organisation developed this matrix which is used in commerce and industry. When working with senior managers in schools who already have quite a high level of understanding of the planning process, we have found this tool to be of particular value. It provides a new way of assembling information and, rightly, promotes considerable discussion about the way forward.

A number of factors are considered and information is placed on one of the two axes of a matrix. When examining a particular aspect of provision, the vertical axis relates to the *competitive position* of the school in relation to other relevant educational provision. The descriptors for this position are: dominant, strong, favourable, tenable or weak. The horizontal axis relates to the *stages of maturity* of the aspect of provision being considered. The descriptors here range from embryonic through growth and mature to ageing. Thus, a blank matrix

	Stages of Maturity			
	Embryonic	**Growth**	**Mature**	**Ageing**
Dominant				
Strong				
Favourable				
Tenable				
Weak				

Competitive position →

Figure 11.12 *Little's Lifecycle Portfolio matrix*

looks like Figure 11.12.

The criteria by which the positions are determined for the *competitive position* axis are:

Dominant:	The organisation often has a quasi-legalised monopoly status.
Strong:	The organisation can follow its own strategies without concern about the competition.
Favourable:	The organisation is one of several leaders.
Tenable:	The organisation's position can be maintained by specialisation or focus.
Weak:	The organisation is too small to survive independently in the long term.

The criteria by which the positions are determined for the *stages of maturity* axis are:

Market growth rate   Spread of market share between competitors
Growth potential   Customer loyalty
Breadth of product lines   Entry barriers
Number of competitors   Technology

The stages of maturity are thus characterised as:

Embryonic: through *growth* and *mature* to: *Ageing:*

- Rapid growth
- Changes in technology
- Fragmented market shares
- Pursuit of new customers

- Falling demand
- Declining number of customers and competitors
- Narrow product line

The Little organisation goes on to suggest strategies for products or services which are located in certain sectors of the matrix. We have adapted their suggestions in the grid in Figure 11.13.

		Stages of Maturity		
	Embryonic	**Growth**	**Mature**	**Ageing**
Dominant	Grow quickly	Grow quickly Attain cost leadership Defend position	Defend position Attain cost leadership Revitalise Grow quickly	Defend position Focus Revitalise
Strong	Differentiate Grow quickly	Grow quickly Catch up Attain cost leadership Differentiate	Attain cost leadership Revitalise Differentiate/ focus Grow with other providers	Hold niche Find niche Hang-in
Favourable	Differentiate Focus Grow quickly	Differentiate/ focus Catch-up Grow with other providers	Hold niche, hang-in Differentiate/ focus/find niche Revitalise Turnaround performance Grow with other providers	Retrench Turnaround performance
Tenable	Grow with other providers Focus	Catch-up Hold niche, hang-in Focus or find niche Turnaround performance Grow with other providers	Turnaround performance Find niche Retrench	Divest parts of the work Retrench
Weak	Find niche Catch-up Grow with other providers	Turnaround performance Retrench	Withdraw entirely Divest parts of the work	Withdraw entirely

Competitive Position

Figure 11.13 *Strategies suggested by Little's Lifecycle Portfolio matrix*

A school would use the matrix to consider an area of its work, such as after-school provision or A level Music. At the local level, the concept could also be used to analyse the position of each school in the district. Whatever the case, the position on the matrix suggests alternative strategies which might be appropriate. The examples below show how this might work in practice.

Case example 11.7: nursery provision for 0 to 4 year-olds on a primary or secondary school site

Greenfield School has a nursery unit which occupies a spare classroom. The nursery has an excellent reputation for developing literacy and numeracy skills. Over the last two years it has proved difficult to recruit good teachers to the main school but the presence of the nursery has been a deciding factor for several staff whose children are aged 0 to 3. Greenfield's position near a commuter station offers significant opportunities. The caretaker's house is available should extra space be needed.

1 *Decide on the aspect* under consideration, in this case the nursery.

2 Using the information gathered from a range of sources during strategic analysis, *decide on the competitive position* of the nursery.

The nursery is one of several in the area which have been quite successful in the last three years in terms of recruitment and reputation. This puts it in a *favourable* position.

3 *Decide the stage of maturity* of the nursery age market in your area.

There seems to be some potential *growth* in this age range because of government initiatives related to education and to women in the workforce.

4 *Place* the nursery *on the matrix*.

In this example, the nursery would be placed at point 1 on Figure 11.14. It may also be appropriate to mark with an arrow the direction in which the aspect of provision seems to be moving on the matrix. The model now offers possible strategies according to the position in the matrix.

5 *Examine the suggested strategies*.

The matrix in Figure 11.13 would suggest that this school should differentiate/focus, catch-up or grow with other providers.

Case example 11.8: GNVQ leisure and tourism

Redroof School has been running GNVQ courses in Business and Finance for three years and started Leisure and Tourism last year. The local FE college has been offering the latter course for two years and has a significant reputation for its provision.

1 *Decide on the aspect* under consideration, in this case the GNVQ Leisure and Tourism.

2 Using the information gathered from a range of sources during strategic analysis, *decide on the competitive position* of this course.

The school has little experience in this subject area. This puts it in a *tenable* position in terms of student recruitment and staff competence.

3 *Decide the stage of maturity* of the market for this course in your area.

This is a relatively new aspect of provision with the likelihood of considerable growth. This places the course in the *embryonic* category.

4 *Place* the course *on the matrix.*

In this example, the course would be placed at point 2 on Figure 11.14. It may also be appropriate to mark with an arrow the direction in which the aspect of provision seems to be moving on the matrix. The model now offers possible strategies according to the position in the matrix.

Competitive Position	Stages of Maturity			
	Embryonic	Growth	Mature	Ageing
Dominant				
Strong				
Favourable		①		
Tenable	②			
Weak				

Figure 11.14 *Positioning the examples of the Lifecycle Portfolio matrix*

5 *Examine the suggested stategies.*

The matrix in Figure 11.13 would suggest that this school should grow with the other providers or focus.

Information from other tools in this section should assist the school to further define the situation and help to focus the decision-making process.

The matrix can now be used to plot the position of the various aspects of your school's provision in order to stimulate debate and discussion about possible strategic options.

Conclusion

This chapter has shown, initially, how to collect data and, in the second part, how to put that data into a usable, analysable form through deploying five strategic analysis tools. It is possible to use some or all of these, although we feel that, in order to obtain a balanced view, schools should use at least three of the tools so that they can bring together information in different sorts of formats.

The first three strategic tools provide three key functions. They provide a means of integrating the data gathered in the data gathering exercises in order to show the current position of key elements of the school's activities. They focus attention on action that might be needed in order to achieve organisational success and they help to articulate what the school believes its strategic direction and products should be in the future.

The fourth tool, Kawasaki's matrix, helps to position various strategic options on a feasibility/desirability dimension which will lead into the choice process. Finally, readers may find Little's Lifecycle Analysis useful in order to suggest strategies which the school could pursue in a range of situations.

References

Abbott, R., Steadman S. and Birchenhough M. (1988) *GRIDS School Handbooks*, 2nd edn, Primary and Secondary versions, York: Longman for the SCDC.

Bowman, C. and Asch, D. (1987) *Strategic Management*, Basingstoke: Macmillan.

Davies, B. (1997) 'Rethinking the educational context: a reengineering approach' in B. Davies and L. Ellison, *School Leadership for the 21st Century: A Competency and Knowledge Approach*, London: Routledge.

Davies, B. and Ellison, L. (1993) 'Parental Choice and School Response', paper presented at the British Educational Management and Aministration Society, National Research Conference, Sheffield, February.

Davies, B. and Ellison, L. (1997a) *School Leadership for the 21st Century: A Competency and Knowledge Approach*, London: Routledge.

Davies, B. and Ellison, L. (1997b) *Strategic Marketing for Schools*, London: Pitman.

Glatter, R., Woods, P. and Bagley, C. (1995) *Diversity, Differentiation and Hierarchy: School Choice and Parental Preferences*, ESRC/CEPAM Invitation Seminar, Milton Keynes, 7–8 June.

Kawasaki, G. (1995) *How to Drive the Competition Crazy*, New York: Hyperion.

Porter, M. (1980) *Competitive Strategy*, New York: Free Press.

West, A. (1992) 'Factors affecting choice of school for middle class parents: implications for marketing', *Educational Management and Aministration*, Vol. 20 No. 4: 223–30.

12

Planning, Doing, and Coping with Change

Michael Fullan

> Few, if any, strategies can be purely deliberative, and few can be purely emergent. One suggests no learning the other, no control.
>
> – Mintzberg (1994, p. 25)

For the growing number of people who have attempted to bring about educational change, 'intractability' is becoming a household word. Being ungovernable, however, is not the same as being impervious to influence. And the inability to change *all* situations we would ideally like to reform does not lead to the conclusion that *no* situation can be changed.

Why Planning Fails

> We trained hard . . . but it seemed every time we were beginning to form up into teams we were reorganized. I was to learn later in life that we tend to meet any situation by reorganizing, and what a wonderful method it can be for creating the illusion of progress while producing confusion, inefficiency, and demoralization.
>
> – Gaius Petronius, A.D. 66 cited in Gaynor, 1977

Understanding why most attempts at educational reform fail goes far beyond the identification of specific technical problems such as lack of good materials, ineffective professional development, or minimal administrative support. In more fundamental terms, educational change fails partly because of the

---

Source: Fullan, M. (2001) *The New Meaning of Educational Change*, 3rd edition. London: RoutledgeFalmer. Edited version.

assumptions of planners, and partly because solving substantial problems is an inherently complex business. These two issues are explored in the next two subsections.

Faulty assumptions and ways of thinking about change

There are three interrelated reasons why most planning fails. It is hyperrational; it fails to take into account local context and culture; it is dangerously seductive and incomplete. In a word, the assumptions of policymakers are frequently *hyperrational* (Wise, 1977, 1988). One of the initial sources of the problem is the commitment of reformers to see a particular desired change implemented. Commitment to *what should be changed* often varies inversely with knowledge about *how to work through a process of change*. In fact, as I shall claim later, strong commitment to a particular change may be a barrier to setting up an effective process of change, and in any case they are two quite distinct aspects of social change. The adage 'Where there's a will there's a way' is not always an apt one for the planning of educational change. There is an abundance of wills, but they are *in* the way rather than pointing the way. As we have seen, a certain amount of vision is required to provide the clarity and energy for promoting specific changes, but vision by itself may get in the way if it results in impatience, failure to listen, etc. Stated in a more balanced way, promoters of change need to be committed and skilled in the *change process* as well as in the change itself.

Lighthall's (1973) incisive critique of Smith and Keith's (1971) famous case study of the failure of a new open-concept elementary school provides strong support for the hypothesis that leadership commitment to a particular version of a change is negatively related to ability to implement it. Lighthall states that educational change is a process of coming to grips with the *multiple* realities of people, who are the main participants in implementing change. The leader who presupposes what the change should be and acts in ways that preclude others' realities is bound to fail. Lighthall describes Superintendent Spanman's first speech to the Kensington school faculty.

> Spanmans's visit to Kensington School was to make a presentation to the 21-member faculty. It was not for the purpose of discussing with them their joint problems of creating a whole new kind of education. His purpose was to express to the faculty parts of his reality; it was not to exchange his for theirs. Inasmuch as it was the faculty who were to carry the educational goals and images of his reality into action – that is, to make much of his reality their realities, too – and inasmuch as no person responds to realities other than his own, Spanman's selection of a one-way form of communication was self-defeating. In order for his reality to become part of theirs he would have to have made part of theirs his (p. 263).

Innovators who are unable to alter their realities of change through exchange with would-be implementers can be as authoritarian as the staunchest defenders of the status quo. This is not to say that innovators should not have deep convictions about the need for reform or should be prepared to abandon their ideas at the first sign of opposition. Rather, innovators need to be open to the realities of others: sometimes because the ideas of others will lead to alterations for the better in the direction of change, and sometimes because the others' realities will expose the problems of implementation that must be addressed and at the very least will indicate where one should start.

Lighthall documents how the superintendent and principal at Kensington continually imposed only their own realities and how their stance led in a relatively short time to disastrous results. Lighthall (1973) observed: 'The tendency is widespread for problem-solvers to try to jump from their private plans to public implementation of these plans without going through the [number of realities] necessary to fashion them in accordance with problems felt by the adult humans whose energy and intelligence are needed to implement the plans' (p. 282). Sarason (1971) states it another way: 'An understandable but unfortunate way of thinking confuses the power (in a legal or organizational chart sense) to effect change with the process of change' (p. 29). In short, one of the basic reasons why planning fails is that planners or decision makers of change are unaware of the situations faced by potential implementers. They introduce changes without providing a means to identify and confront the situational constraints and without attempting to understand the values, ideas, and experiences of those who are essential for implementing any changes.

But what is wrong with having a strong belief that a certain aspect of schooling should be changed? Is it not appropriately rational to know that a given change is necessary and to make it policy if one is in a position to do so? Aside from the fact that many new programs do not arise from sound considerations, there are other more serious problems. The first problem is that there are many competing versions of what should be done, with each set of proponents equally convinced that their version is the right one. Forceful argument and even the power to make decisions do not at all address questions related to the process of implementation. The fallacy of rationalism is the assumption that the social world can be altered by seemingly logical argument. The problem, as George Bernard Shaw observed, is that 'reformers have the idea that change can be achieved by brute sanity'.

Wise (1977) also describes several examples of excessive rationalization, as when educational outcomes are thoroughly prescribed (e.g., in competency-based education) without any feasible plan of how to achieve them. Wise characterizes the behavior of some policymakers as wishful thinking: 'When policy makers require by law that schools achieve a goal which in the past they have not achieved, they may be engaged in wishful thinking. Here policy makers behave as though their desires concerning what a school system should accomplish, will in fact, be accomplished if the policy makers simply decree it' (p. 45). Wise goes on to argue that even if rational theories of education were better developed – with goals clearly stated, means of implementation set out, evaluation procedures stated – they would not have much of an impact, because schools, like any social organization, do not operate in a rational vacuum. Some may say that they should, but Wise's point is that they do not, and wishing them to do so shows a misunderstanding of the existing culture of the school.

The second missing element is the failure of reformers to go to the trouble of treating local context and culture as vital. Micklethwait and Wooldridge (1996) remind us that policymakers often impose ideas without taking into account local context, and that they are very vulnerable to quick fixes. Senge and associates (1999) make a similar point:

> The fundamental flaw in most innovators' strategies is that they focus on their innovations, on what they are trying to do – rather than on understanding how the larger culture, structures, and norms will react to their efforts. (p. 26)

In *What's Worth Fighting for Out There*, Hargreaves and I (1998) argued that we need to take a very different planning approach to so-called resisters because (1) they may have some good ideas, and (2) you ignore them at your peril if they stay around for implementation. There are, in other words, good technical and political reasons for taking resisters more seriously. In some cases, resistance may be a source of learning. Resisters may be right. They may have 'good sense' in seeing through the change as faddish, misdirected, and unworkable (Gitlin & Margonis, 1995). Thus, resistance to change can be instructive. As Maurer (1996) observes:

> Often those who resist have something important to tell us. We can be influenced by them. People resist for what they view as good reasons. They may see alternatives we never dreamed of. They may understand problems about the minutiae of implementation that we never see from our lofty perch atop Mount Olympus. (Maurer, 1996, p. 49)

In a similar vein, according to Heifetz (1994), a counterintuitive rule of thumb is required in order to reject 'one's emotional impulse . . . to squash those in the community who raise disturbing questions. Consequently, an authority should protect those whom he [or she] wants to silence. Annoyance is often a signal of opportunity' (p. 271). It is a mistake for principals to go only with like-minded innovators. As Elmore (1995) puts it: '[S]mall groups of self-selected reformers apparently seldom influence their peers' (p. 20). They just create an even greater gap between themselves and others that eventually becomes impossible to bridge.

This is not to say that resistance should carry the day, but rather that we need more powerful and sensitive strategies to help instigate the learning and commitment that is necessary for actual implementation and sustained impact.

A third serious flaw concerns the seductive nature of planning when one is aching for a clear solution to urgent problems. Our first guideline for action for principals (and all leaders) is 'steer clear of false certainty' (Hargreaves and Fullan, 1998, p. 105). In times of great uncertainty there is an understandable (but dangerous) need to want to know what to do.

Stacey, the 'complexity theorist' explains why:

> We respond to the fact that situations are uncertain and conflictual with a rigid injunction that people be more certain and more consensual . . . This denial of uncertainty itself allows us to sustain the fantasy of someone up there being in control and, perhaps, of things turning out for the best if we simply do what we are told, and so it protects us for a while from anxiety'. However, because that defensive response involves dependency and a flight from reality, it hardly ever works. (Stacey, 1996b, pp. 7–8)

Management, leadership, and change gurus can bring about especially seductive kinds of dependency. Their charismatic authority promises people a way out of the chaos that they feel. Gurus cultivate dependent disciples rather than independent thinkers. In his study of the guru phenomenon, psychiatrist Anthony Storr (1997, p. 223) notes that this is because gurus need the reassurance and sense of certainty that having disciples gives them so they can cope with and put aside their own inner doubts. What disciples get out of the relationship is the comfort of someone else taking responsibility for their decisions. Storr eloquently warns us that 'the charisma of certainty is a snare which entraps the child who is latent in us all'. Disciples of modern gurus, he concludes, are 'looking for what they want in the wrong place'. I think this is what Peter Drucker was getting at when he allegedly said, '[P]eople refer to gurus because they don't know how to spell charlatan'.

False certainty also occurs when you think you have a good idea, but it turns out that it is incomplete. In Hill and Ceho's (1998, pp. 1–10) words, reform theories often have 'zones of wishful thinking'; that is, for the reform to be successful certain things have to happen 'that the reform needs, but cannot cause'. In further work, Hill, Campbell, and Harvey (2000) analyze seven competing reform proposals: standards-based, teacher development, new school designs, decentralization and site-based management, charter schools, school contracting, and vouchers.

In addition to the problem of multiple, disconnected innovation, Hill, Campbell and Harvey conclude:

> We learned that there is a plausible case for each of the proposals: each addresses a real problem and would probably cause real changes in public education if fully implemented.
>
> But we also found that none of the proposals was sufficient because none could deliver all of the changes its proponents intended unless other changes which the proposal itself could not deliver, occurred at the same time. For example, reforms based on teacher training do not create incentives to overcome some teachers' reluctance to put in the time and effort to improve their knowledge and skills. In a similar vein, reforms such as vouchers do not in themselves guarantee that there will be a plentiful supply of high-quality independent school providers or that enough teachers and principals to run such schools exist. (p. 23)

We have, of course, now wandered into the next topic – solving today's educational problem is complex; it *is* rocket science.

Complex problems

Solving complex problems on a continuous basis is enormously difficult because of the sheer number of factors at play. It is further complicated because the *sine qua non* of successful reform is whether *relationships improve*; in fact, we have to learn how to develop relationships with those we might not understand and might not like, and vice versa (Fullan, 2001).

Chaos or complexity theorists put it best:

> Most textbooks focus heavily on techniques and procedures for long-term planning, on the need for visions and missions, on the importance and the means of securing strongly shared cultures, on the equation of success with consensus, consistency, uniformity and order. [However, in complex environments] the real management task is that of coping with and even using unpredictability, clashing counter-cultures, disensus, contention, conflict, and inconsistency. In short, the task that justifies the existence of all managers has to do with instability, irregularity, difference and disorder. (Stacey, 1996a, pp. xix–xx)

Stating the case more fully (and dauntingly), Stacey argues:

A complexity theory of organization is built on the following propositions:

- All organizations are webs of nonlinear feedback loops connected to other people and organizations (its environments) by webs of nonlinear feedback loops.
- Such nonlinear feedback systems are capable of operating in states of stable and unstable equilibrium, or in the borders between these states, that is far-from-equilibrium, in bounded instability at the edge of chaos.
- All organizations are paradoxes. The are powerfully pulled towards stability by, the forces of integration, maintenance controls, human desires for security and certainty, and adaptation to the environment on the one hand. They are also powerfully pulled to the opposite extreme of unstable equilibrium by the forces of division and decentralization, human desires for excitement and innovation, and isolation from the environment.
- If the organization gives in to the pull to stability it fails because it becomes ossified and cannot change easily. If it gives in to the pull to instability it disintegrates. Success lies in sustaining an organization in the borders between stability and instability. This is a state of chaos, a difficult-to-maintain dissipative structure.
- The dynamics of the successful organization are therefore those of irregular cycles and discontinuous trends falling within qualitative patterns. Fuzzy but recognizable categories taking the form of archetypes and templates.
- Because of its own internal dynamics, a successful organization faces completely unknowable specific futures.
- Agents within the system cannot be in control of its long-term future, nor can they install specific frameworks to make it successful, nor can they apply step-by-step analytical reasoning or planning or ideological controls to long-term development. Agents within the system can only do these things in relation to the short term.
- Long-term development is a spontaneously self-organizing process from which new strategic directions may emerge. Spontaneous self-organization is political interaction and learning in groups. Managers have to use reasoning by analogy.
- In this way managers create and discover their environments and the long-term futures of the organizations. (p. 349)

The positive side, or if you like, the 'solution' involves developing learning organizations. In their field book, Senge and colleagues (2000) argue that fiat or command can never solve complex problems; only a learning orientation can:

> This means involving everyone in the system in expressing their aspiration, building their awareness, and developing their capabilities together. In a school that's learning, people who traditionally may have been suspicious of one another – parents and teachers, educators and local business people, administrators and union members, people inside and outside the school walls, students and adults – recognize their common stake in the future of the school system and the things they can learn from one another. (Senge et al., 2000, p. 5)

Complex indeed! Anything else is tinkering.

Success is Possible

Recognizing the limitations of planning is not the same thing as concluding that effective change is unattainable. But in order to determine if planned educational change is possible, it would not be sufficient to locate situations where change seems to be working. We would need to find examples where a setting has been *deliberately transformed* from a previous state to a new one that represents clear improvement. We need to know about the causes and dynamics of how change occurs.

Over the past decade there have been a number of clear examples of how school districts and schools improved the quality of education through a process of deliberate change. The good news is that we have cases at the school level, at the district level and recently at the state level. The bad news is twofold. First, the successful examples are still in the minority in the sense that only a small proportion of schools, districts, and states have been successful in their attempts. The second worry is more disturbing. There is reason to believe that hard-won successes over a period of 5 to 10 years cannot be sustained under current conditions; furthermore, it appears that the accomplishments are real, but superficial. In other words, even the successful cases cannot be expected to last or to be deep.

Be that as it may, successful change is possible in the real world, even under difficult conditions. And many of the reasons for the achievements can be pinpointed. There are classrooms, schools, communities, districts, and states that have altered the conditions for change in more favorable, workable directions. Not every situation is alterable, especially at certain periods of time; but it is a good bet that major improvements can be accomplished in many more settings than is happening at present.

Planning and coping

We have come to the most difficult problem of all. What can we actually do to plan for and cope with educational change? This section contains an overview of the assumptions, elements, and guidelines for action. First, I introduce the topic by indicating some of the basic issues and by noting that advice will have to vary according to the different situations in which we find ourselves. Second, I provide some advice for those who find that they are forced to respond to and cope with change introduced by others. Third, the bulk of the section is addressed to the question of how to plan and implement change more effectively.

In general, there are four logical types of change situation we could face as individuals. These are depicted in Figure 12.1. There are many different specific roles even within a single cell that cannot be delineated here, but people generally find themselves in one of the four situations depending on whether they are initiating/promoting a change or are on the receiving end, and whether or not they are in authority positions. I start with coping, or being on the receiving end of change (cells III and IV), because this is the most prevalent situation.

		Authority position: YES	Authority position: NO
Relation to change effort	Initiator or promoter	I Planner (e.g., policymaker)	II Planner (e.g., developer)
	Recipient or responder	III Coper (e.g., principal)	IV Coper (e.g., teacher)

Figure 12.1 *Change situations according to authority position and relation to the change effort*

Those in situations of having to respond to a particular change should assume neither that it is beneficial nor that it is useless; that much is clear from the previous analysis. The major initial stance should involve *critical assessment*, that is, determining whether the change is desirable in relation to certain goals and whether it is 'implementable' – in brief, whether it is worth the effort, because it *will* be an effort if it is at all worthwhile. Several criteria would be applied: Does the change address an unmet need? Is it a priority in relation to other unmet needs? Is it informed by some desirable sense of vision? Are there adequate (not to say optimal) resources committed to support implementation (such as technical assistance and leadership support)? If the conditions are reasonably favorable, knowledge of the change process outlined in previous chapters could be used to advantage – for example, pushing for technical assistance, opportunities for interaction among teachers, and so on. If the conditions are not favorable or cannot be made favorable, the best coping strategy consists of knowing enough about the process of change so that we can understand why it doesn't work, and therefore not blame ourselves; we can also gain solace by realizing that most other people are in the same situation of nonimplementation. In sum, the problem is one of developing enough meaning vis-á-vis the change so that we are in a position to implement it effectively or reject it, as the case may be.

Those who are confronted with unwanted change and are in authority positions (cell Ill) will have to develop different coping mechanisms from those in nonauthority positions (cell IV). For the reader who thinks that resisting change represents irresponsible obstinacy, it is worth repeating that nonimplementable programs and reforms probably do more harm than good when they are attempted. The most responsible action may be to reject innovations that are bound to fail and to work earnestly at those that have a chance to succeed. Besides, in some situations resistance may be the only way to maintain sanity and avoid complete cynicism. In the search for meaning in a particular imposed change situation, we may conclude that there is no meaning, or that the problem being addressed is only one (and not the most important or strategic) of many problems that should be confronted. The basic guideline is to work on coherence by selecting and connecting innovations, thereby reducing disjointed overload while increasing focus.

We should feel especially sorry for those in authority positions (middle management in district offices, principals, intermediate government personnel in provincial state regional offices) who are responsible for leading or seeing to implementation but do not want or do not understand the change – either because it has not been sufficiently developed (and is literally not understandable) or because they themselves have not been involved in deciding on the change or have not received adequate orientation or training. The psychiatrist Ronald Laing captures this situation in what he refers to as a 'knot':

There is something I don't know
that I am supposed to know.
I don't know what it is I don't know,
and yet am supposed to know,
And I feel I look stupid
if I seem both not to know it
and not know *what* it is *I* don't know.
Therefore, I pretend I know it.
This is nerve-wracking since I don't
know what I must pretend to know.
Therefore, I pretend I know everything.

– R. D. Laing, *Knots* (1970)

This is a ridiculous stance, to be sure, as painful as it is unsuccessful. It can, of course, be successful in the sense of maintaining the status quo. Depending on one's capacity for self-deception, it can be more or less painful as well. In any case, teachers know when a change is being introduced by or supported by someone who does not believe in it or understand it. Yet this is the position in which many intermediate managers find themselves, or allow themselves to be. Those in authority have a need for meaning, too, if for no other reason than that the change will be unsuccessful if they cannot convey their meaning to others.

Planning and implementing change

The implications for those interested in planning and implementing educational change (cells I and II) are very important, because we would all be better off if changes were introduced more effectively. It is useful to consider these implications according to two interrelated sets of issues: What *assumptions* about change should we note? How can we plan and implement change more effectively?

The assumptions we make about change are powerful and frequently subconscious sources of actions. When we begin to understand what change is as people experience it, we begin also to see clearly that assumptions made by planners of change are extremely important determinants of whether the realities of implementation get confronted or ignored. The analysis of change carried out so far leads me to identify ten 'do' and 'don't' assumptions as basic to a successful approach to educational change.

1. Do not assume that your version of what the change should be is the one that should or could be implemented. On the contrary, assume that one of the main purposes of the process of implementation is to *exchange your reality* of what should be through interaction with implementers and others concerned. Stated another way, assume that successful implementation consists of some transformation or continual development of initial ideas.
2. Assume that any significant innovation, if it is to result in change, requires individual implementers to work out their own meaning. Significant change involves a certain amount of ambiguity, ambivalence, and uncertainty for the individual about the meaning of the change. Thus, effective implementation is a *process of clarification*. It is also important not to spend too much time in the early stages on needs assessment, program development, and problem definition activities – school staff have limited time. Clarification is likely to come in large part through reflective practice.
3. Assume that conflict and disagreement are not only inevitable but fundamental to successful change. Since any group of people possess multiple realities, any collective change attempt will necessarily involve conflict. Assumptions 2 and 3 combine to suggest that all successful efforts of significance, no matter how well planned, will experience an implementation dip in the early stages. Smooth implementation is often a sign that not much is really changing.

4. Assume that people need pressure to change (even in directions that they desire), but it will be effective only under conditions that allow them to react, to form their own position, to interact with other implementers, to obtain technical assistance, etc. It is all right and helpful to express what you value in the form of standards of practice and expectations of accountability, but only if coupled with capacity-building and problem-solving opportunities.

5. Assume that effective change takes time. It is a process of 'development in use'. Unrealistic or undefined time lines fail to recognize that implementation occurs developmentally. Significant change in the form of implementing specific innovations can be expected to take a minimum of 2 or 3 years; bringing about institutional reforms can take 5 or 10 years. At the same time, work on changing the infrastructure (policies, incentives, and capacity of agencies at all levels) so that valued gains can be sustained and built upon.

6. Do not assume that the reason for lack of implementation is outright rejection of the values embodied in the change, or hard-core resistance to all change. Assume that there are a number of possible reasons: value rejection, inadequate resources to support implementation, insufficient time elapsed, and the possibility that resisters have some good points to make.

7. Do not expect all or even most people or groups to change. Progress occurs when we take steps (e.g., by following the assumptions listed here) that *increase* the number of people affected. Our reach should exceed our grasp, but not by such a margin that we fall flat on our face. Instead of being discouraged by all that remains to be done, be encouraged by what has been accomplished by way of improvement resulting from your actions.

8. Assume that you will need a *plan* that is based on the above assumptions and that addresses the factors known to affect implementation. Evolutionary planning and problem-coping models based on knowledge of the change process are essential.

9. Assume that no amount of knowledge will ever make it totally clear what action should be taken. Action decisions are a combination of valid knowledge, political considerations, on-the-spot decisions, and intuition. Better knowledge of the change process will improve the mix of resources on which we draw, but it will never and should never represent the sole basis for decision.

10. Assume that changing the culture of institutions is the real agenda, not implementing single innovations. Put another way, when implementing particular innovations, we should always pay attention to whether each institution and the relationships among institutions and individuals is developing or not.

Finally, do not be seduced into looking for the silver bullet. Given the urgency of problems, there is great vulnerability to off-the-shelf solutions. But most external solutions have failed. The idea is to be a critical consumer of external ideas while working from a base of understanding and altering local context. There is no complete answer 'out there'.

References

Elmore, R. (1995). Getting to scale with good educational practice. *Harvard Educational Review*, 66(1), 1–26.

Fullan, M. (2001). *Leading in a culture of change*. San Franciso: Jossey-Bass.

Gaynor, A. (1977). A study of change in educational organizations. In L. Cunningham (Ed.), *Educational administration* (pp. 28–40). Berkeley, CA: McCutcham.

Gitlin, A., and Margonis, R. (1995.) The political aspect of reform. *The American Journal of Education*, 103, 377–405.

Hargreaves, A., and Fullan, M. (1998). *What's worth fighting for out there*. New York: Teachers' Federation; Buckingham, UK: Open University Press.

Heifetz, R. (1994). *Leadership without easy answers*. Cambridge, MA: Harvard University Press.

Hill, P., Campbell, C., and Harvey, J. (2000). *It takes a city*. Washington, DC: Brookings Institution.

Hill, P. and Celio, M. (1998). *Fixing urban schools*. Washington, DC: Brookings Institution

Lighthall, F. (1973, February). Multiple realities and organizational nonsolutions: an essay on the anatomy of educational innovation. *School Review*, 255–87.

Maurer, R. (1996). *Beyond the wall of resistance*. Austin, TX: Bard Books.

Micklethwait, J., and Wooldridge, A. (1996). *The witch doctors: making sense of management gurus*. New York: Random House.

Mintzberg, H. Ahlstrand, B., and Lampei, J. (1998). *Strategy safari: a guided tour through the wilds of strategic management*. New York: Free Press.

Sarason, S. (1971). *The culture of the school and the problem of change*. Boston: Allyn & Bacon.

Senge, P., Cambron-McCabe, N., Lucas, T., Smith, B., Dutton, J. and Kleiner, A. (2000). *Schools that learn*. New York: Doubleday.

Senge, P., Kleiner, A., N., Roberts, C., Ross, R., Roth, G. and Smith, B. (1999). *The dance of change*. New York: Doubleday.

Smith, L., and Keith, P. (1971). *Anatomy of educational innovation: an organizational analysis of an elementary school*. New York: Wiley.

Stacey, R. (1996a). *Strategic management and organizational dynamics* (2nd ed.). London: Pitman.

Stacey, R. (1996b). *Complexity and creativity in organizations*. San Francisco: Berrett-Koehler.

Storr, A. (1997). *Feet of clay: a study of gurus*. London: HarperCollins.

Wise, A. (1977). Why educational policies often fail: the hyperrationalization hypothesis. *Curriculum Studies*, 9(1), 43–57.

Wise, A. (1988). The two conflicting trends in school reform: legislative learning revisited. *Phi Delta Kappan*, 69(5), 328–33.

13

Fair Furlong Primary School: Five Years on

Agnes McMahon

Introduction

Re-visiting Fair Furlong school after a five-year period has been a powerful learning experience.[1] A great deal has happened in the intervening years; the school has gone through some difficult times. Much has changed but there is also much that is familiar. Changes have taken place at national and local levels and in the school itself

Changes in education policy at national level are well documented and it is noteworthy that when the original case study was conducted, the school had not yet been inspected by OfSTED, pupils' test results at Key Stages 1 and 2 were not published and the literacy and numeracy strategies had not yet been introduced. Much more data about school performance and pupil achievement is now available to teachers and the wider community. The major change at local level has been the dissolution of Avon LEA and its replacement by four unitary authorities. Fair Furlong school is now in the City of Bristol authority, and, as might be expected, the establishment of the unitary authority led to some changes in personnel and in the education policy framework. For example, the LEA adviser who now has responsibility for the school was not in this post five years ago.

Information about the developments in the school over the past five years was collected through interviews with three of the four headteachers who have been in post during this time; with a senior member of staff in the LEA; with nine teachers, learning support assistants and school governors, seven of whom were in post when the original case study was produced and with a teacher who had worked at the school over the five-year period but who left in December 1999.

Source: Maden, M. (ed.) (2001) *Success against the odds – 5 Years on*. London: RoutledgeFalmer. Edited version.

Since the first case study was conducted the school has experienced problems and has not been able to sustain the momentum for improved teaching and learning that was evident at that time, although it is now recognised to be on track again and making progress. Why did the school experience these set-backs? The outline of the story is quickly told: Mary Gray, the headteacher who was in post when the first case study was conducted, retired in the summer of 1996. The headteacher who took over the school was not successful in this context and resigned at the end of the 1999 spring term. An acting headteacher was appointed in the Easter holiday but he resigned after less than three weeks in post, at which point the LEA brought in an experienced headteacher from a neighbouring school to take over the leadership of the school. He was in post for two terms until the current (at time of writing) headteacher, Peter Overton, took up his appointment in January 2000. This series of events led to a situation which was described by the OfSTED team who inspected the school in March 2000 as: 'a period of considerable instability caused by difficulties in the leadership and management' (OfSTED, 2000). Standards of pupil achievement declined during the period of instability, although they have now begun to rise again and pupil test scores in summer 2000 were an improvement on the previous year. The OfSTED inspectors concluded that: 'although the school is now making steady improvement, it is not yet an effective school'. They recognised that the newly appointed headteacher had a clear view for the development of the school and was already making considerable improvements and stated that: 'the school now has a good capacity to improve' (OfSTED, 2000). Nevertheless, the school has been judged to have serious weaknesses in the quality of provision and much will have to be done to raise achievement.

How has this situation arisen, when five years ago the school seemed poised to make significant gains in teaching and learning? Many of the teachers and governors who were working in the school at that time are still in post, the community is reasonably stable and there have been no significant changes in the catchment area or in the type of children entering the school. There is no simple answer, rather a combination of factors appearing to have resulted in the school's losing momentum; issues about the pace of change and the management of change have been especially significant. Sustaining improvement and growth is a challenging task in any school; perhaps it is especially challenging in an area of social deprivation.

The School Community

The area in which the school is situated remains one of social deprivation and many families still have to struggle with hardship and poverty. Withywood is in the 16 per cent most disadvantaged wards in England (1998 Index of Local Deprivation). A 1998 study conducted by the University of the West of England noted continuing poverty, ill health, educational under-achievement, long-term unemployment, housing need, crime and drug misuse as problems in the area. Many of the difficulties that the community faced five years ago have not been overcome. The area remains removed from the city's growth areas and road access to the city centre and the motorways is poor, there are no large employers in the area and there is very little inward investment. Approximately 42 per cent of the families in the neighbourhood are in receipt of means-tested council tax benefits (Bristol City Council, Department of the Environment, Transport and Leisure, 1999).

However, there are signs that things are beginning to improve. One very obvious indicator is that several of the tower blocks of flats have been demolished and replaced by low-rise housing, and some of the existing housing stock is being refurbished. The Council's policy is not to house families with young children in the remaining tower blocks. Levels of unemployment in the area have reduced, although many people still travel to work in other parts of Bristol rather than finding jobs locally. A number of people suggested that the area is becoming more settled, families are choosing to stay in the locality, and there are some signs of a market building up in owner-occupied housing.

What is the School Like Now?

Many features of the school are little changed since 1994. Fair Furlong is a large mixed primary school with a nursery class, taking children from ages 3 to 11. In July 2000 there were 345 pupils on roll including 41 in the nursery, a reduction on the 1994 figure of 382. This drop in numbers is partly due to a number of pupils being withdrawn from the school but also to a reduction in the number of school-age children in the community. The majority of the pupils are white (99 per cent) and there are no pupils for whom English is an additional language, a pattern that has not changed over the five years; 41 per cent of the pupils are entitled to free school meals, a reduction on the 1994 figure of 49 per cent. Eleven pupils have Statements (an increase on the number five years ago) and a total of 41 per cent of the pupils have been judged to have special educational needs (1998/99). The OfSTED report on the school noted that the number of pupils with special educational needs was above average, and that 'children start school with well below average skills in all the areas of learning, and that language and literacy skills are particularly poorly developed' (OfSTED, 2000: 13). The attendance rate at the school dropped over the past few years to a low of 88.5 per cent in 1998/99, though it is now improving again.

The school remains predominantly a female environment. With the exception of the male headteacher, all the staff who work in the school are women, a not uncommon pattern in primary schools. The general appearance of the school in the summer term of 2000 was very good. The headteacher in post five years ago had placed a high priority on making the building a good environment for teaching and learning and this appears to have been maintained. The corridors and classrooms are brightly painted with interesting displays of pupils' work, the classrooms seem well resourced, one classroom is now a dedicated information technology suite with fifteen computers for pupils' use. The hedge around the school boundary that was first planted by pupils, parents and teachers in the 1995/96 school year has now grown and most of it is thriving. The most obvious difference is that security measures around the school have been increased. The school had suffered from vandalism, broken windows and theft of equipment for many years and this became worse during the period of instability. In 1999, at the instigation of the acting headteacher, the LEA installed high steel railings around the front of the school and a fence was placed around the whole school perimeter. This increased level of security has reduced the incidence of vandalism experienced by the school.

Visiting the school in the summer term of 2000 was an enjoyable experience. The pupils were friendly and well behaved as they moved around the school and in the playground. The atmosphere during class time was calm and purposeful. The OfSTED inspectors had noted that pupils' attitude to learning and their personal development and relationships were satisfactory throughout the school and that their behaviour was good (OfSTED, 2000). The parents were always very supportive of the school and this support has been maintained.

What Problems Occurred in the School?

The headteacher who was appointed in 1996 was an experienced teacher and a successful headteacher. She had worked in a number of different schools and, prior to taking up her second headship in Fair Furlong, she had been head of a multi-ethnic school in a city in the south-east of England. A stranger to Bristol before her appointment, she had wanted to work in a larger school and a school that had challenge. She saw her priority task in Fair Furlong being to develop the curriculum: 'I gathered from the interview and from the previous head that I was there to develop the curriculum . . . standards were low and I was appointed to take that forward'.

Unfortunately, because of the difficulties that arose in the school, progress on curriculum development was slow. What caused these difficulties? There is no simple explanation – rather a combination of factors seemed to lead to the school going into a downward spiral. All the teachers, learning support assistants and governors who were interviewed in the summer term of 2000 had worked in the school before the appointment of the current head; six of them had been interviewed for the original case study. The two issues consistently cited as contributing to the difficulties in the school were: a decline in the standard of pupil behaviour and problems in communication which had led to a breakdown in relationships between the headteacher and the senior management team. The headteacher's account of the situation would support this analysis but opinions differ about where responsibility for this lay.

The management of pupil behaviour

One of the major problems in the school, reported by all those interviewed, was that over a two-year period there was a serious deterioration in pupil behaviour which contributed to a decline in teaching and learning. Five years ago the school had a clear behaviour policy in place which was based on assertive discipline. Indeed, a similar policy had been adopted by all the schools in the local cluster. In Fair Furlong a key rule for everyone was: 'Everyone will act with courtesy and consideration to others at all time'. This was elaborated in seven supporting statements. The behaviour policy had been developed collaboratively by the staff and was linked to a system of rewards and sanctions which were clearly understood by pupils and staff and were applied consistently. Children who misbehaved had their names written on the board during the lesson and sanctions (e.g. some loss of play time) were applied. The headteacher appointed in 1996 changed this policy in her first year in the school. She was unfamiliar with assertive discipline and became increasingly uncomfortable with it.

The head ended the practice of making children stand up if they misbehaved in assembly and, over the next twelve months, engaged in discussion with LEA personnel and the staff about how the behaviour management policy might be modified. In September 1997 staff were asked to stop putting children's names on the board with a cross beside them to indicate misbehaviour and to work with colleagues in their key stage team to develop alternative sanctions. Children were to be informed of this change in policy by their class teachers. The head wanted the children to take more ownership of their own behaviour and wanted staff to take more responsibility for the management of pupil behaviour in their classrooms rather than passing problems to another member of staff to handle, though she recognised that some teachers found this difficult. Several staff reported that the head wanted to move to a system which placed greater emphasis on self-discipline, negotiation and peer mediation, but their perception was that, although the school rules were unchanged, the sanctions had been removed. The changes were not fully supported by the staff, implementation faltered and pupil behaviour began to deteriorate.

> The new policy, it was a softly, softly, let's all be reasonable about this, policy, which might work if you started it with children in the nursery and grew it with them but you couldn't bring it in here, wham, with the children we have, because they are far too clever and play the game, and we lost every time. Even the good ones became awkward.
>
> (Learning support assistant)

. . . in two or three years. [assertive discipline] had reached a stage where it needed reviewing . . . in the short term it had a very good effect, you could change the behaviour of the children but at the end of the day various people had real concerns that the children didn't own their behaviour, so there was nothing about the children being independent and making choices and that was an issue.

(Teacher who used to work in the school)

The LEA placed a special needs support teacher in the school for one day a week, but, despite this additional help, the standard of pupil behaviour continued to decline for the next couple of years and this led to other problems, not least with teaching and learning: 'the behaviour in the classroom was so bad that you couldn't get on with the teaching' (Class teacher).

Staff morale also declined: 'there was a lot of staff illness in the year before the head left, and people felt very low and depressed, and not feeling valued or achieving' (Class teacher).

Communication

Problems of communication between the head and the senior management team (SMT) appear to have developed during the first year. In 1996 the new headteacher inherited the existing senior management team whose members had worked closely with the outgoing head. She said that she became aware that her management style was very different. Whereas the previous head had very clear ideas about what she wanted to achieve and was ready to lead from the front, feeding in ideas for discussion, she aimed for a collegial approach in which 'people take areas of responsibility and some global responsibility for what is going on and it is a discussion in which I take a lead but people take responsibility within that'. In the event, after discussion with the LEA and the chair of governors, the head decided to restructure the SMT. One change was to include the special educational needs co-ordinator (SENCO), who replaced one of the existing members. This caused a degree of bad feeling, and communication with the staff became more difficult. On another occasion, staff sought union advice on a particular staffing issue and a meeting was held with a national union representative. The head was present at this meeting and said that the experience had been 'amazingly damaging for everyone and for me'. As pupil behaviour continued to deteriorate the head decided to advertise a senior post and seek applications from the staff; this resulted in a member of staff, not at that point a member of the SMT, being appointed as behaviour manager. This teacher supported the head's approach to behaviour management which they tried to implement without the full backing of the staff. Whereas this decision had been a good one for the head – 'I felt I had some support – up till then I felt really isolated' – the communication problems with other members of staff continued. Over the next year, relationships with senior staff continued to decline and fewer SMT meetings were held, although staff meetings were maintained. It appears that the management group effectively became the head, deputy and behaviour manager. The downward spiral in the school was difficult to reverse: because the management of pupil behaviour became a key issue for all the staff, less attention was paid to curriculum innovation and developing teaching and learning strategies; as communication between the head and some of her staff deteriorated, there was less discussion about school policy and less staff ownership of changes that were introduced.

> . . . she had very clear ideas about how she wanted things done and she had a habit of scrapping something and putting something else in place almost immediately without discussion or scrapping something and then never quite getting round to replacing it.
>
> (Class teacher)

At a midpoint in the headship, the SMT members raised their concerns about the management of the school with the chair of governors, who in turn contacted the LEA. The LEA came into the school to review the situation, supported the strategies that the headteacher was putting in place and agreed academic targets with her for school improvement. However, when these were reviewed a year later it was judged that insufficient progress had been made, and the head resigned at the end of the 1999 spring term. She said that she had realised that the school was in 'negative collusion' and felt that she could not take it any further.

Getting Back on Track

The school faced the prospect of going into the 1999 summer term without a headteacher, but the governors, on the recommendation of the LEA, appointed an experienced, retired head from outside the authority as acting headteacher. He began the term but resigned within three weeks. This contributed to a further drop in staff confidence and morale. However, the LEA provided immediate support for the governing body by bringing in the headteacher of a neighbouring primary school on the estate as acting headteacher, and he remained in this post until the current head took over in January 2000. He, the acting head, was – and is – a well-respected head, well known in the community, with eight years' experience of headship in his school and a previous headship in the neighbourhood. He retained the headship of his own school, and the role that he agreed with the LEA and the governors of both schools was 'to go into Fair Furlong to support their staff in sorting out their difficulties'. He began to work immediately with the staff. He closed the school on the Monday after he had been appointed and had a whole day meeting with staff, listening to their accounts of what the problems were and encouraging them to commit to changing the ethos. This seems to have had a cathartic effect:

> He was very good, let us say what we felt, get it off our chests and then said right, that's it, now let's move forward.
>
> (Class teacher)

The acting head brought two members of his own staff with him to the first meeting at Fair Furlong and made it clear that he would not be the only one providing support to the teachers.

> I felt I needed a member of staff, for me one of the problems with the 'superhead' label is just that, the idea that they come in like a knight on a charger to sort things out, and very often from what I can tell they do it on their own . . . I wasn't prepared to do that.
>
> (Acting head)

His immediate priority was to support the teachers in managing pupil behaviour, and he used a number of strategies to do this. One was to provide additional support in ICT. Fair Furlong has a dedicated computer suite, although the ICT curriculum was not being fully implemented in the school at that time. The head brought in a member of his own staff as an ICT co-ordinator to work in the school for a number of hours each day. She was to take half a class at a time to work on an integrated learning system so each teacher had an opportunity to do good work with the remaining half of the class. A firm believer in the importance of ICT – 'in areas like this I think computers are going to be one of the ways of breaking this glass ceiling that we are all hammering at' – he also used the computer room as part of his strategy for managing behaviour.

> A computer room was a wonderful place where you could have control in a relaxed manner that the children respond to – and they are also doing educational work as well. As I patrolled the school, taking children out, they would go into that room sit down at a desk and be perfectly quiet; other children were working and they had no way of responding to an audience or anything else.
>
> (Acting head)

A second major strategy was that he put himself in the forefront of pupil management. He said that the behaviour of Fair Furlong children was always excellent at assemblies. He took the assembly every morning, using this as a means of establishing his own credibility with the children. He then spent the teaching time patrolling the corridors, going into classrooms to assist teachers when required, removing pupils who were being disruptive. He aimed to support individual teachers in the way he felt they needed to be supported rather than attempt to review the whole school policy on behaviour management. He also encouraged the teachers to reinstate the lunchtime and after-school clubs and activities which had not been running for some time. He held detentions at lunchtime:

> . . . to get the rogues off the playground. Pupil behaviour . . . it's the key thing. If you haven't got control of your school in an area like this you don't get anything. You don't get any achievement, or very little – everything is affected, including staff morale. I have never met a professional body of teachers so de-skilled.

> (Acting head)

He felt that it was crucially important to gain the support of the parents in managing pupil behaviour; so he held a meeting with them on the first day, sent a newsletter home to make it clear that he was not prepared to tolerate bad behaviour and called parents into school if a child broke the good behaviour policy. 'In the first week I saw loads of parents'.

Within a few weeks the standard of behaviour began to improve in the school, and teachers regained confidence as they realised that he would provide back-up support. Nevertheless, the time and energy that the staff had to devote to behaviour management meant that little work was done on developing the curriculum, assessment systems and general policy development. Much remained to be tackled.

There were some staff changes in the summer term and a number of new staff were appointed for September 1999. The current headteacher took up his post in January 2000 and eight weeks later the school had a full OfSTED inspection. Although the inspectors judged the school to have serious weaknesses, they recognised that it was poised once again to make significant improvements, and early evidence of this is already becoming apparent.

What can be Learned from this Experience?

Many people suffered because of the difficulties that Fair Furlong experienced: the children, the parents, the headteacher and the staff. No one wanted such a state of affairs to occur, children were unhappy and staff were stressed and demoralised. Why did it happen? The answers are complex and perhaps everyone who experienced it will have a different explanation.

This case study can only present a partial window on events. Nevertheless, even this brief study prompts a number of questions about what are appropriate forms of leadership in urban schools, about how to handle transition from one headteacher to another, about the management of change and about how schools are supported.

Leadership

In the English education system the role of the headteacher is paramount and the headteacher is widely regarded, not least by government, as the key ingredient in an effective school. One potential problem with this view is that too much can be laid at the head's door and insufficient attention paid to the need for everyone to participate in the leadership of the school. The need for the head to be a team builder is often emphasised, but less consideration may be given to the notion of shared leadership (MacBeath, 1998) where the school leader works to maximise the leadership qualities of others. One of the goals of the current head at Fair Furlong is to establish an ethos in the school where the children and staff accept some responsibility for maintaining and improving the school community. Several of the staff who were interviewed clearly supported this view of shared leadership. They suggested that the school needed a leader who would work with them, who would back them up, especially in matters of pupil management, but they recognised that each member of staff also needed to 'do their bit'.

> Schools like this need a kind of leadership that, when that leader leaves, the school doesn't fall apart . . . leadership where the skills to lead the school are passed to other members of staff. For behaviour issues you need someone strong at the top who will go head-on with children and will take them on, because we do have some very challenging children who will go head to head with you. You need someone at the top who will back you and say, that's not acceptable and it will be dealt with, and will deal with it appropriately, but you also need someone who will allow us to manage our subject areas and develop our own professional skills because a lot of the behaviour issues are related to professional practice – children misbehave if you deliver lessons which are at the wrong level. You need someone at the top who will help us develop those professional skills.
>
> (Class teacher)

Several people also argued that, in schools such as Fair Furlong, what was needed was a 'hands-on' form of leadership – 'someone with extra special communication skills' (Class teacher) – who was able to build strong relationships with children and parents as well as the staff; someone who would spend time in the classrooms with the children and the teachers, help with pupil management at break times and be at the school gate to chat to the parents.

> Both of them [current head and acting head] are the same. They've had those children in the palm of their hands when they walk into assembly. The children respect them, they adore them and they are frightened of upsetting them and that sort of very outgoing personality is important in a school like this. That was where the previous head didn't succeed, she was more quiet and calm and not very giving of herself.

(Class teacher)

Changing headteachers

The question of how the transition from one headteacher to another should be handled is not one that has received much attention. A typical pattern is that the incoming head will visit the school on one or two occasions, probably meet the staff and the current headteacher and have access to the paperwork. There is normally little opportunity to do more, not least because they are probably themselves working in another school. This was certainly the case with the head who was appointed to Fair Furlong in 1996. She made two short visits to the school before her appointment, had only a brief meeting with the previous head and wasn't given the keys of the school until her contract started on 1 September. Only when a new school is being established do heads seem to be given a few months to learn about and prepare for the job. There appears to be a widely held assumption that the new headteacher will come in with their own ideas and vision of what needs to be done (which may have been discussed with the governors at interview) and will make a fresh start in the school, rather than work to understand, consolidate and build upon what is already in place.

In Weindling and Earley's (1987) study of secondary headteachers, one of the main problems cited by new heads was 'difficulties caused by the style and practice of the previous head'. By implication this was because it contrasted with what they want to do (Weindling, 1999). Yet the transition stage can be crucial. Mary Gray, the head who was in post in Fair Furlong when the original case study was conducted had achieved a great deal. She had put systems in place in the school which were leading to improvements in teaching and learning; she was respected and well liked by staff, children, parents and the wider community; she played an active role in the cluster group for local headteachers; and in very many ways she was a hard act to follow. It cannot be easy taking over a school from a head recognised to be very successful.

> She [the incoming head] wanted to stamp her own personality on the school. She tried to change too many things too quickly, though this wasn't obvious at the time.

(Class teacher)

Mary Gray had taken the school forward a long way, but she recognised that much remained to be done. Her successor was judged to have the skills necessary to make the next leap forward, focusing on the curriculum and standards of teaching and learning, but her management style and ways of working with staff were different. How does a school community, especially the staff, learn to adapt to different leadership styles? How can two different management styles be made to gel? Should more time be allowed for the transition process? Should provision be made for incoming heads to spend preparatory time in the school observing systems, talking to people and gaining a fuller understanding of the way the school is working before taking up the appointment?

Supporting headteachers

Fair Furlong school is situated in a disadvantaged urban area. Life is difficult for many families and the children bring problems with them into school. In such schools, teachers and headteachers have to work especially hard to make the school effective. They have to work together inside the school but they also need access to other forms of support. Successive government policies over recent years have led to a diminution of the LEA role in relation to schools. Schools have more responsibility for self-management and can buy in professional help, but are less likely to have an LEA adviser coming into the school on a regular basis to monitor and support their work, not least because there may be fewer advisers in post. In the case of Fair Furlong, the LEA did provide support and acted quickly to bring in an acting headteacher in the 1999 summer term. Their effective intervention was noted in the OfSTED report (OfSTED, 2000).

Headteachers may also look to colleagues in neighbouring schools for support. Fair Furlong has not been the only school in the neighbourhood to experience difficulties and one positive outcome has been to strengthen the cluster of local schools. There are twelve schools in the cluster and the headteachers meet on a fortnightly basis. Could they have been more supportive when Fair Furlong was experiencing difficulties? In the event they were unaware of any problems. The headteacher commented:

> They are a group of very professional people and I have a high regard for them. They were very well established and perhaps if I had felt comfortable in going to them and saying what was happening, I am sure they would have been supportive.
> Because I was new to the area, because they had worked together, they were unaware this was happening . . . it's a difficult thing to share . . . it's a very personal thing.
>
> (Headteacher 1996–99)

The headteachers and governors recognise that they are facing the same issues in the same area and have now committed themselves to working on problems in a collaborative fashion. They have drawn up a joint school development plan for the cluster with additional specific targets for individual schools, they have planned in-service training for subject co-ordinators from all the schools for the next year. The current headteacher in Fair Furlong is an active member of the cluster group and sees it as a key means of providing support for school development.

Teachers' professional development

Good teaching is central to pupil achievement. All teachers have had to develop new skills and expertise in response to the multiple innovations in curriculum and assessment; teachers in challenging schools need to be especially skilled. Excellent teaching and classroom management can stimulate and engage children, but, when classes become disruptive, teachers experience stress, their morale drops and this is likely to have a negative effect on their practice. In February 2000, the OfSTED inspectors judged that the quality of teaching was satisfactory overall and some was very good or excellent. Examples of good teaching were seen from all teachers. In the last year there have been staff changes at Fair Furlong and a number of young teachers with good subject knowledge and skills and fresh ideas have been appointed and this is reported to have had a positive impact on the school as a whole. The current head is actively working to promote continuing professional development for the staff, supporting their attendance at in-service courses, working with them in the classrooms and encouraging discussion about how to improve teaching and learning. His prime focus is on school improvement and how best to achieve this.

There is an underlying question about how best to promote continuing professional development for teachers. In recent years most teachers have experienced only short (e.g. half-day) training courses related to specific innovations rather than more sustained educational opportunities (e.g. long courses, periods of secondment) which might have a more positive effect on their practice in the longer term (McMahon, 1999). A number of the teachers at Fair Furlong are very experienced and have taught in the school for many years. The challenge that they and many other teachers face is how to keep their practice fresh and innovative and be themselves responsive to change. Over the five-year period the school did have a number of strategies in place which help to develop professional experience (e.g. taking responsibility for teaching a different age group, classroom observation with feedback, mentoring schemes, INSET courses) but this may not be sufficient. After many years in the classroom teachers may gain much more benefit from periods of secondment, business placements, study visits, etc., and the government appears to recognise this (DfEE, 2000).

Management of pupil behaviour

Every school has to resolve the question about what are the most appropriate ways of managing pupil behaviour but the challenge this poses will be greater in some schools than in others. The difficulties in Fair Furlong arose in part because staff held different views about how the children's behaviour should be managed. A central school-wide system for behaviour management clearly can work very well but a view was also expressed that it may be de-skilling for individual teachers who simply apply the system rather than engage with the underlying issues.

The governors

The governors of Fair Furlong School are committed and loyal and several have worked for the school for many years; many of them come from the local community. Should they have been more aware of the problems that the school was experiencing and have intervened more quickly? Perhaps. The OfSTED inspectors (OfSTED, 2000) reported that the governors had not ensured that identified weaknesses had been addressed but recognised that this was due in part to difficulties in communication with the head and noted that they are now making significant improvements. However, it can be argued that the responsibility placed on governors for the management of schools is too great. This is certainly the view of the National Primary Heads Association which stated that: 'the expectations placed on governors, unpaid and often in full-time employment, were totally unrealistic and needed to be reassessed' (Education and Employment Committee, 1998, para. 51).

Concluding Note

School improvement is not easy. The history of Fair Furlong over the past few years illustrates how hard it can be to sustain improvement and how quickly a school ethos can change. There are lessons to be learned from this experience, certainly for the staff of this school and possibly for others who might find themselves facing similar difficulties. A key underlying message is that the transition from one head to another is in itself a major innovation for a school and it needs to be carefully planned, managed and supported.

▮ Editors' note

1. This chapter is taken from a collection of follow-up case studies of eleven successful schools in disadvantaged areas. The schools were originally studied in the mid-1990s (NCE, 1996), and revisited five years later. National Commission on Education (1996) *Success against the odds*. London: Routledge.

▮ References

Department for Education and Employment (2000) *Professional Development: Support for Teaching and Learning*, DfEE 0008/2000, London: DfEE.

Education and Employment Committee (1998) *Ninth Report: The Role of Headteachers Volume 1*, London: HMSO.

Hartcliffe and Withywood Community Partnership (1999) *Working Together for Change: Funding Bid for Single Regeneration Budget Round 5*, Bristol City Council.

MacBeath, J. (1998) (ed) *Effective School Leadership: Responding to Change*, London: Paul Chapman Publishing.

McMahon, A. (1999) Promoting continuing professional development for teachers: an achievable target for school leaders? In: T. Bush, L. Bell, R. Bolam, R. Glatter and P. Ribbins (eds) *Educational Management: Redefining Theory, Policy and Practice*, London: Paul Chapman Publishing.

OfSTED (2000) *Inspection Report: Fair Furlong Primary School*, London: OfSTED.

Weindling, D. (1999) Stages of headship. In: T. Bush, L. Bell, R. Bolam, R. Glatter and P. Ribbins (eds) *Educational Management: Redefining Theory, Policy and Practice*, London: Paul Chapman Publishing.

Weindling, D. and Earley, P. (1987) *Secondary Headship: The First Years*, Windsor: NFER-Nelson.

Part 4

Educational Improvement

Reform, Accountability and Strategic Choice in Education

Tim Simkins

Introduction

A dominant theme of the discourse of the educational reforms of recent years has been that of institutional autonomy. A plethora of terms have been used to describe this phenomenon. In addition to the term autonomy itself, we have had delegation, devolution and decentralisation. For schools the terms 'self-management, 'school- or site-based management', 'local financial management' and 'local management' have all been used; for colleges the dominant term has been 'incorporation' (Bullock and Thomas, 1997; Abu-Duhou, 1999; Leithwood and Menzies, 1998; McGinn and Welsh, 1999; Fullan and Watson, 2000). Some terms have been preferred at particular times in the history of reform, and some have been preferred in some countries rather than others.

All the terms imply the redistribution of power within an education system in ways which enhance the importance of the individual school or college *vis-á-vis* the wider systems, national and local. However, in some ways the concept of organisational autonomy is an unhelpful one. First, it suggests a degree of freedom which few if any organisations in the modern world can achieve. Secondly, certainly in England and Wales, it overemphasises one aspect of what has been a multifaceted reform process, aspects of which have had very different concerns. And, thirdly, it reifies the school or college as an organisation over and above the individuals and groups both inside and outside who have a stake in, and influence over, the purposes and processes of education.

Source: Commissioned.

We need, therefore, to consider institutional autonomy in a wider context and to ask deeper questions about it. This chapter will attempt to do this, suggesting, in particular, that accountability in its many and changing forms is a more helpful construct for understanding recent processes of policy change in education. The following discussion explores the ways in which changing ideas about accountability have been embodied in the reform process, the ways in which these have reconstituted power relationships between key actors, and the implications of these changes for the kinds of strategic choices available to those responsible for strategy in schools and colleges. The argument is grounded in the experience of Great Britain, and of England and Wales in particular. However, while Britain – like all nations – is unique in the particular combination of policy changes that it has experienced, many of the themes identified here will have resonance in many other national contexts across the world.

Power in the Educational System

A useful way of exploring this issue is to distinguish between 'criteria power' and 'operational power' (Winstanley *et al.*, 1995). Criteria power refers to the ability of organisational stakeholders to define the aims and purposes of a service, to design the overall system within which it is provided, to set or influence the performance criteria which providers must satisfy and to evaluate their performance in relation to these criteria. Operational power, in contrast, refers to the ability of stakeholders to provide the service itself or to decide how it is provided, and to change the way in which it is delivered, through the allocation of limited resources or by using relevant knowledge and skills. In other words, criteria power is concerned with determining purposes and frameworks relating to the 'what' and 'why' of service provision, while operational power is concerned with the 'how' of service delivery.

Using this framework, we can identify a number of ways in which the nature and distribution of power in education in England and Wales have changed over recent years:

- *Central government*, previously limited in power in relation to major aspects of educational policy and practice, has considerably increased its criteria power, both directly and through agents such as Ofsted[1] and the funding councils[2], so that it is now the key actor in relation both to the determination of policy objectives nationally and the establishment of operational frameworks through which these policies are carried out.
- *Local education authorities (LEAs)* have perhaps been the main losers. Colleges have been removed from their control while, in the schools sector, they have found themselves squeezed between an increasingly

powerful central government drawing criteria power to itself and developments in relation to local management which have transferred operational power to the level of the school.

■ *Teachers* have lost criteria power. The influence of the teacher unions on national policy has been significantly reduced, while national developments in relation to curriculum and testing have limited teachers' freedom in the classroom. Local management of schools and incorporation of colleges[3] have enhanced the power of governing bodies and senior managers, rendering the role of 'ordinary' teachers in the development of school or college policy more problematic.

■ *Parents and employers* have seen their operational power increased in various ways, particularly through the power to exercise choice between institutions and through representation of parents and employers, respectively, on school and college governing bodies.

■ *Students* remain largely formally disempowered within the system, depending on the willingness of other parties – such as parents when choosing schools, or governors, senior managers and teachers when determining school or college policy – to recognise, and take account of, their interests, although developments in further education such as the FE Charter[4] may be modifying this.

This analysis emphasises two important points about the reforms. The first – their simultaneous decentralising and centralising tendencies – is something of a paradox, although one which characterises the experience of reform right across the public sector (Hoggett, 1996). Thus, while a number of parties may have had their *operational* power increased – particularly governors and senior managers of schools and colleges – criteria power has been drawn much more firmly into the centre, as will be seen shortly. Viewed in this context, increased autonomy, while significant, is severely constrained. The prime areas of freedom lie partly on the edges of the 'what' – determining aspects of the character of the organisation and of policy beyond those established centrally. Primarily, however, they are concerned with the 'how' of management: the organisation of the school or college, its students and its curriculum, the teaching and learning process, the deployment of resources in the pursuit of its objectives and the ways in which it manages its relations with the outside world.

Secondly, the reforms have significantly changed the formal pattern of power at the level of the institution itself, with teachers seeing their power reduced while governors, senior managers and some external stakeholders have all had their power increased significantly. How these shifts in power actually work out in practice, however, depends very much on local circumstances and in particular on the ability and willingness of the various parties to make effective use of the potential they now have to influence policy and practice at institutional level. The outcomes of such processes will have a major influence on how self-management works in practice.

Changing Patterns of Accountability

Thus the world of power relationships in which educational organisations now operate is extremely complicated. For every area of increased power there seems to be a corresponding area in which additional external controls and constraints have been imposed. A key issue here for schools and colleges, as for other public sector organisations, is that of accountability.

Accountability is a complex issue and it can take many forms (Kogan, 1986; Poulson, 1996; Riley, 1998). In its pure form accountability of party A to party B requires three things: first, an expectation that A will act in ways which are consistent with the legitimate requirements of B; secondly, that A will render some form of account to B for their performance; and, thirdly, that B may exercise sanctions over A if A fails to conform to B's expectations. This might be termed the 'hard' form of accountability. In many areas, however, while there may be a clear understanding that party B has a legitimate right to influence the behaviour of A, this is not accompanied by any means of ensuring compliance or punishing non-compliance. This might be called 'soft' accountability and its effectiveness will depend on the degree to which party B is able to use the influence strategies available to it to convince party A that compliance will be worth while.

It can be argued that the dominating government concern which underlay the reforms was that pre-existing accountability mechanisms within the educational system were too soft, and consequently that new, harder control mechanisms needed to be established.

The challenge to professional control

Traditionally in education, professionals have had the primary responsibility for determining the core activities of the service. The *professional* model of accountability is based on the assumption that quality in the educational system is best ensured by granting autonomy to teachers, advisers and others who have been trained in, and have access to, relevant bodies of professional knowledge and whose professional ethic leads them to act always in the interest of their 'client' – the pupil or student. The yardstick of quality under this model is good practice which is defined by the profession and moderated by processes of peer review, through professional networks of information and exchange, perhaps supported by inspection and advisory teams that operate primarily to monitor and disseminate good practice. At the level of the school or college it is embodied in concepts of 'collegial' governance through which responsibility for policy and its implementation rests with the teaching staff acting together in the interests of the students.

It can be argued that this approach to accountability dominated educational practice at least to the end of the 1970s, and it has been the increasingly emphatic challenge to it which has characterised the policy debate of the later years of the 20th century (Ranson, 1994; Bottery, 1999; Hargreaves, 2000). Indeed, within policy circles there has developed a widespread view that professional accountability is so soft that it is tantamount to an absence of any real accountability at all, or, in a less extreme view, that professional accountability alone is insufficient to ensure that the educational provision responds adequately to the complex demands of a modern economy and society. Such suspicion of professional autonomy is not, of course, confined to education: it can be found in the health and social services and elsewhere (Exworthy and Halford, 1998), although it is perhaps in education that the dominant role of the professional has come under greatest challenge. Pressures have grown, therefore, to find other accountability mechanisms which can reduce professional power and increase the influence of other stakeholders in the educational system. The education reforms have emphasised three of these: government regulation, community empowerment through governing bodies, and the marketisation of the educational system through increased 'customer' choice and the encouragement of increased competition between schools and colleges.

State control: the role of central government

Education – at least in the public sector – is clearly a legitimate concern of the political process and hence of representative bodies established to express the public interest. In this country, since the 1944 Education Act, formal political responsibility for education has been shared between central government, the local education authorities and school and college governing bodies, although in practice the latter had little power until the 1980s. Of course, the authority of each level of representative government derives from a rather different definition of political legitimacy, and there have always been areas of ambiguity, overlap and tension between their powers and aspirations, not least when different political groups have been in control at the different levels. Nevertheless, prior to the 1980s, the relationship between their respective powers and responsibilities remained fairly stable (Thody, 1992). The Education Acts of the 1980s and 1990s, however, have shifted the balance decisively away from the local authorities. Powers of governance now lie primarily with the other two legal 'partners', namely, central government and governing bodies.

First, a multitude of powers now lie directly with central government and its agents. It was common prior to the 1980s to argue that the secretary of state's powers were primarily indirect and negative: he or she could steer change through some powers of resource control and the ability to refuse permission for particular developments. He or she had very few positive powers, however, and had little involvement in particular in curriculum matters. A major sea change, however, came about with the Education Reform Act 1988, the Further and Higher Education Act 1992, and subsequent legislation. For the first time the broad pattern of educational provision was to be managed within a strong framework established centrally.

Over recent years central government has actively and increasingly exercised its powers in five main ways. It has:

1 used legislation and regulation to determine much more broadly than in the past the *aims and purposes* of the service and, in the case of schooling, the *content* of education in particular through the National Curriculum and testing;
2 used legislation to influence profoundly the *organisation of the system* and the position of individual schools and colleges within it: it determines the types of schools and colleges that there shall be, the terms on which each shall be funded, and the ways in which they shall be governed and held to account;
3 used legislation and regulation to redistribute *rights and responsibilities* within the system, determining the powers of governing bodies, of parents and of key para-governmental organisations, such as Ofsted and the funding agencies;
4 used a variety of *resourcing mechanisms*, particularly the regulation of formula-funding regimes and the provision of earmarked funding streams to influence school and college priorities; and
5 sought to influence the discourse about *educational practice and performance* through the publication of information about the performance of individual schools and colleges, through the process of inspection with its associated sanctions for organisations deemed to be 'failing', and in some cases – for example, the literacy and numeracy hours[5] – through more direct intervention in the organisation of teaching.

Viewed from this perspective, one of the areas of choice facing the individual school or college is the response to the regulatory framework within which it must operate. What position will be taken on its character and governance, given the range of opportunities provided for in legislation? To what degree and in what ways will it develop its curriculum provision in ways that respond to the values, priorities and needs of those whom it serves, given the framework provided by national curricula and tests and examinations? And how will it establish and present its own unique character both internally and to the world outside, given the standardised frameworks provided by the process of inspection and by the legal requirements to present certain kinds of information in particular ways? These are fundamental questions: the ways in which they are tackled will go a long way in providing the basis upon which other choices can be built.

The educational organisation in the community: empowered governing bodies

In addition to enhancing its own powers, central government has legislated to change the constitution and increase the powers of school and college governing bodies. The empowerment of governing bodies prior to 1988 was an evolutionary process, dating back at least to the 1970s and one in which a number of LEAs played a major part. However, the reforms of the late 1980s saw a radical move forward. The 1988 and 1992 Acts fully incorporated college governing bodies, while granting school governing bodies responsibility for all major personnel decisions, for the management of block budgets running to millions of pounds in many cases, and for the management of premises. This redefined the local government of education profoundly. Power was transferred towards the specific stakeholder groups represented on governing bodies and away from the wider local community as represented by the local education authority.

Governing bodies can conceive their roles in a number of ways. Writing about schools before the reforms, Kogan *et al.* (1984) suggested four such roles:

1 The *supportive* governing body which looks beyond the school to generate political and other support for the school's activities.
2 The *mediating* governing body which promotes a consensus between the various local stakeholder interests, hearing and testing different viewpoints in an attempt to ensure that the school system is operating smoothly.
3 The *advisory* governing body which provides a sounding board for professionals within the school and provides advice where required.
4 The *accountable* governing body which expects the professionals to render an account to it and makes judgements about the performance of the school in relation to policies and expectations established nationally and locally.

None of the school governing bodies in Kogan *et al.*'s study played an accountable role: 'They were not seen in this way by appointing authorities, by schools, or indeed by the majority of their own membership, and lacked the authority, resources and, for the most part, inclination for such a role' (ibid., p. 164). The clear expectation now, of course, is that this should be the primary role played by all governing bodies, and they have been provided with the powers and authority to play it. However, the granting of *de jure* powers and responsibilities does not, in itself, guarantee that these will be fully exercised *de facto*. Indeed, the evidence suggests that despite the expectations placed upon them by the government and others, there is considerable variability in the degree to which governing bodies exercise the accountability role in its full sense. The majority are continuing to play one or more of the other roles, whose potential value of course does not decrease as a result of the higher profile given to the accountability role (Deem *et al.*, 1995; Gleeson and Shain, 1999a).

In reality, therefore, even in relation to the accountable role, the way in which a governing body conceives and plays its role is a matter of considerable choice. How far, for example, should governors initiate policy and how far should they act as validators of policies that are designed primarily by the senior managers and the staff of the organisation? The factors which will influence the role which a governing body actually plays include the types of individuals who are elected and co-opted to it, their expectations about what they should do and how they should behave, and the kinds of pressures that the governors face from inside and outside the organisation.

Schools and colleges in the market: competition and customers

Unlike the models of accountability considered so far, the market model is not concerned with the rearrangement of formal roles and power *within* the educational system. Rather it is concerned to establish a competitive environment within which schools and colleges are compelled to respond to the wishes of their 'customers' through the operation of market forces. According to this model, accountability relationships can be established directly with those who use public services without the need for other groups, such as the government, community representatives or professionals, to interpret their needs for them (Chubb and Moe, 1990). The purest expression of this model in education occurs in those areas, such as the private schools and training sectors, where services are supplied at full cost to those who are able and willing to pay. Such an approach to accountability requires a number of conditions for it to work effectively, namely:

■ a number of *supplier organisations* with the capacity to meet customer requirements on a competitive basis;
■ individuals, who can act as *customers* in the market for services;
■ an *information system*, which informs potential customers about the nature and quality of the services on offer; and
■ a *resource-based link* between customers and suppliers so that changing patterns of demand result in changes in the flows of resources to suppliers.

Where these conditions exist, it is argued, there is no need for any socially or institutionally agreed measure of educational quality to be established because quality is equated with customer satisfaction and those schools and colleges that attract students and hence prosper in the market will be self-evidently of high quality.

The educational reforms have contained elements which reflect all these requirements. First, there has been an attempt to establish a diversity of institutional provision through a variety of strategies for encouraging schools and colleges to seek 'special' status' – city technology colleges, specialist schools, city academies and so on.[6] Secondly, schools and colleges have been placed firmly in the marketplace by linking resources to enrolment through the operation of formula budgeting and by creating competitive pressures through increasing parental and student choice. Thirdly, requirements have been established that certain kinds of information on policies, provision and performance in examinations and inspections are published in order, it is argued, to facilitate processes of choice.

However, despite these developments, the market, like that in other areas of public provision, remains a 'quasi-market' (Le Grand and Bartlett, 1993) with two highly significant characteristics. First, the market operates under a high degree of regulation. As has already been seen, the secretary of state delimits (for the state sector of education at least) what products shall be available in the market (through the National Curriculum and through curriculum policies in post-16 education), who shall be allowed to enter the market and on what terms (through the power to regulate the establishment, merger and closure of institutions), what 'prices' shall be charged (through placing constraints on funding formulae), and what information shall be made available to customers. The consequences of powers such as these are considerable: relatively minor changes can have major effects on the terms on which institutions compete so that some are advantaged – intentionally or unintentionally – in relation to others.

Secondly, the nature of the market varies from area to area: different 'local competitive arenas' (Woods *et al.*, 1998) vary enormously in the nature and degree of competition which are placed upon schools within them. For some – for example, some primary schools in rural areas – choice and competition may have little meaning. For others – for example, some comprehensive schools and colleges in urban areas – they may literally be a matter of life and death. Schools and colleges in different market circumstances, therefore, will face different degrees of market pressure and constraint and this will affect their attitude to the management of their external relationships, and particularly their conception of 'marketing'. Some, no doubt, will find the market pressures so strong that their freedom of movement is severely limited. For others, though, their response to the 'marketplace' will be a major indicator of the choices which they make about the kind of institution they wish to be. For example, are they seeking to develop and project a distinctive character, and, if so, what and how? How big do they wish to be? And what kind of student intake do they wish to have (Bagley *et al.*, 1996; Foskett, 1998)?

Of course, choices in these areas cannot be made without also taking a view about the kind of relationships that are to be developed with other institutions. In particular, how far should market pressures be accepted and competitive success sought within the local arena? Or how far should attempts be made to reduce the pressures of competition by seeking collaborative strategies with others in the area? In some areas and at some times there may be little choice about such matters; at others real choices will exist which raise fundamental questions about the school's or college's values.

■ Metaphors for Change

It can be seen, therefore, that the professional model of accountability has been challenged from three directions: increased central government control, increased community participation through governing bodies, and increased marketisation of the educational system through enhanced competition and customer choice. Taken together they have established quite new frameworks of discourse about education policy (Ball, 1990). Beyond this, however, each of these major changes in patterns of accountability provides important choices at the level of the school or college: about the kind of organisation it should be and the relations that it should have with its key stakeholders. These choices can perhaps be best expressed, as Glatter (1991; Glatter and Woods, 2001) argues, through a number of organisational images which underlie different aspects of the reform.

First, the school or college might be viewed as a *local outlet* for a range of curricular products largely specified by the distant central office of the relevant government ministry or agency. Viewed in this way the prime purpose of the organisation is to deliver a product – the nationally defined curriculum and specified examination/test outcomes – in ways which meet local needs and expectations while maintaining the essential integrity of the product. Secondly, it might be viewed as a *participatory community*. From this perspective, the empowerment of governing bodies is seen as a means through which stakeholders drawn both from within the organisation and, more important, from the wider local community can enable it to develop in ways which reflect and respond to local priorities and concerns. Finally, the school or college may be viewed *as a separate business* operating in a competitive market whose purpose is to provide products and services which individual consumers value and to market these in ways which will ensure that these 'customers' choose this school or college over others.

Each of these images is, in fact, a metaphor which illuminates particular aspects of the complex world which schools and colleges now inhabit and emphasises some power relationships over others. Each embodies an important truth and important policy values in relation to the place of the individual institution within the broader system. Such metaphors are extremely powerful in informing and guiding our thinking, as Morgan (1997, p.4) argues:

> [A]ll theories of organisation and management are based on implicit images or metaphors that lead us to see, understand and manage organisations in distinctive yet partial ways . . . the use of metaphor implies *a way of thinking* and *a way of seeing* that pervade how we understand our world generally.

Thus metaphors may either constrain our thinking – if we are imprisoned in one image of the organisation to the exclusion of others – or they can liberate us to develop new insights and perspectives.

For those responsible for governing and managing schools and colleges, therefore, an understanding of such metaphors and their implications increases the power to choose the kind of organisation that they wish to create. In particular, it helps to sharpen up thinking about desirable roles and relationships. For example, are governors local guardians of nationally determined expectations of education, representatives of the wider community which they serve, or are they a board of directors whose prime concern is to ensure the success of the institution in the marketplace? Are parents or students loyal clients dependent on the professional expertise of teachers to do the best for them, customers who can best influence schools and colleges by shopping around and exercising the option of 'exit' if they are dissatisfied, or partners or citizens who are expected, and expect, to influence the school or college through the exercise of informal or formal 'voice' (Hirschman, 1970)? And are senior staff leading professionals aspiring to develop a shared educational enterprise through building collegial relationships with colleagues, or executives managing the human resources of the institution towards organisational goals established at the apex of the institution or outside it? These are profound questions. The ways in which schools and colleges resolve them will help to determine the character of the education system for years to come.

Trends and issues

So far we have outlined four modes of accountability: the professional mode which dominated the educational system until the 1980s, and the three modes – central government control, community participation and market pressures – which governments since 1988 have sought to use to supplement, or to counteract, professional power. These modes of accountability are summarised in Table 14.1. As this table shows, each mode empowers different key actors, embodies different mechanisms of influence, conceives in different ways those whom education is primarily designed to serve, implies different success criteria and relies on different underpinning metaphors.

Table 14.1 *Four modes of accountability*

Accountability mode	Key actors	Influence mechanisms	Dominant conception of those to be served	Success criteria	Metaphor for school or college
Professional	Teachers	Peer review	Clients requiring a professional service	Good practice; meeting individual student needs	Collegium
Government control	Government	Legislation; regulation; inspection	Subjects on whose behalf government acts	Conformance with policy	Local branch of national organisation
Community participation	Community representatives	School governance	Citizens actively involved in governance	Satisfaction of interests	Participatory community
Market pressure	Consumers	Choice	Customers choosing a service provider	Competitive success	Competitive business

The problems which such diverse and competing pressures place on public sector 'human service organisations' are well described by Kouzes and Mico (1979). Schools, colleges and similar organisations are potentially in a state of continuous tension between the various legitimate demands which are placed upon them, and their leadership and management involve a balancing act of strategic choices that is often far more complex than private sector organisations typically encounter. Viewed over the longer term – and thinking about the future – two major themes arise from this analysis.

First, the balance between the various accountability pressures has changed, is changing, and can be expected to continue to change over time. The dominant policy theme of the Conservative governments that were in office from 1979 to 1997, and especially during the Thatcher years, was to reduce the degree of government control over provision of public services and to empower individuals. This implied 'setting institutions free', under the guidance of empowered governing bodies with enhanced lay membership (parents in schools and employers in colleges) within an increasingly marketised environment. Some important aspects of central control were also developed – particularly the National Curriculum and testing and the revised inspection system – but the philosophical thrust was towards deregulation. From the mid-1990s, however, and especially during the years of the Labour government, the pendulum has swung increasingly towards central direction. The emphasis on competition among schools and colleges has been replaced by greater emphasis on collaboration, although parental choice remains an important theme and organisational diversity is a growing one. However, within the schools sector both LEAs and governing bodies are increasingly being co-opted as agents of central government, delivering national policies against centrally determined targets. Rewards and punishments for individual institutions linked to performance are replacing, or significantly modifying, the pressures of the marketplace. Similarly, many in the colleges sector see the funding councils as much more centralist than the LEAs they replaced. There seem to be two reasons for these developments: an impatience with the assumed imprecision and unpredictability of indirect market accountability mechanisms; and concern about some of the equity effects of quasi-market solutions to the 'problem' of educational quality. However, it is difficult and dangerous to generalise, let alone predict, where the 'roller coaster' of educational policy will travel next and how the balance between central direction, community control and market pressures will evolve in future.

The second major theme concerns the ways in which these *external* pressures interact to influence the *internal* accountability arrangements in schools and colleges. We have discussed the external challenges to the professional domain within schools. Many argue that these changing external pressures are having a profound impact on the internal accountability regimes of public sector organisations, including those in the education sector. This arises because government direction, empowered governing bodies and market competition all emphasise the corporate dimension of accountability, focusing on the school or college as an organisation as the prime focus for assessing performance and rendering accounts. A major consequence of this corporate focus has been an increased emphasis on institutional 'management' – and latterly 'leadership' – as the dominant vehicle for ensuring that professional autonomy and judgement are harnessed to broader 'corporate', and hence national, purposes. There is a suspicion of 'collegial' methods of shared responsibility favoured by professionals. These, it is argued, do not provide sufficiently strong levers for assuring and improving performance.

The increasing emphasis on management and leadership in education, as elsewhere in the public sector, is often linked to the rise of 'managerialism' – a set of beliefs about how organisations should be run (Pollitt, 1993; Clarke and Newman, 1997). Some of the ways in which the managerialist model differs from the more traditional 'bureau-professional' model (Clarke and Newman, 1997) are set out in Table 14.2. There has been much debate about the degree to which managerialism is embedding itself within schools and colleges. Many aspects of the recent changes suggest an increasing trend in this direction (Simkins, 2000). These include the development of organisational mission statements, of school development plans, college strategic plans and marketing strategies, an emphasis on the achievement of clearly defined short-term targets and the use of quantified performance indicators to monitor these, and the introduction of particular managerial approaches drawn from the private sector, such as Investors in People and the European Quality Framework. At the level of individuals, staff appraisal, more flexible salary structures and performance-related pay for senior staff also provide considerable opportunities for the extension of 'managerialist' approaches (Gleeson and Husbands, 2001).

Table 14.2 *Bureau-professionalism and managerialism*

Characteristic	Bureau-professionalism	Managerialism
Attachments	Client-centred professional service values	Over-riding values and mission of the organisation
Decision-making	Bureaucratic rules plus professional discretion and judgement	Managerial discretion and techniques
Agendas	Assessed needs of individual clients and client groups	Organisational objectives and outcomes; deployment of resources
Norms	Needs and rights of clients	Efficiency; organisational performance; customer orientation

Source: Simkins, 1999, p. 272

Nevertheless, the pattern of change is not a simple one. First, organisational and leadership responses to external pressures can take many forms (Hall, 1997). A 'hard' approach is to set up clearly defined, hierarchical structures of managerial accountability, design performance indicators to enable success or failure to be clearly identified, and to use staff appraisal and performance-related pay and other tools of 'performance management' to reward those who perform well. Softer approaches are less concerned with such techniques: their emphasis is on the establishment of a strong achievement-orientated culture within which all members of the organisation are encouraged to accept responsibility for ensuring quality of performance. These more sympathetic approaches, too, seek to subordinate the role of the professional *qua* professional to that of the organisation's mission expressed through leadership and managerial structures. They do, however, provide stronger possibilities for developing management and leadership approaches that draw more sensitively on the expectations and values of professionals.

Secondly, organisational responses will depend very much on context. The external environments facing institutions differ between sectors. Despite the common trends outlined in this chapter, the regulatory regimes facing schools and colleges differ considerably (Simkins, 2000). Within sectors, too, local circumstances, such as the degree of local competition or the attitudes and values of governors, can have a major effect on perceptions of strategic possibilities. Furthermore, the policy context is changing over time. The hyperactivity of policy-makers and the changes in emphasis of successive governments have already been noted. In these circumstances it is not surprising that research suggests that leadership and management approaches have changed in their turn (Grace, 1995; Withers, 2000; Gleeson, 2001).

For these reasons, it is dangerous to draw conclusions too readily about the internal consequences for schools and colleges of the changing patterns of external accountability pressures. Local and temporal contexts matter, and so do the values and preferences of leaders, managers and others within the school or college.

Conclusion

The nexus of accountabilities that schools and colleges now have to manage is greater than ever. A balance has to be sought among the ever-changing external constellation of demands from central government, from the community and from individual clients/customers. Internal accountability arrangements have to respond to these pressures while embodying values and ways of working that will maintain the commitment and ensure the effectiveness of all those working within the organisation. Figure 14.1 summarises this complex picture.

Figure 14.1 *Tensions in external and internal accountability*

Strategic choices in this context cannot avoid fundamental questions about the determination of guiding values in the education system. Value tensions can occur in all kinds of ways. For example, a teacher may feel that compliance with certain curriculum requirements deriving from the central government regulation would be inconsistent with his or her judgement of what is best for his or her students; a headteacher or principal may feel that he or she has to take decisions as a 'manager' in the interests of 'efficiency' which are not consistent with his or her professional duty to his or her colleagues or students; in a governing body conflict may arise because a chair of governors feels that the college principal is usurping the governors' legitimate policy-making role; or decisions by head or governors about individual pupils with particular difficulties or needs may be coloured by their potential impact on the school's image in the 'marketplace'.

Such tensions are never fully resolved because they embody competing concepts of legitimacy within any area of public service. They are worked out in practice through legislative frameworks which place duties and constraints on the organisations and individuals involved, through organisational structures which create frameworks for interaction, and through management processes which the parties concerned use to negotiate their roles in any particular context. They present particular challenges for organisational leaders (Leithwood, 2001), completely reframing the debate of the 1970s and 1980s around the tension between the roles of 'leading professional' and 'chief executive' (Hughes, 1985). Alongside – and related to – these challenges for leadership is the need for renewed debate about the nature of professionalism (Gleeson and Shain, 1999b; Hargreaves, 2000). The search for modes of organisation that retain the core professional values while meeting external demands for effective and efficient management will be a key challenge of the coming years.

Notes

1. Ofsted (Office for Standards in Education): the agency with responsibility for inspecting schools on behalf of the government, recently charged with inspecting colleges also.
2. Funding councils: government funds for post-school education are provided through agencies. The Learning and Skills Council has replaced a number of funding mechanisms for further, adult and work-based education, including the Further Education Funding Councils. Universities receive government funds primarily through the Higher Education Funding Councils.
3. Local management and incorporation: terms used to describe the resource and other management powers granted by law to schools and colleges, respectively.
4. FE Charter: the requirement placed on colleges to provide statements about their responsibilities to their clients within a national framework provided by the Charter for Further Education.
5. Literacy and numeracy hours: teaching requirements imposed on schools to contribute to the government's aim of increasing performance in these basic skills.
6. City technology colleges, specialist schools and city academies: some of the mechanisms through which government has sought to encourage schools to seek unique identities, often involving specific funding together with an expectation that additional funding is obtained from the private sector.

References

Abu-Duhou, I. (1999) *School-Based Management*. Paris: Unesco/IIEP.

Bagley, C., Woods, P. and Glatter, R. (1996) Barriers to school responsiveness in the education quasi-market. *School Organisation* 16(1): 45–58.

Ball, S. (1990) *Politics and Policy Making in Education: Explorations in Policy Sociology*. London: Routledge.

Bottery, M. (1999) *Professionals and Policy: Management Strategy in a Competitive World*, London: Cassell.

Bullock, A. and Thomas, H. (1997) *Schools at the Centre? A Study of Decentralisation*. London: Routledge.

Chubb, J. and Moe, T. (1990) *Politics, Markets and America's Schools*. Washington, DC: The Brookings Institution.

Clarke, J. and Newman, J. (1997) *The Managerial State: Power, Politics and Ideology in the Remaking of Social Welfare*, London: Sage.

Deem, R., Brehony, K. and Heath, S. (1995) *Active Citizenship and the Governance of Schools*. Buckingham: Open University Press.

Exworthy, M. and Halford, S. (eds.) (1998) *Professionals and the New Managerialism in the Public Sector*. Buckingham: Open University Press.

Foskett, N. (1998) Schools and marketisation: cultural challenges and responses. *Educational Management & Administration* 26(2): 197–210.

Fullan, M. and Watson. N. (2000) School-based management: reconceptualising to improve learning outcomes. *School Effectiveness & School Improvement* 11(4): 453–74.

Glatter, R. (1991) 'Boundary management and the new order', *Management in Education*, 5(4) 27–9.

Glatter, R. and Woods, P. (2001) Reframing the governance of schooling. Paper presented at the Annual Conference of the American Educational Research Association, Seattle.

Gleeson, D. (2001) Style and substance in educational leadership. *Journal of Education Policy* 16(3): 181–96.

Gleeson, D. and Husbands, C. (2001) *The Performing School: Managing Teaching and Learning in a Performance Culture*. London: RoutledgeFalmer.

Gleeson, D. and Shain, F. (1999a) By appointment: governance, markets and managerialism in further education. *British Educational Research Journal* 25(4): 545–61.

Gleeson, D. and Shain, F. (1999b) Teachers' work and professionalism in the post-incorporated further education sector. *Education and Social Justice* 1(3): 55-64.

Grace, G. (1995) *School Leadership: Beyond Educational Management*. London: Falmer Press.

Hall, V. (1997) Managing staff. In B. Fidler *et al.* (eds.) *Choices for Self-Managing Schools: Autonomy and Accountability*. London: Paul Chapman Publishing.

Hargreaves, A. (2000) The four ages of professionalism and professional learning. *Teachers and Teaching: History and Practice* 6(2): 151–81.

Hirschman, A.O. (1970) *Exit, Voice and Loyalty: Responses to Decline in Firms, Organizations and States*. Boston, MA: Harvard University Press.

Hoggett, P. (1996) New modes of control in the public service. *Public Administration* 74: 9–32.

Hughes, M.G. (1985) Leadership in professionally staffed organisations. In M. Hughes *et al.* (eds.) *Managing Education: the System and the Institution*. London: Holt Education.

Kogan, M. (1986) *Education Accountability: An Analytic Overview*. London: Hutchinson.

Kogan, M., Johnson, D., Packwood, T. and Whitaker, T. (1984) *School Governing Bodies*. London: Heinemann.

Kouzes, J. and Mico, P. (1979) Domain theory: an introduction to organizational behaviour in human service organizations. *Journal of Applied Behavioral Science* 15(4) 449–69.

Le Grand, J. and Bartlett, W. (eds.)(1993) *Quasi-Markets and Social Policy*. London: Macmillan.

Leithwood, K. (2001) 'School leadership in the context of accountability policies. *International Journal of Leadership in Education* 4(3): 217–35.

Leithwood, K. and Menzies. T. (1998) A review of the research concerning the implementation of school-based management. *School Effectiveness & School Improvement* 93: 233–85.

McGinn, N. and Welsh. T. (1999) *Decentralization of Education: Why, When, What and How?* Paris: Unesco/IIEP.

Morgan, G. (1997) *Images of Organization* (2nd edn). London: Sage.

Pollitt, C. (1993) *Managerialism and the Public Services* (2nd edn). Oxford: Blackwell.

Poulson, L. (1996) Accountability: a key-word in the discourse of educational reform. *Journal of Education Policy* 11(5): 579–92.

Ranson, S. (1994) *Towards the Learning Society*. London: Cassell.

Riley, K. (1998) *Whose School is it Anyway?* London: Falmer Press.

Simkins, T. (1999) Values, power and instrumentality: theory and research in education management. *Educational Management & Administration*, 27(3) 267–83.

Simkins, T. (2000) Education reform and managerialism: comparing the experience of schools and colleges. *Journal of Education Policy* 15(3): 317–32.

Thody, A. (1992) *Moving to Management: School Governors in the 1990s*. London: David Fulton.

Winstanley, D., Sorabji, D. and Dawson, S. (1995) When the pieces don't fit: a stakeholder power matrix to analyse public sector restructuring. *Public Money and Management* 15(2): 19–26.

Withers, B. (2000) The evolution of the role of the principal in further education: a follow-up study. *Research in Post-Compulsory Education* 5(3): 371–89.

Woods, P., Bagley, C. and Glatter, R. (1998) *School Choice and Competition: Markets in the Public Interest?* London: Routledge.

School Effectiveness and Improvement: The Story so Far

Peter Mortimore and John MacBeath

We have learned from school effectiveness and improvement research so far:

- that school education cannot compensate for society and that in making high demands of teachers and raising our expectations of schools we must have scrupulous respect for the evidence on socio-economic inequality and the changing nature of family and community life;
- that schools can make a difference and that being in an effective as against a less effective school is a crucial determinant of life chances for many individual young people;
- that 'effects' are complex and multilayered and that while schools of themselves can make a difference there are even more significant effects at the level of department and classroom;
- that children experience schools differently; that achievement is not a simple linear progression but subject to ebbs and flows over time and in response to the influence of the peer group and pupils' own expectations on the basis of gender, race and social class;
- that the context of national culture is a powerful determinant of parent, student and teacher motivation and that school improvement requires more than simplistic borrowing of remedies from other countries;
- that we are learning, and still have a lot to learn, about how schools improve and what kind of support and challenge from external sources is most conducive to their effective development;

Source: MacBeath, J. and Mortimore, P. (eds.) (2001) *Improving School Effectiveness*. Open University Press. Edited version.

- that a salient dimension of school improvement is helping schools to be more confident in the use of their own and other data, more self-critical and more skilled in the use of research and evaluation tools;
- that we will only make dramatic advances in educational improvement, in and beyond schooling, when we develop a deeper understanding of how people learn and how we can help them to learn more effectively.

The Unequal Society

Our country has been exceptional in that the difference between the 'haves' and 'have nots' seems to have resulted from official policies designed to lift the constraints affecting the rich. These policies have sought to penalise the poor in the interest of freeing them from the so-called 'dependency culture'. Britain stands out internationally, along with New Zealand, in having experienced the largest percentage increase in income inequality between 1967 and 1992.

(Mortimore and Whitty 1997: 2)

In recent decades many countries, the United Kingdom included, have witnessed a progressive rise in standards of living. However, this statistical mean conceals the fact that the number of people living in poverty has increased threefold since 1979. The distance between rich and poor, privileged and underprivileged has grown progressively during the Thatcher and post-Thatcher years and the proportion of children living in poor households is now 32 per cent, compared to the European Union average of 20 per cent.

Schools may require, but cannot provide, the prior childhood experiences that lay the foundations for success. They can seek, but cannot vouchsafe from parents, the promise of continuing support for children's emotional stability and academic achievement. Without that, children can find themselves swept along by a sequential age- and competence-related curriculum and, as well documented by Robert Slavin (1995), a self-generating downward spiral of low self-esteem, low achievement and reduced motivation. The direction of the spiral may be reversed when schools reach out to families and communities in new ways with new insights into learning. The good news, as Slavin and others have shown, is that schools can make a difference.

■ Schools can Make a Difference

From a commonsensical point of view it is obvious that schools make a difference, that from entrance at the age of 5 to exit at the age of 18, an educational transformation has taken place.

The unambiguous finding from three decades of studies across the world (Brookover *et al.* 1979; Rutter *et al.* 1979; Mortimore *et al.* 1988; Scheerens 1997) is that schools do indeed make a difference. While social background continues to play a strong influential role, schools are not helpless in promoting educational and social mobility. In other words, there is a 'school effect'. While studies between and within countries come to different conclusions about the magnitude of the school effect, there is a broad consensus that it lies somewhere in the region of 5 to 15 per cent. That is, with all other factors held constant, there is a 5 to 15 per cent variance between more and less effective schools.

This is, on the face of it, perhaps disappointing. However, the *School Matters* study (Mortimore *et al.* 1988) found that disadvantaged students did make more progress in more effective schools than their counterparts in the least effective schools. When translated into life chances for a pupil, or cohort of pupils, its significance becomes more graphically apparent. For example, in England this could be translated as a difference for the average pupil of seven grade Cs instead of six grade Es at GCSE (Thomas and Mortimore 1994).

In Scotland, studies at Edinburgh's Centre for Educational Sociology (Gray *et al.* 1983; Cuttance 1988; McPherson 1992) translated effectiveness as gaining one or more 0 Grades (GCSEs) more than expected. In the Netherlands it is described in terms of pupils in a five-ability stream school performing at two streams higher (Brandsma and Dollard 1996).

Findings such as these reflect the methodology of mainstream school effectiveness research which looks for 'outliers', that is, unusually effective schools, comparing these either with the norm or with schools at the opposite polarity – particularly ineffective schools. It is from these more effective schools that factors of effectiveness are derived. While less attention has been given to the characteristics of ineffective schools, research in this area may, in the long term, prove equally instructive.

Characteristics of effective and ineffective schools

Studies of effectiveness are now so numerous that it would take a voluminous publication to list them all. A 1997 review by Bosker and Scheerens of seminal studies (those meeting specific methodological criteria) listed 719 factors that had been found to be associated with effectiveness. In a meta-analysis (Sammons *et al.* 1996), these were reduced to 11 salient factors:

 1 professional leadership;
 2 shared vision and goals;
 3 a learning environment;
 4 concentration on learning and teaching;
 5 high expectations;
 6 positive reinforcement;
 7 monitoring progress;
 8 pupil rights and responsibilities;
 9 purposeful teaching;
10 a learning organization;
11 home–school partnership.

To what extent can we then characterize ineffective schools as lacking in these 11 features? It is, as Myers argues (1994), not that simple. She describes 'troubled' schools as having 'antithetical' characteristics, their cultures a product of myriad influences at work. 'Troubled' schools in her study (1996) tended to have their own individual clustering of factors, a dynamic mix of student ambivalence, low staff expectations, a pervasive negative ethos, weak or inconsistent leadership.

These find close echoes in other studies. Rosenholtz (1989) compared high consensus ('moving') and low-consensus ('stuck') schools, finding in the latter a lack of attachment, more concern with their own identity than with a shared community of purpose. Their school environments were 'unfree' and characterized by boredom, punitiveness and self-defensiveness. Gray and Wilcox (1994) conclude: 'We still suspect that there are problems and barriers to change which are specific to "ineffective" schools but which the research has not yet teased out' (p. 16).

Reviewing his own research, Reynolds (1995) suggests that it is easy, and mistaken, to make assumptions about what ineffectiveness is and what the differences are between failure on the one hand and lack of success on the other: '. . . people like me have implicitly back-mapped the characteristics of the effective school on to the ineffective school, thinking that what the ineffective school has is the absence of things that make the effective school effective . . . We have, in short, only viewed failure as not being successful, not as failure' (pp. 66–7).

We have not given sufficient attention to the possibility that ineffective schools are driven by factors still to be explained and with an internal dynamic still to be unravelled. Whether our focus is on effectiveness, ineffectiveness or the transition between them, we have had to move on from correlational studies to enquire more deeply into the how rather than the what, not simply what the characteristics are but how they are acquired or lost. Not simply what do effective and ineffective schools look like but how do they get that way?

Where Do Effects Lie?

Knowing, and being able to demonstrate, that schools can and do make a difference was an important step. However, the general finding that schools matter is tantalizingly elusive because it leaves a host of unanswered questions. We have needed to know more about where effects lie and we have had to test more rigorously what might be hidden more deeply within the 'school effect'.

Consistently outstanding and unambiguously awful schools are the exception. Schools as we know them tend to be a complex mix of good, less good and, occasionally, very bad teachers. In some countries we would find it difficult to detect any overall school effects at all because they could provide little more than a uneven profile of different classes, held together by a common heating system and connecting corridors. In such schools, we might well find very wide differentials between the performance of one class and another, but little influence over and above that which could be ascribed to the school as such.

Schools in the United Kingdom, whether primary, secondary or special, are rarely an aggregation of effective teachers or effective departments. They are led and managed and have whole-school policies, development plans and staff development sessions. There is synergy, and sometimes entropy, at school level, a whole that may either be greater or lesser than the sum of its parts. In other words the school as an organization may add value to that of its individual members or, on the other hand, may subtract value. It may enhance and multiply the skills of its members, or may stifle and inhibit their mutual growth.

In loosely coupled, or virtually uncoupled, schools with little interclass or interdepartmental collaboration, we might expect to find a very large variation in the performance of pupils; in other words, a high degree of inconsistency within the school as a whole. In a well led and managed school, in contrast, we would hope to see less variation and greater consistency both across the school and over time as children move through it year on year – in other words, a quite clearly distinguishable 'school' effect.

This 'consistency' measure has been the focus of considerable research in recent years and is of most relevance to systems, such as in the United Kingdom, where the cross-fertilization from classroom to classroom, subject to subject, is seen as important in enhancing effectiveness at whole-school level, and feeds back down into improved performance at classroom and individual pupil levels.

Teacher effects

The individual classroom and the individual teacher provide a useful starting point for examining effectiveness. An ideal scenario for the researcher would be in a school where children had the same teacher from 6 until 16, as is the case in many schools in Denmark. We might expect to find over a ten-year period a sharp and increasing divergence between effective teacher A and ineffective teacher B which, assuming two comparable classes, might tell a powerful story. We might, on the other hand, find a growing convergence, suggesting other influences at work – school effects or perhaps departmental effects.

Comparison of two, or more, teachers over a lengthy period would offer a measure of two key factors in the assessment of effectiveness – consistency and stability. The different achievements between teacher A's and teacher B's pupils at a given point in time would measure consistency while the degree of variance over time would provide us with a measure of stability. In practice, both consistency and stability measures are needed if we are to understand the strength of individual teacher effectiveness.

Dutch researchers (Luyten and Snidjers 1996) were able to study two samples of pupils, one which had the same teacher in grades 7 and 8, the other with two teachers in each grade. They concluded that variation is reduced by 20 per cent if the teacher stayed with the class and that 80 per cent of the variation across grades might be attributable to quality differences among teachers.

What most of the research appears to agree on is that teacher effects are powerful and that they are not limited to the time period which pupils spend with that particular teacher. Research tends to confirm what we would expect from anecdotal experience of our own children or our own personal experience – the impact of an effective primary school teacher lingers on into secondary (Sammons *et al.* 1994).

Departmental and subject effects

In secondary schools teachers are members of subject departments. There is normally a subject leader or head and a collegial team that can provide an important locus for sharing of practice, for monitoring, for quality assurance and for professional development. So, we would expect to find at departmental level some effect greater than that of the individual teachers. One study (Luyten 1994) reported a 40 per cent variance at subject department level, with only 15 per cent of the variance attributable to the whole-school effect. In other words, subjects (or departments) make more of a difference to individual achievement and progress than does the particular school attended.

Caution has to be exercised in making such a judgement, however, because we also know something about the different nature of subjects. Children come virtually brand new to some school subjects while others have a longer gestation in their home education. So, for example, reading shows a weaker school effect than mathematics because reading and pre-reading skills are often accomplished before a child starts school while the same is less true for mathematics. This was a finding of Mortimore and his colleagues (1988) and a clear conclusion of our research a decade later.

A number of studies in secondary schools (Smith and Tomlinson 1989; Thomas 1995b) found that there was a generally positive correlation among different subjects and between individual subject departments and whole-school effectiveness. But these correlations were not consistently high, some departments within a school being significantly more effective than others. Similarly, across a whole sample of schools, some subjects tended to correlate more consistently with whole-school effects. English and science, for example, related more closely to the composite GCSE score than other subjects. In Scotland there was a similar finding in a 1987 study (Cuttance) and in 1989 (Willms and Raudenbush).

Whole-school effects

As the department can add value to the achievements and effects of individual teachers, so the school may be more than a collection of subject enclaves. It may create a synergy, a whole-school effect, by drawing strengths from each department, cross-fertilizing and amplifying best practice across the school. Alternatively, improvement may come from the top down, from directive leadership, school policies, a vision or plan to which departments and teachers 'sign up'. In either case the school effect is of the further value added by the organization as a whole, through its ethos, culture, policy and planning.

Once classroom and departmental effects have been taken into account, most studies tend to show a relatively small school effect. However, the more we move towards a learning organization, the less easy it will become to separate out specific school effects from departmental and classroom effects. In a highly collaborative school in which people teach together and learn together, the differentiation of specific influences will be more difficult to locate. The further we move away from the model of the individual teacher in her classroom, towards teamwork, shared responsibility and corporate professional development, the less easy it will be to isolate the specific contribution of the individual teacher.

The high-achieving teacher may not easily be separated from the context in which the achievement takes place. This is why the rewarding of individual achievement, either through 'Platos' (teaching awards) or through performance-related pay, is problematic and resisted by schools which see themselves as collectives and see their achievements as jointly owned.

▌ Children Experience Schools Differently

Effective schools tend to be good for all their students while all students tend to perform poorly in ineffective schools. While that was a clear finding from the junior Schools Study in 1988 (Mortimore *et al.*) and in a follow-up ESRC study (Thomas *et al.* 1995a), this is, like many findings, a generalization which is tested by its exceptions. A more recent study (Sammons *et al.* 1998) did find exceptions to the 'rule'. That general principle, sound and common-sensical as it seems, does not appear to hold true in every context or country and may perhaps be subject to change along with changes in the political and cultural climate. For example, pressure on schools to invest heavily in those students most likely to show transparent returns (borderline A–C GCSE students, for example) might achieve that goal at the expense of others who would thrive in a school stronger on learning support.

Some studies have reported varying effects for different types of students. In Scottish schools, Raudenbush and Willms (1988), for example, found that some schools were effective for students of high ability but not low ability and vice versa. In another study, Willms and Kerr (1997) found that some schools were better for girls and some better for boys or for some social groups as against others.

In another study, Pam Sammons and her colleagues (1998) have explored the 'differential effectiveness' of schools, showing that not only do some groups of pupils perform better than others but that they do so at different times in their school cycle. Some pupils show spurts of achievement while others reach a plateau and stay there. Others actually regress. Some pupils do well in some subjects and not others, with individual teachers and not with others. In our research as in other studies, we found that girls tend to out-perform boys, in some cases allowing boys a head start but gradually overtaking them. There were complex patterns of achievement which became more discernible as pupils moved up through the system.

The evidence from both our research and the Sammons study suggests that the longer pupils stay in school, the more pronounced becomes the influence of social class. Is this a school effect or a background effect? That is, does the social background which pupils bring with them exert itself more strongly over time, or is a school constructed in such a way as to accentuate the difference progressively?

While we are able to separate out social class, ethnicity and gender for the purposes of research, it is also clear that it is the interrelationship of these that is truly significant and how they play themselves out in the day-to-day life of classrooms and schools.

> The experience of a low attaining English middle-class girl with parents of Indian background needs to be probed with a more textured understanding of peer group affiliation, racial and sexual harassment, ascribed roles, sub-cultural tensions and parental and teacher expectations. High achieving, African-Caribbean boys may experience particularly acute difficulties in adjusting to the different expectations of peers, teachers, their families and the group identity which defines them not only as a threat to the authority of teachers but to that of the police and others in positions of power.
>
> (MacBeath 1999: 22)

A review of research (Gillborn and Gipps 1998) provides a rich and detailed picture of the intersect between individual experience and school life. Drawing on both school effectiveness research and ethnographic studies, the authors conclude that we have still some way to go in understanding how the internal culture of the school works and how it connects, in multiple, interwoven strands, to the world outside.

Martin Thrupp (1999) has criticized effectiveness research for its blindness to the importance of 'social mix', arguing that the key to our understanding is limited only by our ability to probe with enough sensitivity the complexity of peer social interaction. This thesis receives overwhelming support from Judith Harris (1998) in her controversial book *The Nurture Assumption*. Her contention, supported by a considerable body of research, is that the child's identity as a person, her capacity as a learner and her motivation as a student come from the way in which she defines herself within the immediate peer reference group. Gender, race, ability, class, 'academic' or 'non-academic', anti-school or pro-school may be the salient characteristics of one's identity, but only when school structures and the nature of the school social mix push that feature into social prominence.

In an all-girls school, gender is not a salient feature, just as race is not a salient feature in an all-black school and the undesirable status of 'swot' has less currency in a school where selection is by ability. However, in a large racially and socially heterogeneous comprehensive school what becomes a salient feature of a pupil's self-definition arises from a complex social dynamic, constantly shifting as new friendships form and old ones disappear, as the social mix of the school and peer group changes or stabilizes. In Harris's thesis young people's most essential experience of schooling is one of defining and redefining themselves in relation to their peers.

Children experience schools differently because they meet different teachers and engage in different ways with the curriculum, but the alliances they form with others may, in the end, prove to be equally or even more powerful in shaping their expectations of achievement. In fact the compositional, or contextual, effect has been recognized by effectiveness researchers for some time. It was identified in a 1985 study in Scotland by Willms and his colleagues at the University of Edinburgh (Willms and Cuttance 1985) and returned to in subsequent studies. In 1997 Willms described how the contextual effect had become highlighted and intensified as a consequence of interschool mobility: 'When a pupil with an advantaged background transfers from a low social class to a high social class school, the contextual effect is strengthened for the chosen school and weakened for the school the child left' (Willms 1997: 3).

'We do not fully understand the contextual effect', concluded Willms' team, warning that there may be spurious effects due to inadequate statistical models, 'but taken together with the evidence from other sources we can conclude that it exists and may even be much more powerful than we had previously thought'.

A study in Grampian schools was unequivocal in its conclusions about the contextual effect. The researchers (Croxford and Cowie 1996) reported: ' . . . serious inequalities in pupils' examination results. The attainment of an average pupil may be raised or lowered by two or three Standard Grades [GCSE equivalent] by differences in school social context' (p. 5).

It is clear that the subcultural dynamics identified by Hargreaves (1967) in his *Social Relations in a Secondary School* are still as powerfully at work. It is a challenging area for further in-depth inquiry not just by researchers but more critically by schools themselves as they become more experienced and expert in self-evaluation.

■ National Cultural Context is a Powerful Determinant

As school effectiveness studies have become more international we have become more aware of those aspects of effective schools that 'travel' across cultures and those that don't. Factors such as home–school partnerships and purposeful teaching, for example, appear to have strong international currency, but deeper probing reveals the extent to which structural features of different national systems play a significant part. Scheerens *et al.*'s (1989) reanalysis of data from the Second International Mathematics and Science study found that in some countries there were relatively small differences between one school and the next while in others there was a much higher level of variance. In systems that were vertically differentiated, that is systems in which pupils entered different tracks or schools at a given age, there were large differences in the mean achievements of pupils across schools. This was true of Belgium and the Netherlands, for example.

In more horizontally integrated, or 'comprehensive', systems where pupils moved up together within the same structure (Scottish, American, Swedish, Finnish and New Zealand schools, for example), there were relatively small differences between schools but relatively large differences between classes within schools. France, Canada and Israel belong to this second group insofar as there is relatively little variance between schools, but they also reveal comparatively little variance among classes within schools.

In a case study of Singapore and London schools, the research team draw four key lessons (Mortimore *et al.* 2000: 142):

- There is no single recipe for turning a school around but there are common elements which include motivating staff, focusing on teaching and learning, enhancing the physical environment and changing the culture of the school.
- Improvements must fit in with the grain of society rather than go against it. Indiscriminate borrowing may not achieve the desired results.
- Resources in themselves do not guarantee improvement but help convince staff, parents and students that society believes in the school and is willing to invest.
- Change has to be carried out by the school itself. Friends are important, but change has to come from within.

Sensitivity to history and context does not preclude learning from other countries. Indeed, in a context of globalization this is becoming an educational imperative. But in any borrowing, whether inter-classroom or inter-school, national or international, the message is 'watch and learn, don't copy'.

How Schools Improve

Schools change over time. Headteachers come and go. Good teachers are promoted out of the classroom. Weaker teachers sometimes replace stronger ones. Student cohorts change with housing and demographic shifts. Some schools lose direction while others grow in confidence. Schools are subject to so many external pressures that for some it is a difficult task to maintain stability, let alone demonstrate improvement.

One way in which effectiveness researchers have tried to measure stability and improvement is through fluctuations in examination performance. In a 1995 ESRC study (Sammons *et al.* 1995) it was found that schools' results tended to be relatively stable over time (a correlation of 0.8) but that there was variation within subject departments (correlations between subject and whole-school of between 0.38 and 0.92). Gray and his colleagues (1999a) found a progressive rise over the decade of the 1990s in examination performance, with one in ten schools improving at a rate 'ahead of the pack'. Underlying this analysis the research team make a crucial distinction about improvement, identifying tactics, strategies and capacity as three key distinguishing measures of sustainability. Improvement, as measured by student performance, was in most cases at the tactical level – that is, focusing teachers' energies and efforts on how to improve performance. The strategic schools had longer term goals and had delved deeper into student learning. The capacity-building schools were a small minority. They had gone beyond incremental change to restructuring with an emphasis on collegial self-evaluation.

Drawing on Hopkins's (1994) definition of school improvement as 'a strategy for educational change that enhances student outcomes as well as strengthening the school's capacity for handling change' (p. 3), we may posit a two-dimensional matrix, with the vertical axis representing low to high student outcomes and the horizontal measuring low to high capacity for handling change. The improving school, by definition, is located in the high-outcome/high-capacity quadrant, the 'ineffective/stuck' school in the low-outcome/low-capacity quadrant. As Gray *et al.* (1999b) suggest, schools that have and use outcome data in a positive, active way to enhance the capacity of the school as an organization are those most likely to be truly self-improving in the longer term.

Fullan (1995) described the notion of inclusive self-improving schools as 'a distant dream'. Certainly researchers, critical friends and school development teams have found the job of improvement less easy than the politicians would like. These improvement efforts have, however, furnished us with a fairly extensive lexicon of obstacles to improvement. One project (Reynolds 1991, 1992), which failed to 'turn round' a school in Wales, provides some useful insights into blocks to improvement. These included:

- teachers projecting their own deficiencies on to children or their communities;
- teachers clinging on to past practices;
- defences built up against threatening messages from outside;
- fear of failure;
- seeing change as someone else's job;
- hostile relationships among staff;
- seeking safety in numbers (a ring-fenced mentality).

These features were not hard to identify in some of the schools in which we worked as critical friends. Drawing on Senge's (1990) notion of 'organizational learning disabilities' we identified eight of these (MacBeath 1998) which were so ingrained in the school culture that they militated against any notion of a quick fix.

School improvement is a slow process because it is about maturation. David Hargreaves (1999) uses the horticultural metaphor of sowing, germinating, thinning, shaping and pruning, showing and exchanging, to describe the process of improvement. We may add to that the most delicate and subtle aspect of progress: grafting – the process by which an organism allows an external source to take root and flourish, and forever change its organic nature. Where there was clear evidence of growth in our schools, it was in those schools where good ideas were able to take root and flourish.

We were to discover the truth of Argyris and Schön's (1978) dictum that organizations are often less knowledgeable and skilful than their members, and sometimes 'cannot seem to learn what everybody knows' (p. 71). But organizations can also have a collective wisdom that exceeds that of their individual members. A vital indicator of a school's capacity for improvement is its increased learning ability, because as we move towards the learning organization, the culture of the school becomes the knowledge carrier, spanning generations of staff. Writing about 'the attrition of change', Dean Fink (1999) comments:

> Change has to be built into the processes. Change identified with a person has the roots of its own destruction. There has to be loyalty to broader issues. Life cycles of many 'lighthouse' schools have been shortened because people could not shift loyalties from the individual to broader concepts.

> (Fink 1999: 277)

The challenge of continuous improvement is to marry culture and structure. Structures without an underpinning culture of improvement are doomed to be ineffective. Strong cultures without sustaining structures will not survive from one generation to the next.

Schools Becoming Confident, Self-critical and Skilled in Evaluation

Policy makers have been keen to rank schools, to pinpoint weaknesses and identify areas for improvement. They have been slower to put the tools in the hands of schools themselves, despite the fact that tools of self-evaluation are potentially powerful. A more cynical view might be that it is precisely because of their power that they are best left in the hands of those with a need to circumscribe and control teachers and teaching.

School self-evaluation is, however, developing an unstoppable momentum and schools are gradually becoming more confident in the use of data, more self-critical, more skilled in the use of research and evaluation tools. It is increasingly commonplace for schools to have attainment data for all of their students, including value-added data at the level of the individual pupil, class, department or whole school. With these data at their disposal teachers have the means to track the progress of their pupils and to make more informed and skilled interventions.

This tells only a part of the story, however, and schools more advanced in self-evaluation complement the quantitative data with deeper qualitative probes. For example, using performance data as a basis for sampling, teachers can systematically examine students' work across subjects, across classes and across teaching staff. This may reveal inconsistencies at individual student level, pointing to differential quality of teachers or departments. For example, a student may perform well in one subject but not in another, or with one teacher but not another. Effectiveness researchers are accustomed to uncovering such differential effects, but when used at school level by teachers for teachers it is salutary and revealing. The sensitivity of such self-evaluation within a school presupposes either a very high level of openness and trust among a staff or requires the support of a critical friend to help in the interpretation of data and may require him or her to mediate the impact of unwelcome news.

Schools are also increasingly likely to have attitudinal data from parents, students or staff. This is typically gathered through questionnaires, sometimes complemented by interviews or focus groups. Schools are becoming increasingly skilled in the customizing of questionnaires or other research tools and often benefit from a resident expert who has taken a course, has statistical expertise or a research background. All of these methodologies, once the sole province of researchers, are now accessible by teachers and management. Again, the support and guidance of a critical friend can help to avoid some of the pitfalls and hazards of home-made research tools or unscientific modes of data collection.

The most powerful use of data for school self-evaluation is as a tin opener for analysis and discussion within a staff, a management team, a group of students or parents.

It is significant that teacher evaluations of Ofsted, however negative, are consistently positive about the *Ofsted Framework for School Inspection* (Gray and Wilcox 1997). This is in large part because it puts into the hands of teachers a tool they can use for themselves, whether in preparation for inspection or their own self-evaluation. In a study for the National Union of Teachers (MacBeath 1999) the Ofsted framework was used in a playful way to explore what these criteria really meant to people and how important they were in the daily life of the school. Working with Ofsted criteria and ranking them in order of importance for a school was engaging for people, not only because it began to give them some sense of ownership, but because it generated dialogue and exposed different viewpoints. People did not immediately agree as to what words meant or how important things were. But they didn't want to arrive at a consensus that concealed their differences. They wanted to find patterns of meaning which lay in the spaces between words. This is one of the strengths of self-evaluation and where it takes root. 'A culture attuned to the multiplicity of particulars or differences, in which it seeks to find patterns, may process information more easily than a culture searching for universal and uniform attributes' (Hampden-Turner and Trompenaars 1993: 114).

External evaluators are sometimes prone to make claims for objectivity, as if their vantage point is a more elevated and panoramic one, more far-seeing in its vision than those inside the school, with all the subjective attachments which that implies. However, Hampden-Turner and Trompenaars warn: 'The problem with "objectivity" is that those who claim to have it believe they need to look no further, need listen to no one else, and never alter their convictions. They have the "data" or the "givens". But those pursuing polyocular knowledge will never be satisfied, never know enough' (1993: 114–15).

Clumsy as it may be, the term 'polyocular' draws our attention to the multi-faceted nature of knowledge and the deficiencies inherent in singular ways of seeing. When we open up the school to different ways of seeing we have to acknowledge our neglect of the student insight, the student voice. Jean Rudduck's (1996) approach to school improvement through student participation has seemed at times like a single strand in the school improvement tapestry but helpfully reminds us of the inner struggles and search for meaning which tend to elude more quantitative approaches:

Our broad understanding of what pupils have told us in interviews is that the conditions of learning that are common across schools do not adequately take account of the social maturity of young people, nor of the tensions and pressures they feel as they struggle to reconcile the demands of their social and personal lives with the development of their identity as learners.

(Rudduck *et al.* 1996: 10)

As we begin to appreciate how students make meaning of their school life we learn how different the school can be for different children. Qualitative researchers such as Dennis Thiessen (1995), Michael Fielding (1999) and Susan Groundwater-Smith (1999) have shown us that there are still deeper layers to be explored. Thiessen (1995) draws distinctions between 'knowing about students' perspectives', 'acting on behalf of students' perspectives', and 'working with students' perspectives'. We are increasingly skilled in the first of these – and in speaking on their behalf. We have to become better at the third of these – helping students to speak for themselves and to work with them in the business of school improvement. Groundwater-Smith has added a fourth level to Thiessen's trilogy – 'acting with students in partnership, to improve and change their lifeworld conditions' (1999: 4).

■ Deeper Understanding of How People Learn

The more we peel back the layers of effective, and less effective, schools, the closer we get to the core of what makes a school work – a commitment to, and joy in, learning. The more we do this with anticipation of surprise, the greater our chance of discovering something new and challenging, perhaps even in the most unlikely of places.

Every year brings new discoveries, sometimes adding scientific endorsement to grandmother's claims (carrots, greens and cod liver oil), often shattering old myths. Year on year we contest prior assumptions about under-achievement, learning difficulties or bad behaviour. Year on year new etiologies are found. With each new discovery the convenient labelling of children by ability or potential is exposed and evidence produced to demonstrate its insidiously destructive effects.

We know more today than we did in the past about the relationship of mind and body, thought and action, emotion and reason, physical and psychological health, what we eat and what we are (see, for example, Ornstein 1993; Le Doux 1997; Martin 1997). Yet we are still on the verge of plumbing their mysteries. We have little knowledge of what school learning people actually draw on in their daily lives. We do not have measures of the resilience or durability of knowledge. We do not as yet have a theory of learning and until we do our theories of teaching will always be tentative and propositional. This may be viewed not as a problem or matter for regret but as an exciting, continuing challenge.

In their document *Teaching for Learning* (SCCC 1997), the Scottish Consultative Council on the Curriculum suggests the following set of questions for teachers to put to themselves on a regular basis:

- How often do I encourage pupils to think for themselves and try out new ideas?
- What techniques do I use to help learners be more aware of how best they learn and why?
- What assumptions do I make about the individual learner when I teach?
- On what are these assumptions based?
- How would I describe the climate I am trying to establish in the classroom?
- What do I say and do to establish this climate?

These questions provide a stimulus for teachers to probe more deeply into their classroom practice, emphasizing the importance of having tools that can assist in that quest for more effective learning. Again borrowing from the researchers' repertoire, observation is being used increasingly frequently, either for performance monitoring by management, for peer assessment or, more occasionally, by students. The SCCC set of questions suggests a form of reflection, or observational framework, which focuses on learning rather than teaching, that is on what the pupils are doing rather than on what the teacher is doing. This is not only less threatening to teachers but, entered into in a spirit of inquiry, may lead to significant discoveries about the how, when and what of learning.

References

Argyris, C. and Schön, D. (1978) *Organisational Learning: A Theory of Action Perspective. Reading,* MA: Addison Wesley.

Brandsma, H.P. and Dollard, S. (1996) The effects of between-school differences in effectiveness on advice for secondary education for individual pupils, *School Effectiveness and Improvement.* NYP.

Brookover, W. et al. (1979). *School Social Systems and Student Achievement; Schools Can Make a Difference.* New York, NY: Praeger.

Croxford, L. and Cowie, M. (1996) *The Effectiveness of Grampian Secondary Schools.* Grampian Regional Council. Edinburgh: Centre for Educational Sociology.

Cuttance, P. (1987) *Modelling Variation in the Effectiveness of Schooling.* Edinburgh: Centre for Educational Sociology.

Cuttance, P. (1988) Intra-system variation in the effectiveness of schooling, *Research Papers in Education,* 3: 183–219.

Fielding, M. (1999) Students as radical agents of change: a three year case study. Paper presented at the British Educational Research Association, University of Sussex, September.

Fink, D. (1999) The attrition of change, *School Effectiveness and School Improvement,* 10(3): 269–95.

Fullan, M.G. (1995) *Successful School Improvement,* 2nd edn. Buckingham: Open University Press.

Gray, J. and Wilcox, B. (1994) *The Challenge of Turning Round Ineffective Schools.* Buckingham: Open University Press.

Gray, J. and Wilcox, B. (1995) *Good Schools, Bad Schools.* Buckingham: Open University Press.

Gray, J., McPherson, A. and Raffe, D. (1983) *Reconstructions of Secondary Education.* London: Routledge and Kegan Paul.

Gray, J., Hopkins, D., Reynolds, D. *et al.* (1999a) *Improving Schools: Performance and Potential.* Buckingham: Open University Press.

Gray, J., Reynolds, D., Fitzgibbon, C.T. and Jesson, D. (eds) (1999b) *Merging Traditions: The Future of Research on School Effectiveness and School Improvement.* London: Cassell.

Groundwater-Smith, S. (1999) Students as researchers: two Australian case studies. Paper presented at the British Educational Research Association, University of Sussex, September.

Hampden-Turner, C. and Trompenaars, L. (1993) *The Seven Cultures of Capitalism.* New York, NY: Doubleday.

Hargreaves, D.H. (1967) *Social Relations in a Secondary School.* London: Routledge and Kegan Paul.

Hargreaves, D.H. (1999) *Creative Professionalism: The Role of Teachers in the Knowledge Society.* London: DEMOS.

Harris, J.R. (1998) *The Nurture Assumption.* London: Bloomsbury.

Hopkins, D. (1994) Towards a theory for school improvement. Paper presented to ESRC Seminar Series on School Effectiveness and School Improvement, University of Newcastle Upon Tyne, October.

Le Doux, J. (1997) *The Emotional Brain.* Allendale, PA: Touchstone Books.

Luyten, H. (1994) *School Effects: Stability and Malleability.* Enschede, the Netherlands: University of Twente.

Luyten, J.W. and Snidjers, T.A.B. (1996) School effects and teacher effects in Dutch elementary education, *Educational Research and Evaluation*, 2, 1–24.

MacBeath, J. (1998) 'I didn't know he was ill': the role and value of the critical friend, in L. Stoll and K. Myers (eds) (1998) *No Quick Fixes: Perspectives on Schools in Difficulty*. London: Falmer Press.

MacBeath, J. (1999) *Schools Must Speak for Themselves*. London: Routledge.

MacBeath, J. (ed) (1998) *Effective Leadership: Responding to Change*. London: Paul Chapman Publishing.

McPherson, A. (1992) *Measuring Added Value in Schools*, briefing no. 1. London: National Commission on Education.

Martin, P. (1997) *The Sickening Mind*. London: Flamingo.

Mortimore, P. and Whitty, G. (1997) *Can School Improvement Overcome the Effects of Disadvantage?* London: Institute of Education.

Mortimore, P., Sammons, P., Stoll, L., Lewis, D. and Ecob, R. (1988) *School Matters: The Junior Years*. Somerset: Open Books (reprinted in 1994 by Paul Chapman Publishing, London).

Mortimore, P., Gopinathan, S., Leo, E. *et al.* (2000) *The Culture of Change: Case studies of Improving Schools in Singapore and London*. London: Institute of Education.

Myers, K. (1994) Why schools in difficulty may find the research on school effectiveness and school improvement inappropriate for their needs. Unpublished paper for doctoral thesis. London: Institute of Education.

Myers, K. (1996) *School Improvement in Practice: Accounts from the Schools Make a Difference Project*. London: Falmer Press.

Ornstein, R. (1993) *The Roots of the Self*. San Francisco: Harper & Row.

Raudenbush, S.W. and Willms, J.D. (1988) Procedures for reducing bias in the simulation of school effects. Paper presented at the American Educational Research Association, New Orleans, April.

Reynolds, D. (1991) Changing ineffective schools, in M. Ainscow (ed.) *Effective Schools for All*. London: Fulton.

Reynolds, D. (1992) School effectiveness and school improvement: an updated review of the British literature, in D. Reynolds and P. Cuttance (eds) *School Effectiveness: Research, Policy and Practice*. London: Cassell.

Reynolds, D. (1995) The effective school: an inaugural lecture, *Evaluation and Research in Education*, 9 (2): 57–73.

Rosenholtz, S.J. (1989) *Teachers' Workplace: The Social Organization of the School*. New York, NY: Longman.

Rudduck, J. Chaplain, R. and Wallace, G. (1996) *School Improvement: What can Pupils Tell Us?* London: Fulton.

Rutter, M., Maughan, B., Mortimore, P. and Ouston, J. with Smith, A. (1979) *Fifteen Thousand Hours: Secondary Schools and their Effects on Children*. London: Open Books.

Sammons, P., Hillman, J. and Mortimore, P. (1994) *Key Characteristics of Effective Schools: A Review of School Effectiveness Research*. London: Office for Standards in Education.

Sammons, P., Hillman, J. and Mortimore, P. (1995) Accounting for variations in academic effectiveness between schools and departments: results from the 'Differential Secondary School Effectiveness' project – a three-year study of GCSE performance. Paper presented at the European Conference on Educational Research/BERA Annual Conference, Bath, September.

Sammons, P., Mortimore, P and Thomas, S. (1996) Do schools perform consistently across outcomes and areas? in J. Gray, D. Reynolds, C. Fitz-Gibbon and D. Jesson (eds) *Merging Traditions: The Future of Research on School Effectiveness and School Improvement*. London: Cassell.

Sammons, P., Smees, R., Thomas, S., Robertson, P., McCall, J. and Mortimore, P. (1998) The impact of background factors on pupil attainment and progress in Scottish schools: a summary of findings. Paper presented at the International Congress for School Effectiveness and Improvement, University of Manchester, January.

Scheerens, J. (1997) Theories on effective schooling, *School Effectiveness and School Improvement*, 8(3): 220–42.

Scheerens, J., Vermeulen, C. and Pelgrum, W. (1989) Generalisability of instructional and school effectiveness indicators across nations, *International Journal of Educational Research*, 13(7): 789–99.

Scottish Consultative Council on the Curriculum (1997) *Teaching for Effective Learning*. Dundee: SCCC.

Senge, P. (1990) *The Fifth Discipline: The Art and Practice of the Learning Organisation*. New York, NY: Doubleday.

Slavin, R. (1995) Success for all: restructuring elementary schools. Paper presented at the International Congress for School Effectiveness and Improvement, Leeuwarden, January.

Smith, D. and Tomlinson, S. (1989) *The School Effect: A Study of Multi-Racial Comprehensives*. London: Policy Studies Institute.

Thiessen, D. (1995) Whose voices? Whose perspectives? Some challenges in understanding the curriculum experiences of primary pupils. Paper presented at the European Conference in Educational Research, Seville, September.

Thomas, S. (1995a) *Considering Primary School Effectiveness: An Analysis of 1992 Key Stage 1. Results, The Curriculum Journal*, 6(3): 279–95.

Thomas, S. (1995b) Differential secondary school effectiveness. Paper presented at the Annual Conference of the British Educational Research Association, Bath, September.

Thomas, S. and Mortimore, P. (1996) Comparison of value-added models for secondary school effectiveness, *Research Papers in Education*, 11 (1): 5–33.

Thrupp, M. (1999) *Schools Making a Difference: Let's Be Realistic*. Buckingham: Open University Press.

Willms, J.D. (1985) The balance thesis – contextual effects of ability on pupils' 'O' grade examination results, *Oxford Review of Education*, 11 (1): 33–41.

Willms, J.D. (1987) Parental choice and education policy, *CES Briefing*, 12, August.

Willms, J.D. and Kerr, M. (1987) Changes in sex differences in school examination results since 1975, *Journal of Early Adolescence*, June.

Willms, J.D. and Raudenbush, S.W. (1989) A longitudinal hierarchical linear model for estimating school effects and their stability, *Journal of Educational Measurement*, 26 (3): 209–32.

16

School Effectiveness and School Improvement: Critique of a Movement

Janet Ouston

Introduction

This chapter is a work in progress, in fact it has been in progress for many years since I started to worry about the validity and impact of the body of work called School Effectiveness and School Improvement (SESI). It is deliberately not a research review, although it will draw on some research to illustrate the argument. It is a personal reflection on why I have spent so long being concerned about something that nearly everyone else in education seems to have taken for granted as self-evidently true. It feels a bit like being that small boy in the Hans Anderson story – what sort of clothes is this emperor actually wearing? Rather than getting pulled too deeply into the nitty-gritty of research findings I want to take a more distanced perspective, to look at this remarkable forest rather than at the individual trees.

It should also be kept in mind that this chapter was written from outside SESI, not from within. SESI is often called a 'movement' which seems to indicate that it has progressed from being a 'field of study' which Vaill (1991, 64) defines as having divergent views and debates to a 'cult' where 'one either buys the approach or one doesn't'. This is one of my concerns about its impact, and one I will return to later. I am very aware that many of the reservations set out in this chapter have been made elsewhere by, for example, Silver (1994), White and Barber (1997) and Slee, Weiner and Tomlinson (1998) among many others, and that I have not done justice to others' work, nor adequately acknowledged their influence on my thinking.

Source: Bush, T., Bell, L., Bolam, R., Glatter, R. and Ribbins, P. (eds.) (1999) *Educational Management: Redefining Theory, Policy and Practice*. London: Paul Chapman Publishing. Edited version.

Critiques of SESI can be seen as falling into three categories: the first concerns the validity of research on differential school effectiveness, the second its implications for 'school improvement' and the third its impact on education more widely. They are sometimes run together in an unhelpful way. Here they will be treated separately.

■ School Effectiveness

During the 1970s I was a member of a research team which undertook a study of students attending 12 secondary schools in south London, following their progress from the last year in primary school to the end of compulsory schooling (Rutter, Maughan, Mortimore, Ouston and Smith, 1979). Using the best analytic techniques available at the time, we concluded that schools differed from one another both in their 'raw' outcomes (of attendance, in-school behaviour, examination results and delinquency) and after they had been 'adjusted' for attainment and behaviour at the end of primary school. We then related these differences to aspects of the internal life of the schools and created one of those now familiar lists of 'features of effective schools'. (It should be noted in passing that there is a PhD in analysing those lists and the operational definitions used to create them. I returned to *Fifteen Thousand Hours* for the first time for many years recently, to check what we had written about leadership. I was amazed that leadership is not discussed and headteachers are only mentioned in passing: 'obviously the influence of the headteacher is very considerable' (203). But since then leaders have been exhorted to be 'strong', 'firm', 'professional', 'purposeful', 'participative' – in fact almost anything except 'invisible'.)

None of the *Fifteen Thousand Hours* team were school management specialists – did such people exist in the 1970s? Methodologically, we were influenced by Brown's (1966) research on the relationships between ward practice in psychiatric hospitals and patients' recovery, and by Newman's (1972) study of crime and the design of public housing estates in the US. Far from being managerial, which was a criticism made at the time, it was an attempt to encapsulate school life from the perspective of teachers and students using a quantitative methodology. But it was used in an increasingly managerialist political context to support a managerial approach.

The research was published in 1979, a year which was an important turning point in the wider political scene. The election of the Conservative government led to the massive changes in society, in particular in the public sector. Our study of schools in south London created a surprising amount of interest nationally and internationally. While it had been out of tune with the 1970s, it fitted, and helped to create the educational *zeitgeist* of the early 1980s. The message of the research, and of other school effectiveness studies, seemed simple, and fitted – and still fits – the political climate.

Very early on I had two serious doubts about the interpretation of the findings. Did these features of effective schools really relate to all schools or just to the inner city? I have since commented on this (Ouston, 1993) and others have also raised the same question (see for example Brown. Duffield and Riddell, 1995). The second concern was about cause and effect, which in real organisations are inextricably entwined. As all undergraduate psychology students know, one cannot argue causation from correlation. Were the features of what became known as 'effective' schools the result of being effective or the cause of effectiveness? As Stoll and Fink (1996, 29) say 'This is a continuing challenge for researchers'.

A trivial example to illustrate this issue is that of the house-plants. The effective schools were pleasant places to be in. They were clean and cared for and had plants in classrooms. If one had cleaned the classrooms of the less effective schools and given each teacher a house-plant would the exam results have improved? I doubt it: the house-plants would probably have died. But this question raised much more serious questions in its wake. Being good social scientists we set out to try to disentangle causes from effects by working intensively with schools committed to improvement and recording what happened. The results were very disappointing, although we learned a lot along the way (Maughan, Ouston, Pickles and Rutter, 1990; Ouston, Maughan and Rutter, 1991).

Looking back I can see that we were very naïve. The problem with the research was that the schools were so complex, and nothing happened rationally in the way that we thought it might. Even given goodwill and hard work, change didn't happen as we hoped and planned. And it was almost impossible to track. We were asking a question that I think no one has cracked in the rigorous way we sought, and it may actually be uncrackable: how do changes in the management of a school lead to changes in student outcomes, and how can you see that happening in real time? We then did the next best thing, which was to do a retrospective case study of schools that had changed over the previous ten years. Here the task is so much simpler because you start from known 'starting' and 'end' points and the historical perspective allows you to ignore all the clutter and noise of real institutions at work. I learned from this that schools are extremely difficult to conceptualise, and that one has to have theory – both personal theory and public theory – to guide interpretation. I realised too that there could be many theories that might be useful for this purpose, but that all of them were enormously more complex than our simple, rational, model of organisational change.

So professionally I moved away from school effectiveness to school management where at least one could think in higher-order concepts such as organisational systems, authority, power and values. But this is running ahead, of the argument. To sum up:

Researchers in school effectiveness have proposed that:

■ schools differ from each other in their achievements
■ it is possible to 'adjust for' prior attainment, or social factors, and rank
  schools according, to how successful they are in promoting students' progress
■ it is possible to relate these rankings to internal features of the schools.

If these conclusions are not valid, either conceptually or technically, then the whole of SESI is in difficulties. If schools don't differ, or we can't measure these differences reliably, then the lists of the features of effective schools have little justification. Much work in this area (e.g. Gray and Wilcox, 1995; Goldstein and Spiegelhalter, 1996; and Croxford and Cowie, 1996) has argued that adjusted differences between schools are very small, that the majority of schools cannot be distinguished from one another. Croxford and Cowie, in their study of 38 Grampian secondary schools, estimated a difference of one grade between the average leaver in the most effective school compared to the least effective after adjusting for social factors. Only three schools were significantly above average, and four significantly below. The remaining 31 schools were indistinguishable. Goldstein and Spiegelhalter similarly conclude from their data that:

> two thirds of all possible comparisons (between schools) do not allow
> separation. Thus, even with the input adjustment, the use of rankings to judge
> differences between institutions may have a limited utility. A ranking . . . may
> allow us to isolate some institutions, at the extremes, as candidates for further
> study. In other words we can use such rankings as screening instruments, but
> not as definitive judgements on individual institutions.

(397)

Gray and Wilcox (1995) reported that, in their study, school factors might be seen to account for four grade points between the average student in the 'best' and 'worst' schools. They also argue that most schools are indistinguishable from each other.

In all these studies differences between schools were reduced considerably when adjustments were made for differences in intake: these might be in prior attainment, in social class, or in family poverty. In the analysis of exam results from 32 schools Sammons, Thomas and Mortimore (1997) showed that making such adjustments reduced differences, but shifted only six 'middling' schools from below to above average or vice versa. Gray and Wilcox made a similar point:

in 20 years of reading research on the characteristics of effective schools . . . they
had not come across effective schools where the environment was poor, where
the roof needed repair, or where the school had serious staffing difficulties.

(21)

Reviewing several studies Stoll and Fink estimate that 8–14 per cent of the
variance in pupils' achievement is attributable to school factors. They con-
cede that these are not very large, 'but it may turn out to be the crucial
difference between success and failure' (Stoll and Fink, 1996, 37). Should
such small effects have had such a major impact on educational thinking?

■ Ecological Correlations

There is an apparent contradiction in much of the published research on
school effectiveness. Some researchers claim that the differences between
schools are rather small once prior attainment and/or social factors have
been taken into account. Others – mainly policy-makers – argue that differences between 'similar' schools in attainment can be quite large. So it is
frequently argued by policy-makers (for example, DfEE, 1997a) that schools
with similar percentages of students claiming free school meals (a measure of
family poverty) have very different outcomes. Can both of these findings be
correct? Policy-makers seem unaware of the misleading results that may arise
from correlating averages with averages which were first pointed out by
Robinson (1950) – an example in education would be relating the proportion
of students taking free meals with the proportion attaining particular exam
or test scores. Researchers have increasingly moved to using individual level
data and multi-level modelling (Goldstein and Spiegelhalter, 1996) while
policy-makers have continued to use potentially misleading school level
data. Fitz-
Gibbon (1996) provides several interesting illustrations of the consequences
of these different approaches.
   At this point we are probably justified in concluding that:

■ Differences between schools in their raw scores can be considerable, and
   that these relate in the main to social factors and prior achievement.
■ Adjustments reduce the size of differences between schools but may not
   change their outcome positions relative to other schools.
■ The adjusted differences between the most effective and the least effective
   schools are relatively small. It should be noted that most writers on SESI
   accept this point, but go ahead as if they were much larger!

Decisions on what should be seen as appropriate measures to use to 'adjust' exam scores are critical. Girls do better than boys, just as the socially advantaged do better than the disadvantaged. Should we, for example, use gender as one of the individual 'measures' we use to adjust exam scores? Or are we happy to accept that girls do better than boys? If we adjust for gender, gender differences may become invisible. Would this matter? This is a serious issue because the current notion of 'adjusting for social factors' has led some to the misunderstanding that social factors don't matter: any school can achieve anything, and 'poverty is no excuse'. Paradoxically it may also have led to a lowering of expectations of schools serving socially disadvantaged communities. Some inner city schools receive two conflicting messages: that they are failing to achieve national averages, and that they are doing really well on 'value-added' measures. While both may be true, neither helps schools do as well as they can for their students.

■ Features of Effective Schools

Given that the differences between schools in their adjusted outcomes are small, and that most schools cannot be distinguished from each other, how does it come about that many different research groups come up with similar lists of features? There are two possible explanations for this: first the dominance of 'SESI thinking' has led researchers to look for similar factors. It is worth bearing in mind that many school effectiveness studies in the UK were undertaken before the introduction of LMS and open enrolment. A study by Sammons, Thomas and Mortimore (1997), however, comes up with some similar features to those identified in the Rutter *et al.* (1979) study almost 20 years earlier. But they overstated the similarities: we didn't refer to shared vision, clear leadership, or parental involvement. It is not surprising that they didn't identify any items concerned with LMS and open enrolment as they do not appear to have included these items in their questionnaires.

But the more likely explanation of this finding is that these small differences between schools will only be partly explained by the 'features of school effectiveness'. We have, therefore, a very relatively weak explanation of small differences. So what is it that researchers keep picking up? Because differences between schools are attenuated, but not otherwise changed, the effects recorded may in fact be those that relate to absolute differences between schools in outcomes rather than adjusted differences.

A typical list of 'features of effective schools' includes:

- professional leadership: strong, purposeful, involved
- shared vision and goals
- a learning environment
- concentration on teaching and learning
- explicit high expectations
- positive reinforcement
- monitoring progress
- pupil rights and responsibilities
- purposeful teaching
- a learning organisation
- home–school partnerships.

(from Barber *et al.*, 1995)

These bring to mind a similar list published by Peters and Waterman (1982):

- managing ambiguity and paradox
- a bias for action.*
- close to the customer.*
- autonomy and entrepreneurship
- productivity through people*
- hands on, value driven*
- stick to the knitting*
- simple form, lean staff
- simultaneous loose–tight properties.

The asterisks indicate possible overlaps between the Barber *et al.* list, and Peters and Waterman's list. In fact Peters and Waterman's list might be more appropriate to schools in the current political context, in particular 'managing ambuity and paradox', 'autonomy and entrepreneurship' and 'simultaneous loose–tight properties'.

To conclude this section, it has been argued that social factors are such powerful influences that they are the main determinants of the individual achievement. When exam outcomes are adjusted for social factors many of the differences between schools are reduced but their general pattern (e.g. above average, below average) is not changed. It was then suggested that the lists of 'features of effective schools' were very similar to that reported by Peters and Waterman in their study of effective companies. This may reflect the fact that what is being evaluated is not the value-added effectiveness of the school, but its unadjusted performance. However, if these are not very different, it will make little difference to features identified. The features themselves are also rather unsurprising: a school with 'academic emphasis' seems very likely to have better average attainment than one without; and that 'good' leadership is better than 'bad' leadership even if the definitions are a bit slippery.

School Improvement

There is no reason for the theory and practice of improving schools to be related to research on school effectiveness. Indeed, many theories of the management of change are built on quite different foundations. But school improvers have claimed that the links are important, and even that they should be stronger than they are.

Returning to reconsider our early school improvement project, we assumed – like others – that schools were rational organisations, that their processes were linear, and their feedback loops were negative. Given these assumptions the implementation of change should have been straightforward. All that had to be done was to get less successful schools to look like successful schools and all would be well. The SESI movement has progressed since then, with researchers (e.g. Stoll and Fink, 1996) appreciating that studying features of effective schools may not help. To use a medical metaphor: telling a person with bronchitis that fit people can breathe easily and run up and down stairs doesn't help in their current situation. There has to be a theory about how the sick person might regain health. But the popular presentation of SESI, in for example *Governing Bodies and Effective Schools* (Barber *et al.*, 1995) presents lists of features of effective schools under the heading 'what makes an effective school'. Perhaps the section should have been called what *describes* an effective school.

The school improvement literature includes discussions of the importance of school culture, vision, leadership, pedagogy and so on. Great emphasis is placed on school development planning, and more recently on target setting and self-evaluation. But there is rarely any attempt at developing a dynamic model of school processes although it is frequently mentioned as being desirable. It is my increasingly strongly held belief that one should not attempt to change an organisation without some prior understanding of how it functions, of the key parts of the system and how they inter-relate. One can, of course, change organisations without this understanding, and the outcomes may be positive, but this is accidental rather than intentional. They will also be very vulnerable to adverse outcomes which no one predicted. (Sharp-eyed readers will notice the beginning of the influence of Deming's (1993) ideas at this point!)

Guides to school improvement have a conceptual hole at their centre. They never seem to offer help in answering three key questions, *what will you do to improve? how?* and *why?* Two publications are taken as examples. A TES article by Myers (1998) offers guidelines on all aspects of running an improvement project: the administration and management of the project, selecting schools, appointing staff, publications, training and many other important tasks are covered. But not these key questions. The gap is also seen in *Setting Targets for Pupil Achievement* (DfEE, 1997b) where stage four of the 'five-phase cycle for school improvement' is 'what must we do to make it happen?' (5). But when one turns to the detail of this phase it is expanded to:

> 'What will be done?
> Who will be responsible for ensuring the action takes place?
> What resources and support will be needed?
> What will the timetable be?'
>
> (9)

Governors are offered no help about how to decide 'what will be done?'.

It is difficult to resolve these issues because they require answers which build on a theory of schools as organisations, on individual and social psychology, and on the causal links between school management, classroom practice and learning. Effective change is very context dependent. Teachers need to develop their own theory, to understand why certain practices are successful. A data-base of this kind certainly might help by suggesting some alternatives for action. Using small scale innovations which are reviewed and modified, appropriate initiatives can be developed. Deming (1993) called this the plan–do–study–act cycle. He was not proposing end-of-programme evaluation, but very frequent formative review: plan it, do it, review and study it, and change it. Then do it again, and again. The 'study' phase is of critical importance as it is here that personal theory and understandings are developed. As Mary Marsh (in Ouston, 1997) explained:

> So what it is that you are trying to do often is much less important than how you're trying to do it, and that's the bit you need to get right. Yes, you've got to set clear targets and objectives, but you shouldn't spend weeks developing elaborate ones. Keep it snappy, short, focused, and get on with it. Do it and review it. 'Is it working? No, it isn't. What do we do next?' So it's much more immediate and not so large scale.
>
> (143)

Deming proposed that the management of continuous improvement requires four sets of underpinning concepts:

■ That organisations are interlinked systems, where actions in one area will have consequences elsewhere.
■ That all systems have outcomes which fluctuate over time. Improvement must be interpreted against this background variation.

■ That one has to develop and test out a theory of how and why innovations will lead to particular outcomes.

■ That one has to have a knowledge of psychology, which will lead to an understanding of how all the people in the system will respond to the innovation.

School improvement writing assumes that schools are rational organisations and that rational planning models – such as school development planning – are appropriate. But many writers have argued that chaos theory (Stacey, 1992) or the idea of the learning organisation (Senge, 1990), may provide more useful insights. Surprisingly, Fullan's challenging book *Change Forces* (Fullan, 1993) has made little impact on mainstream school improvement writing. Fullan argues that a new approach is needed to educational change which takes account of the rapidly changing context. He argues against the current emphasis on vision and strategic planning, and against strong top-. down leadership, rationality and accountability. He proposes that in the current context teachers need a personal moral purpose and need to themselves be change agents. He quotes Block (1987, 97–8):

> Cultures get changed in a thousand small ways, not by dramatic announcements from the boardroom. If we wait until top management gives leadership to the change we want to see, we miss the point. For us to have any hope that our own preferred future will come to pass, we provide the leadership.

(14)

Stacey (1992) also argues that decision-making should be devolved, and diversity encouraged. The extent to which these less-rational approaches are appropriate to schools has been discussed in Ouston (1998a).

Impact of SESI on Education More Widely

SESI has had a huge influence on national education policy. It has become part of 'what everybody knows' about education and it is very difficult to discuss or argue against – there is no alternative valid language for debate outside the academic world and not much within. The SESI discourse runs throughout the education policies of recent governments, and seems to have been adopted without hesitation by teachers, governors, parents and academics.

Ball (1990) wrote about the 'discourse of derision' in education in the late 1980s. The school improvement movement can be seen as a contributor to this discourse. Does 'school improvement' mean that all schools need improving, is the message that all schools are weak? It was often said that

LMS centralised decision-making and devolved blame. LMS and the discourse of derision have created a blame culture, and SESI has enhanced this by creating the impression that schools and, in particular, headteachers are entirely responsible for their educational outcomes.

The SESI movement has over-emphasised the role of the head (or leader) and top-down management. This too has meshed with the political climate. The shift to a managerialist view of schools has led to an increasing gap between the managers and the managed (Clarke and Newman, 1997; Whitty, Power and Halpin, 1998). In NPQH (TTA, 1997), for example, headteachers are required to 'lead, motivate, support, challenge and develop staff to secure improvement' (7). The headteacher 'creates an ethos' and 'provides educational vision' (6). There is little space for collaboration or for encouraging the diverse and self-motivated body of teachers, who Fullan (1993) argues are needed for the future. Many years ago Torrington and Weightman (1989) commented that the emphasis on the headteacher-as-leader in their research schools was far in excess of that found in organisations outside education. They questioned 'this dangerous dependence on one person' (230).

A major outcome of the school effectiveness movement and its interpretation by policy-makers has been the emphasis on using examination and test results as the major performance indicators for schools – a good school has become one with good exam results. Nuttall once distinguished between high and low stakes measures of performance. League tables are high stakes, and, as Deming (1993) pointed out, such performance indicators will lead to a distortion of educational processes. Their impact is discussed in Ouston, Fidler and Earley (1998).

Definitions of school effectiveness reflect the political and cultural frameworks within which policy-makers set priorities. They are open to examination, evaluation and change. As an example, we can consider the contrasts between English and Japanese educational priorities. The Japanese are trying to move away from an examination driven system because of its narrowing and inflexible impact on education while we are moving towards it in order to increase literacy and numeracy. Each country's policy-makers seem intent on revisiting the educational history of the other (Ouston, 1998b) in order to promote their current, different, definitions of 'educational effectiveness'. The time has come to examine critically our taken-for-granted defiinitions. Are the research findings as firmly based as we think? What are the costs and benefits of our approaches to school effectiveness and school improvement? What are the opportunity costs? What values underpin our practice? How will these influence the lives of the young people currently in school? There are important and difficult questions to be asked about 'good' education and how it is to be achieved.

There is a serious question to be confronted. How much improvement can schools reasonably expect in the attainment of their pupils? It seems likely that any particular school's examination results will be constrained by its intake; and it seems realistic to assume a band of performance within which the majority of schools will lie.

Students must be given the opportunity for high achievement, but many years ago Jencks (1972) argued that even if schools had little long-term impact on students' lives their immediate effects are important:

> Some schools are dull, depressing, even terrifying places, while others are lively, comfortable, and reassuring. If we think of school life as an end in itself rather than as a means to some other end, such differences become enormously important. Eliminating these differences would not do much to make adults more equal, but it would do a great deal to make the quality of children's (and teachers') lives more equal.
>
> (256)

Schools – particularly those serving disadvantaged families – need to be respectful, values-based, exciting environments for children to grow up in. These may offer all kinds of positive outcomes in addition to the acquisition of examination results. This is an important challenge for all teachers including those with management responsibilities, and one that requires a high quality of management knowledge, understanding and skills.

References

Ball, S.J. (1990) *Politics and Policy Making in Education*, London: Routledge.

Barber, M., Stoll, L., Mortimore, P. and Hillman, J. (1995) *Governing Bodies and Effective Schools*, London: DfEE.

Block, P. (1987) *The Empowered Manager*, San Francisco: Jossey Bass.

Brown, G.W. (1966) *Schizophrenia and Social Care*, Oxford: Oxford University Press.

Brown, S., Duffield, J. and Riddell, S. (1995) School effectiveness research: the policy makers' tool for school improvement? *European Educational Research Association Bulletin*, 1, 1, 6–15.

Clarke, J. and Newman, J. (1997) *The Managerial State*, London: Sage.

Croxford, L. and Cowie, M. (1996) *The Effectiveness of Grampian Secondary Schools*. Report of a research programme undertaken by Grampian Regional Council and the Centre for Educational Sociology, Edinburgh. Edinburgh: CES.

Deming, W.E. (1993) *The New Economics for Industry, Government and Education*, Cambridge, MA: MIT.

DfEE (1997a) *Excellence in Schools*, London: DfEE.

DfEE (1997b) *Setting Targets for Pupil Achievement: Guidance for governors*, London: DfEE.

Fitz-Gibbon, C. (1996) *Monitoring Education: Indicators, Quality and Effectiveness*. London: Cassell.

Fullan, M. (1993) *Change Forces: Probing the Depths of Educational Reform*, London: Falmer.

Goldstein, H and Spiegelhalter, D.J. (1996) League tables and their limitations: statistical issues in comparisons of institutional performance, *Journal of the Royal Statistical Society, Series A*, 159, 3, 385–443.

Gray, J. and Wilcox, B. (1995) *Good School, Bad School*, Buckingham: Open University Press.

Jencks, C. (1972) *Inequality: A Reassessment of Family and Schooling in America*, London: Penguin Books.

Maughan, B., Ouston, J., Pickles, A. and Rutter, M. (1990) Can schools change? I: Changes in outcomes, *Journal for School Effectiveness and Improvement*, 1, 3, 188–210.

Myers, K. (1998) Improve and feel no pain, *Times Educational Supplement*, 15 May 1998, 28.

Newman, O. (1972) *Defensible Space*, New York: Macmillan.

Ouston, J. (1993) Management competences, school effectiveness and education management, *Educational Management and Administration*, 21, 4, 212–21.

Ouston, J. (1997) Chapter 8: Mary Marsh in conversation with Janet Ouston, in P. Ribbins (ed.) *Leaders and Leadership in the School, College and University*, London: Cassell.

Ouston, J. (1998a) Managing in turbulent times, in A. Gold and J. Evans (1998) *Reflecting on School Management*, Lewes: Falmer.

Ouston, J. (1998b) Educational reform in Japan: some reflections from England, *Management in Education*, 12, 5, 15–19.

Ouston, J., Fidler, B. and Earley, P. (1998) The educational accountability of schools in England and Wales, *Education Policy*, 12, 1–2, 111–23.

Ouston, J., Maughan, B. and Rutter, M. (1991) Can schools change? II: Changes in practice, *Journal of School Effectiveness and Improvement* 2, 1, 3–13.

Peters, T.J. and Waterman, R.H. (1982) *In Search of Excellence*, New York: Harper and Row.

Robinson, W.S. (1950) Ecological correlations and the behavior of individuals, *American Sociological Review*, 15, 351–7.

Rutter, M., Maughan, B., Mortimore, P., Ouston, J. and Smith, A. (1979) *Fifteen Thousand Hours*, London: Open Books.

Sammons, P., Thomas, S. and Mortimore, P. (1997) *Forging Links: Effective Schools and Effective Departments*, London: Paul Chapman Publishing.

Senge, P. (1990) *The Fifth Discipline*, New York: Doubleday.

Silver, H. (1994) *Good Schools, Effective Schools: Judgements and their Histories*, London: Cassell.

Slee, R., Weiner, G. with Tomlinson, S. (1998) *School Effectiveness from Whom? Challenges to the School Effectiveness and School Improvement movements*, London: Falmer.

Stacey, R. (1992) *Managing Chaos*, London: Kogan Page.

Stoll, L. and Fink. L. (1996) *Changing our Schools: Linking School Effectiveness and School Improvement*, Buckingham: Open University Press.

Teacher Training Agency (TTA) (1997) *National Professional Qualification for Headship*, London: TTA.

Teacher Training Agency (TTA) (1997) *National Standards for Headteachers*, London: TTA.

Torrington, D. and Weightman, J. (1989) *The Reality of School Management*, Oxford: Blackwell.

Vaill, P.B. (1991) *Managing as a Performing Art: New Ideas for a World of Chaotic Change*, San Francisco: Jossey Bass.

Whitty, G., Power, S. and Halpin, D. (1998) *Devolution and Choice in Education: the School, the State and the Market*, Buckingham: Open University Press.

White, J. and Barber, M. (eds.) (1997) *Perspectives on School Effectiveness and School Improvement*, London: Institute of Education.

17

Effectiveness and Improvement: School and College Research Compared

Paul Martinez

Background

For many years there has been an explosion of interest in two related areas of research: school effectiveness and school improvement. The first attempts to answer the question: What are the factors that are associated with effective schools? The second has a focus on the ways that schools improve to become more effective. Both traditions are inspired by the belief that schools 'can make a difference'. In other words, they are premised on the belief that some schools and some departments within schools perform better than others and that teachers, heads of departments and head teachers can develop and implement measures to improve performance or, alternatively, to maintain existing high levels of performance.

This research effort is substantial, growing in volume, supported by a number of dedicated research centres in universities and international in scope. Similar research efforts are being undertaken throughout the English-speaking world and beyond. Comprehensive introductions to this work can be found in Reynolds (1990), Reynolds *et al.* (1997), Sammons *et al.* (1997), Mortimore (1998), Gray *et al.* (1999), Sammons (1999), Macbeath & Mortimore (2001). A convenient introduction and overview written for an intended further education audience has been produced by Somekh *et al.* (1999).

In the context of this considerable research effort in the school sector, a number of further education (FE) researchers have identified the absence of a research culture in further education (Brotherton, 1998; Elliot, 2000). Indeed, one article noted the 'dearth of research to date on college effectiveness' (Cunningham, 1999, p. 403).

Source: Research in Post-Compulsory Education, Vol. 7, no. 1, 2002, pp. 97–118. Edited version.

The purpose of this chapter is to compare and contrast the literatures of school effectiveness and improvement with similar research in the college sector. It does so by way of.

- a brief summary of the research base and main conclusions from the literature on schools
- a more comprehensive review of research on colleges
- a consideration of key differences in focus between school and college research
- some suggestions concerning opportunities for exchange between school and college-based research traditions.

In terms of scope, the chapter concentrates on British research on schools, colleges, adult education services and government funded, work-based training schemes. It excludes research that looks at improvement and effectiveness issues within higher education.

School Effectiveness Research

The literature of school effectiveness is firstly concerned with the outcomes of education and making comparisons between schools. In the words of Somekh *et al*:

> a more effective institution is typically defined as one whose students make greater progress over time than comparable students in comparable institutions.
>
> (Somekh *et al*, 1999, p. 25)

School effectiveness studies generally:

- seek to answer the question: what factors are associated with an 'effective school'?;
- define effectiveness in terms of the whole school;
- focus on quantitative measures of outcomes, such as academic performance and attendance;
- seek quantitative measures of inputs and processes that can be related to outcomes;
- seek to compare schools on the basis of quantitative measures, and identify the variables which schools can control and which distinguish high from low performing schools;
- employ relatively sophisticated research techniques including multi-level modelling and value added methodologies.

There appears to be a certain amount of agreement over issues thrown up by research to date, and how these might be addressed. Thus, problems associated with a 'top-down', whole institutional focus with its implicit reliance on the views of the head and senior teachers (Ouston, 1999) are being addressed by work at departmental and subject level (Harris *et al.*, 1997; Sammons *et al.*, 1997; Busher & Harris, 2000). The difficulty caused by the failure of quantitative research to replicate findings from qualitative research concerning the role of school leaders (Scheerens & Bosker, 1997) appears to have been resolved by the development of more sophisticated conceptual models and the application of robust quantitative research techniques (Hallinger & Heck, 1998).

The growing maturity of the field can be illustrated by reference to the increasingly nuanced discussion of issues such as school context and pupil intakes. In the domain of research, at least, the old arguments around the impact of economic and social deprivation on school performance have given way to more fruitful discussions of how best to make like-for-like comparisons which will control for independent variables as far as possible (Mortimore, 1998; Sammons, 1999). Indeed, the school effectiveness field might be said to be mature in that meaningful discussions of methodology can take place on the basis of a substantial amount of shared theory (e.g. Ouston, 1999).

Effectiveness research has paid attention to all phases of schooling from nursery to sixth form. It has an international dimension with British researchers increasingly engaged in a dialogue and in collaborative research with researchers from abroad, notably North America, Europe and Australasia. Further evidence of the relative maturity of school effectiveness research can be found in the meta-studies that have appeared. These studies typically propose theoretical frameworks based on syntheses and evaluations of scores and sometimes hundreds of research projects (Wang *et al.*, 1993; Creemers, 1994; Scheerens & Bosker, 1997).

In terms of the messages coming out of this research, there appears to be a broad consensus around a number of factors that have a significant impact on school outcomes. Different researchers place their emphasis slightly differently but the following list of factors drawn from Reynolds *et al.* (1997) and Mortimore (1998) is reasonably typical:

- leadership;
- shared vision and goals;
- a learning ethos and environment;
- high quality teaching and learning;
- high expectations by staff of pupils;
- positive reinforcement;
- close monitoring of pupil progress;
- pupil rights and responsibilities;
- purposeful teaching.

Finally, and perhaps most importantly, the fundamental issue raised by Reynolds many years ago that effectiveness research 'has had much more to say about what makes a "good" school than about how to make schools "good"' (Reynolds, 1990, p. 23), is being addressed by a growing convergence between school effectiveness and school improvement research (e.g. Gray *et al.*, 1999; Sammons, 1999; MacBeath and Mortimore, 2001).

School Improvement Research

School improvement research is concerned with the question of how schools might become better or more effective.

> School improvement is about raising student achievement through focusing on the teaching-learning process and the conditions which support it.
>
> (Hopkins *et al.*, 1994, p. 3)

School improvement, too, has an extensive literature, to which Stoll & Fink (1996) provide a convenient introduction.

The great strength of school improvement research and presumably the source of its continuing attraction for practitioners is that it is:

■ motivational and inspiring;
■ richly illustrated with examples of 'what works';
■ representative of the views of practitioners.

There are some indications, however, that school improvement is a less mature field of research than school effectiveness. Many of the publications take the form of case studies of action research (e.g. Bowring-Carr and West-Burnham, 1999) and suffer the problems associated with such an approach, notably difficulties of generalisation. More generally, some school improvement research has been criticised for being 'lightly empirical and naively quantitative', too reliant on ex post facto explanations and poorly predictive in terms of 'what works' (Gray, 2000, p. 1).

These weaknesses are currently being addressed through efforts to:

■ apply more quantitative research techniques
■ make more explicit and consistent reference to work on school effectiveness
■ develop and apply more rigorous yardsticks of improvement including tests and exam results (e.g. Gray *et al.*, 1999; MacBeath and Mortimore, 2001).

What improving schools seem to have in common is that they share:

- a proactive and shared approach to planning;
- an ethos or culture that favours improvement;
- leadership throughout the school which focuses on the quality of teaching and learning and promotes and facilitates professional discussion around improvement;
- specific interventions to boost exam performance (Somekh *et al.*, 1999).

Research on College Effectiveness

There is quite a substantial volume of research which addresses issues of college effectiveness (CE), but researchers and practitioners may have to look quite hard to discover it, since most of it is not published at all or because it exists in the 'grey' literature of unpublished research dissertations and presentations and papers at conferences.

In comparison with effectiveness research on schools, most of this research addresses issues of effectiveness only indirectly. Indeed, it could be said to be addressing two more preliminary questions: what are the causes of student failure and, by extension, what variables are most significant in accounting for student outcomes (attendance, retention, achievement and attainment)? Notable exceptions to this general observation can be found in work on value added and on differential achievement in colleges whose students are recruited predominantly from areas of high social deprivation.

The discussion which follows attempts to:

- provide an introduction to some of the research which is not in, or is only partly in, the public domain;
- summarise the findings of the research;
- assess the strengths and weaknesses of CE research to date.

Research within individual institutions is by far the largest category of research. It is being generated by individual colleges and adult education services as they attempt to identify the reasons for drop out and exam failure in order to develop improvement strategies. Because it is usually intended for internal consumption and use, the work is largely unknown and unseen outside the originating institutions.

Institutionally based research takes many and diverse forms but the most common include: research undertaken as part of a programme of postgraduate study (MA, MEd, MBA and, occasionally, DEd); surveys of withdrawn students often accompanied by staff surveys; reports produced for management purposes (typically combining analyses of data and student surveys); and research commissioned by a college from an external agency.

The questions addressed most frequently in college effectiveness research are:

- What causes student withdrawal?
- Which causes of withdrawal are within the influence or control of colleges?
- What makes the most difference to student completion and withdrawal?
- Where should colleges concentrate their energies to make improvements?

At the beginning of the 1990s, the prevailing view, faithfully reflected in an authoritative report from Her Majesty's Inspectorate (1991), was that drop out was largely due to factors external to colleges. The main thrust of CE research since then has been to displace that view.

Demographic factors

In Britain, withdrawn students do not have a markedly different profile from completing students in terms of age, ethnicity or gender (Martinez, 1995; Martinez, 1997b; Martinez and Munday, 1998; Stack, 1999).

Unlike schools, colleges do not have entitlement to free school meals to serve as a convenient indicator of social class. The proxy indicator used in the further education sector is therefore the relative economic and social deprivation of the electoral ward where a student lives. Research has demonstrated, however, that social deprivation measured in this way correlates poorly with retention and achievement across the college sector as a whole (Davies & Rudden, 2000, p. 2). A relationship has been identified, but only in the 10% of colleges which recruit the highest proportion of their students from deprived postcodes. Even in this minority of colleges, variations in the demographic composition of the student intake seem to account for no more than 50% of the variation in college performance as measured by the achievement of qualification aims (Davies, 2000). The only study which has asserted a significant 'postcode impact' (Vallender, 1998) did not consider any intervening variables, notably mode of attendance, level of programme or subject/curriculum area.

Student motivation

While college improvement (CI) research has shown consistently that efforts to improve or maintain student motivation can lead to better retention and achievement (Martinez, 1997, 2000), research on college effectiveness suggests strongly that the initial motivations of students as expressed by their reasons for enrolling, aspirations, expectations of college etc, do not vary significantly between students who subsequently stay and students who leave (Martinez, 1995, 1997a; Lamping and Ball, 1996; Kenwright, 1997; Further Education Development Agency [FEDA], 1998). A detailed study that explored student self-esteem and action-control beliefs with a relatively small sample of successful and unsuccessful students, did not find any marked differences between them (Stack, 1999).

Student decision making

Medway & Penney (1994) were among the first to suggest that the student decision making process could be characterised as a continuous weighing of the costs of continuing with or abandoning a programme of study and that decisions to leave resulted 'from rational decisions to respond to the difficulties [students] faced' (Medway & Penney, 1994, p. 38). These early conclusions have been borne out by subsequent research. Using a variety of methods and with samples of up to 9000 students, CE research has shown that college students have complex and multiple reasons for withdrawing from programmes of study and that decisions to withdraw can be seen as rational and positive from the point of view of students (Martinez, 1995; Crossan, 1996; Adamson *et al.*, 1998; FEDA, 1998; Martinez & Munday, 1998; Searle, 1998; Bloomer & Hodkinson, 1999; Adamson & McAleavy, 2000; Freeman, 2000).

Several studies show that students usually leave courses for several reasons (Medway & Penney, 1994; Martinez, 1995; Kenwright, 1997; Vick, 1997). One implication of this finding is that the widespread practice of recording only one, or the 'main' reason for student withdrawal by colleges, officially sanctioned by the Further Education Funding Council (FEFC, 1996, p. 4), misrepresents the student decision making process and gives a false picture of reasons for withdrawing (Martinez, 1995; Kenwright, 1996; Hooper *et al.*, 1999).

In terms of the reasons given by students for withdrawing the conclusions of a number of different studies are remarkably consistent. Causes of dropout fall into three broad categories: college-, work- and personal/family-related (Bale, 1990; BTEC, 1993; CSET Lancaster University, 1994; Martinez, 1995; Kenwright, 1996; FEDA, 1998; Strefford, 1999; Adamson & McAleavy, 2000; Davies *et al.*, 2000).

College-related issues

Studies which limit themselves to surveys of withdrawn students can indicate the range of causative factors and can identify those factors that are college related (Bannister, 1996; Barrett, 1996; North Tyneside College, 1997; Adamson *et al.*, 1998; Gill, 1998; Hall & Marsh, 1998; Longhurst, 1999; Strefford, 1999; Adamson & McAleavey, 2000; Davies *et al.*, 2000; Freeman, 2000). Depending on the sample size and the degree of sophistication of the research design, this can produce valuable information and insights. However, the absence of control groups of completing and successful students can make it difficult to:

■ control and interpret attitudinal data derived from samples of withdrawn students;
■ understand why the great majority of students complete their programmes;
■ identify what is making the most difference to completion and withdrawal.

These issues have been addressed in a number of larger scale studies (Medway & Penney, 1994; Kenwright, 1997; Martinez, 1997b; FEDA, 1998; Martinez & Munday, 1998; Responsive College Unit, 1998; Davies, 1999). These studies show that withdrawn students are most strongly differentiated from completing students by:

■ their evaluations of and attitudes towards college-related issues;
■ lower levels of satisfaction with certain aspects of their experience of college.

Specifically, withdrawn students tend to be less satisfied than completing students with:

■ the suitability of their programme of study;
■ the intrinsic interest of their course;
■ timetabling issues;
■ the overall quality of teaching;
■ help and support received from teachers;
■ help in preparing to move on to a job or higher qualification.

Withdrawn students are, moreover, much less willing to recommend the college to others (Medway & Penney, 1994; Kenwright, 1997; Martinez, 1997b; FEDA, 1998; Martinez & Munday, 1998; Davies, 1999).

The same studies demonstrate that withdrawn students are *not* strongly differentiated from completing students by:

■ the extent of their satisfaction with college facilities (canteen, toilets, classroom accommodation, equipment, library, workshop accommodation, etc.);
■ their personal circumstances (the incidence of personal, family or financial difficulties, their travel costs, and ease of their journey to college).

Further, the incidence of financial hardship does not seem to be strongly associated with decisions to drop out in order to gain employment (Martinez & Munday, 1998, p. 29). The Responsive College Unit with a sample of almost 6000 students came to virtually identical conclusions using a longitudinal research design (1998). It found, in addition, that neither part-time work nor 'external time commitments' correlated strongly with drop out.

The research in the Isle of Wight College (Medway & Penney, 1994) and the research conducted by Davies with a large sample of colleges and school sixth forms (Davies *et al.*, 1998), suggests that the same sorts of factors which are closely associated with withdrawal, are also associated with unsuccessful completion (where students complete their programme but fail to gain the intended qualification). The earlier study concluded that:

. . . the factors affecting non-completion were the same factors which led to unsuccessful completion. Half of unsuccessful completers would have left before completion if an acceptable alternative opportunity had arisen.

(Medway & Penney, 1994, p. 36)

Most CE researchers have found significant differences between the views of students and staff. With some notable exceptions, staff tend to emphasise those factors associated with student withdrawal over which they feel they have little or no control, including the nature of the student intake, resources and college policies (CSET Lancaster University, 1994; Martinez, 1995, Kenwright, 1996; FEDA, 1998; Gill, 1998; Davies *et al.*, 2000).

The more quantitative and larger scale research tends to emphasise the importance of teaching, learning and the support processes. The smaller scale, often more qualitative CE research, provides some more detailed findings about these processes. This research points to the importance of information, advice and guidance processes to help place students appropriately on courses. For younger full-time students, the issue does not appear to be lack of access to advice but rather its quality (Lea, 2000). According to Wardman & Stevens (1998, p. 5):

Most of this group [of withdrawn students] had experienced some elements of careers education, at least one careers interview and had completed at least one career action plan . . . the research suggests that there is scope to improve the quality of guidance. . .

The leading longitudinal study of drop out found that students who felt well informed about their course were less likely to withdraw (Responsive College Unit, 1998). Conversely, studies of withdrawn students have found evidence of:

■ poor, inadequate or inappropriate advice and guidance (Medway & Penney, 1994; Borrow, 1996; McHugh, 1996; Brown, 1998; Hooper *et al.*, 1999; Davies *et al.*, 2000; Little, 2000);
■ poor advice services for adult and continuing education students (Kenwright, 1996; Martinez, 1996; Clarke, 1997; Vick, 1997);
■ problems encountered by students who apply late or who join courses after their commencement (Brown, 1998; Hall & Marsh, 1998; Martinez & Munday, 1998);
■ poor (not to say hazardous and occasionally negligent) course choice decisions on the part of some students (Foreman-Peck, 1999),
■ indiscriminate recruitment (Sommerfield, 1995);
■ insufficient understanding by some students of the demands of their course (for example the balance of practical and classroom work, assessment requirements and the balance of different components of the course) (FEDA, 1998, pp. 40–1; Lea, 2000).

Teaching and learning

Student withdrawal and unsuccessful completion appear to be associated with a number of different aspects of teaching and learning. In no particular order of priority, these would include:

- uninspiring, 'boring' or poorly structured teaching (Medway & Penney, 1994; Borrow, 1996; Kenwright, 1996; Lamping & Ball, 1996; Vick, 1997; Martinez & Munday, 1998);
- poor group ethos or group dynamics (Borrow, 1996; Kenwright, 1996; Lamping & Ball, 1996; Hall & March, 1998; Martinez & Munday,1998; Hooper *et al.*, 1999);
- poor course organisation in terms of changes to the advertised programme, timetable, rooming or staff and inadequate liaison within the teaching team (Borrow, 1996; Kenwright, 1996; Lea, 2000);
- inadequate or poor course design (Martinez, 1997a, 2000; Martinez & Munday, 1998; Holy Cross College, 1999; Davies *et al.*, 2000);
- excessive or poorly scheduled assessment (Borrow, 1996; Adamson *et al.*, 1998; Brown, 1998; Hall & Marsh, 1998; Martinez & Munday, 1998; Wardman & Stevens, 1998);
- inappropriate or inadequate induction (Martinez & Munday, 1998; Responsive College Unit, 1998);
- large gaps in student timetables (Kenwright, 1997; Martinez & Munday, 1998);
- a mismatch between the largely 'activist' and 'hands-on' learning preferences of students and the more theoretical preferences of teachers (Askham Bryan College, 2000; Blaire & Woolhouse, 2000).

Value added research

The college research which most closely resembles the school effectiveness research can be found in discussions of value added approaches and in work on colleges which recruit their students from particularly deprived catchment areas.

Value added research in colleges is based on the exploration of significant relationships between prior attainment at GCSE and subsequent performance at A/AS level. This work is still in its infancy in the sense that the only large-scale studies to date have concentrated on methodological issues, particularly different ways of calculating value added scores, and consequent implications for the construction of 'league tables' of institutional performance expressed in value added terms. Some preliminary work has also been undertaken on the relative performance of different types of educational institutions and on the performance of students by gender (O'Donoghue *et al.*, 1997; Yang & Woodhouse, 2000). Some further work on the relationships between GCSE and GNVQ has been undertaken (Martinez & Rudden, 2001). Such studies have not progressed to a consideration of the processes that give rise to the value added outcomes. Indeed, the only work to date which moves beyond a consideration of patterns of performance to the reasons for such patterns can be found in occasional small scale studies based on individual A level subjects (Holy Cross College, 1999; Little, 2000; Solihull Sixth Form College, 2000).

The other college research which closely resembles school effectiveness research can be found in work by the Learning and Skills Development Agency which explores issues of effectiveness in colleges serving particularly deprived catchment areas. Based on analyses of the detailed student data set contained in the Individualised Student Record, Davies and Rudden (2000) conclude that a 'college effect' accounts for around 50% of the variation in college performance and that the main distinctive features of the more effective colleges in the sample are the relative maturity and sophistication of their improvement strategies (Davies, 2000).

Work based training

There is a much smaller body of work devoted to work based training schemes (Department for Education and Employment (DfEE), 1999a, b, c, 2000). Given the paucity of this research, it is unfortunate that its methods are relatively unsophisticated. All of these reports place great reliance on interview evidence from staff and managers. One of the reports (DfEE, 1999c) is based solely on such interviews. Another (DfEE, 1999a) is based largely on focus group, discussions with just 85 former trainees. A third (DfEE, 1999b) includes a telephone survey of some former trainees but its methodological information is so scant (it does not even give the number of telephone interviews), that it is impossible to form any judgement concerning the validity and reliability of its findings. Only one of these studies (DfEE, 2000) includes a relatively large survey of non-completers (772 respondents). None of these reports attempts to improve the interpretation of information from withdrawn trainees by making comparisons with evidence drawn from a control group of successful or continuing trainees.

■ The Limits of College Effectiveness Research

With the exceptions noted above, the dominant model of CE research is that it:

- seeks to answer the question: why do students drop out or fail to achieve their qualification goals?;
- focuses primarily on the student experience;
- is inspired by and intimately associated with efforts to *improve* colleges;

- attempts to *infer* messages about organisational effectiveness through interpretations and evaluations of the student experience;
- is driven largely by practitioner concerns (and is often undertaken by practitioners);
- focuses on full-time, younger students.

Leaving aside the lack of research on adult learners, the main limitation of this research is that it does not give rise to the ability to make robust like-for-like comparisons between colleges or indeed component parts of colleges. It is not, therefore, possible to identify in a *systematic* way the variables which colleges control and which distinguish high from low performing colleges, nor to identify the variables which are most critical.

This has implications for both policy makers and practitioners. Uncertainty remains concerning key processes and variables that colleges need to focus on in order to be or, indeed, become more effective. Specific questions that have yet to be answered include:

- Are the CE findings to date equally valid for all types of college, all types of student and all types of qualification?
- What is the relative weight or importance of the different process variables?
- What characterises an ineffective college?
- How different are the factors that contribute to effectiveness at course, programme, curriculum area, department, faculty and whole college level?
- How much do support processes (advice and guidance, recruitment and selection, tutoring, financial and welfare services etc) contribute to college effectiveness?

Research on college improvement

There is now a substantial body of college improvement (CI) research that quite closely resembles school improvement research. We have already noted that the field of school improvement research is less mature than that of school effectiveness research. The same applies to college improvement research, which takes the form of case studies and occasional syntheses of case studies.

One of the largest bodies of institutional research comprises a group of over 160 case studies from English colleges. The case studies present and reflect on the experience of projects to improve achievement and/or retention undertaken as part of the Raising Quality and Achievement (RQA) programme led by the Learning and Skills Development Agency. The case studies are drawn from a wide cross section of colleges and their content is equally varied. Some strategies have been developed and implemented across a whole college; others are implemented within departments or programme areas and still others are based in individual courses. Case studies from the projects can be searched and downloaded from the RQA website (www.rqa.org.uk).

Three reports are available which provide syntheses of the RQA case studies (Martinez, 2000, 2001b; Cousin, 2001). There are a small number of other syntheses based on college case studies outside the RQA programme (Kenwright, 1997; Martinez, 1996, 1997a; National Audit Office, 2001).

The case studies have all the weaknesses and strengths associated with an action research approach. They are empirically based, collaborative ventures led by practitioners which are intended to make a difference in the real world. They have a strong focus on improvement and the transfer of successful practice, together with a level of detail sufficient to facilitate replication and transfer and to allow practitioners to make their own judgements about relevance. Almost all of the RQA case studies have been evaluated against measures of effectiveness (retention, achievement and attainment). They are also variable in their method, the rigour of analysis and sometimes the robustness of their data. It is difficult, moreover, to derive generalisations concerning 'good' (still less 'best') practice, transferability to different contexts and, sometimes, cause and effect relationships. They do not distinguish easily those strategies that have had a particularly large impact on retention/achievement and those with a relatively small impact. Finally, because of a reluctance to report on improvement efforts that have failed to achieve their objectives, improvement case studies invariably lack a control group of colleges where improvement efforts have failed.

Two broad sorts of findings emerge from this work, concerning the content of improvement strategies and the process of designing and implementing such strategies.

Content of improvement strategies

In terms of content, there is a high degree of complementarity between CE and CI research. The former identifies problems and implicitly predicts that their resolution will give rise to greater effectiveness as expressed by student retention and achievement. In many ways, the CI research validates these predictions.

Whether implicitly or explicitly, most CI research assumes a process model of the student experience which extends from initial contact, advice and guidance, to recruitment and selection, student preparation, induction, initial assessment, teaching and assessment, learning support, tutoring and on-line programme support, and which ends with progression. The syntheses of college improvement studies cited above largely agree in their conclusions that colleges can improve by:

■ improving and extending advice and guidance services;
■ recruiting with integrity;
■ paying particular attention to the early stages of programmes of learning (student induction, initial assessment and the establishment of group ethos and identity);
■ establishing a close relationship with students through tutoring which is focused on student progress;

- closer monitoring and follow up of poor attendance;
- early identification of under performing students or students who are 'at risk';
- the early diagnosis of student requirements for basic skills and additional learning support and the provision of such support as far as possible within student learning programmes;
- the development of a curriculum framework (structure of the college year and college week, balance of teaching and independent learning and appropriate curriculum offer) which is appropriate for a college's intended students;
- a variety of mechanisms to maintain or improve student motivation including parental involvement, peer support and prizes and ceremonies;
- target setting allied with formative assessment and feedback;
- improvements to teaching strategies.

While many of the improvement strategies in colleges are broadly similar to those identified in the literature on schools, three stand out as being different (Martinez, 2000):

- threshold (advice, guidance, recruitment and induction);
- tutoring;
- curriculum.

The particular emphasis on threshold strategies is easily explained by differences between schools and colleges. For most schools, recruitment, course placement, induction, and starting pupils off on a programme of learning are seen as relatively unproblematic. CE research has shown consistently that many students experience substantial difficulties both before and immediately after enrolment.

The role of personal tutor seems to be more fully articulated than in schools. It involves an oversight of the whole of the student's progress, close liaison with subject tutors and teachers, and both pastoral and academic responsibilities. In terms of curriculum, CI research has tended to emphasise the greater degree of discretion and choice that colleges have in respect of their curriculum framework.

CI research also differs from that of schools in terms of the unit of analysis. Whilst school research tends to take the school as its focus, CI research has a rather heterogeneous and eclectic focus on a variety of different levels within the college, from individual courses to the whole college by way of programmes, departments, schools and faculties.

Notwithstanding the general agreement about the sorts of strategies which have been most successful in securing improvements, CI researchers have emphasised that there are no 'magic bullets', 'single solutions', 'one best way' or 'golden rules' (Kenwright, 1997; Martinez, 2000, 2001b; Cousin, 2001).

Process of college improvement

Common features of college improvement processes seem to include.

- a commitment to 'put students first';
- pro-active leadership which focuses on student success *and* which seeks to engage and motivate staff;
- effective and self critical teaching teams;
- a substantial investment in and commitment to professional development;
- a strong orientation towards research in general and action research in particular;
- well-developed and mature management information and quality assurance systems which command the respect of their users (Martinez & Munday, 1998; Martinez, 2000, 2001b, Cousin, 2001).

Beyond these generalisations, the processes by which colleges improve are almost as varied as the ways in which they improve. Improvement strategies can be top-down, bottom-up or indeed shared. They can be led by a variety of different post holders, from teachers and team leaders to student services managers, to quality assurance directors, to principals and deputy principals. Indeed, 'the way that strategies to raise achievement are inspired, researched, designed, implemented and evaluated varies considerably from college to college and even within the same college' (Martinez, 2000, p. 90).

▌ Conclusions: Research and Policy Issues

This brief comparison of school and college effectiveness and improvement research suggests that there are some significant differences. Each has its strengths, but each might also have something that could be usefully shared with the other. It is notoriously difficult to 'sing the music of the future', but the comparison may help to suggest some fruitful priorities for research. The remainder of this chapter identifies some of the ways that first school and then college research might be enriched and extended in the light of the comparisons made in this chapter. Where relevant, it also reflects on implications for policy and practice.

Given the longer history and greater maturity of schools research, particularly school effectiveness research, it seems likely that most of the potential for transfer will be from school to college research. There are, however, a number of areas where the flow could run in the other direction.

School research and policy issues

A significant difference between school effectiveness (SE) and CE research is that the former has been developed largely by academic researchers, the latter largely by practitioners. This has two main implications. First, there is a wider gap between SE and SI research than between their equivalents in the college sector. Second, SE research tends to focus on the whole school and to rely heavily on evidence derived from senior staff. These considerations suggest that school research could be enriched by:

- more practitioner research;
- wider dissemination;
- research in individual subjects and departments;
- pupil surveys.

The heterogeneity and wealth of college practitioner research suggests strongly that much could be done by research sponsors and, for that matter, by head teachers to encourage more practitioner research in school effectiveness. Indeed, it is difficult to see how school projects to raise standards can be undertaken without some initial internal research of this sort. Universities and research agencies, moreover, could provide wide access to the outcomes of such research perhaps on the model of the website college development projects mentioned earlier.

There is evidence from both CE and CI research that variable patterns of performance can subsist over time not only between different curriculum areas in the same college but between different courses in the same curriculum area in the same college. CI research, moreover, demonstrates that many successful improvement strategies are highly specific to their own context. College research would therefore lend weight to the argument that even greater school research efforts need to be concentrated on individual subjects and departments. Presumably, this would apply particularly to secondary schools.

The reasonably well-developed and sophisticated methods developed in the college sector to research pupil attitudes and experience could enrich research in schools. Colleges have demonstrated that data from students' surveys and focus groups can be of great value, particularly to the investigation and problem formulation aspects of school improvement projects (Cousin, 2001).

College research and policy issues

The limits of CE research to date suggest that college researchers need to extend their methods to embrace some of the approaches developed and applied successfully in the school sector. The increasing size of colleges, the diversity of their student populations and the wide variety of their institutional missions, suggest that something akin to the research framework developed within the school effectiveness tradition is required to provide answers to questions which are becoming increasingly pressing:

- What best distinguishes effective from ineffective colleges?
- How different are the characteristics of effectiveness in different types of colleges, for different types of students and in different types of qualification?
- How different are the factors that contribute to effectiveness at different organisational levels within a college?

Comparisons with school research also suggest that college researchers need to be more willing to engage in discussions of methodology. This conclusion actually bears more on policy than on the dispositions of individual researchers. The Department for Education and Skills (DfES), Learning and Skills Council and the Learning and Skills Development Agency between them sponsor most CE and CI research. If more methodological discussion and rigour are required, it falls to the sponsors of research to include that requirement in their research programmes.

Value added methods offer a relatively well-tried and tested method that could be extended to enrich both CE and CI research. More widespread use of value added methods will depend primarily on two policy decisions: the type of value added reporting which the DfES plans to introduce in the post-16 sector and the extent to which DfES (or Learning and Skills Council) is prepared to support college and school sixth forms in their improvement activity through the provision of value added data. In this respect, the very detailed staff development manual produced by the Scottish Executive (2000) in both paper and electronic forms, could serve as a model for England.

The scope of college research needs to be extended. The focus of college research must widen to embrace not only the part-time, mainly adult students, who make up the great bulk of college populations, but also the increasing number of students who access college through work-based, distance and open learning routes and through outreach centres. The prime responsibility to ensure that this occurs falls partly on the major sponsors of research and partly on college managements which, until now, have tended to focus their improvement efforts on younger, full-time students.

The brief consideration of the volume of CE and CI research and also its limited accessibility (particularly CE research), indicates a need both to:

- synthesise, summarise and make more widely available the research that has already been completed;
- ensure that more unpublished and 'grey' literature enters the public domain.

Again, these are as much policy as research issues. The major sponsors of post-16 research need to commission summaries of available research for intended use by practitioners. With the ready availability of Internet publishing, moreover, there is really no excuse for so much college research to remain inaccessible.

Two apparently technical issues, finally, need to be addressed. Each has a mixture of policy and research aspects. In terms of college administrative systems, the current policy which requires colleges to capture and record a single reason for student withdrawal is indefensible. Colleges need to establish valid ways of identifying any and every reason which might contribute to a student's decision to withdraw. Secondly, the research and policy communities need to establish a convenient indicator for social deprivation, which is at least as valid as the free school meals indicator used in school research.

To summarise, there is quite a substantial body of effectiveness and improvement research in colleges which bears comparison with research in the school sector. The improvement literatures are broadly comparable in terms of their methodologies and findings. The effectiveness literatures are different. CE research is more closely linked to efforts to improve colleges, but compared with SE research is less capable of making a like-for-like comparison and systematically identifying factors contributing to effectiveness in different types of college, for different types of students and at different levels of college organisation. The comparison suggests not only that there is scope for schools and college researchers to learn from each other but, in a number of areas, research and policy issues are linked. Progress in research issues along some of the lines suggested here will either not be accomplished at all or will be accomplished much more slowly without the implementation of changes recommended to universities, sponsors of college research, the Learning and Skills Council, DfES and college and school managers.

Acknowledgement

I am indebted to Tim Simkins for his detailed comments on earlier drafts of this chapter.

References

Adamson, G. and McAleavy, G. (2000) Withdrawal from Vocational Courses in Colleges of Further and Higher Education in Northern Ireland, *Journal of Vocational Education and Training*, 52, pp. 535–53.

Adamson, G., Archibold, J., McAleavy, G., McCrystal, P. and Trimble, T. (1998) *An Investigation Designed to Improve the Effectiveness of Further Education Provision by Reducing Non-completion Rates on GNVQ/NVQ courses in Colleges of Further Education in Northern Ireland*. Belfast: Department of Education for Northern Ireland.

Askham Bryan College (2000) Raising Quality and Achievement Development Project Case Study (published at www.rqa.org.uk).

Bale, E. (1990) Student Drop Out From Part-time Courses of Non-advanced Further Education. MPhil thesis, Bedford College of Higher Education.

Bannister, V. (1996) At-risk students and the 'Feel Good Factor'. MBA dissertation, Further Education Development Agency.

Barrett, J. (1996) *Lifelong Learning: Creating Successful Adult Learners*. Southend: South East Essex College.

Blaire, T. and Woolhouse, M. (2000) Learning Styles and Retention and Achievement on a Two Year A Level Programme in a Further Education College. Paper presented at the annual Further Education Research Network Conference, December.

Bloomer, M. and Hodkinson, P. (1999) *College Life: The Voice of the Learner*. London: Further Education Development Agency.

Borrow, L. (1996) Staying Power: A Customer Service View of Retention in Further Education. MBA dissertation.

Bowring-Carr, C. and West-Burnham, J. (1999) Managing Learning for Achievement, *Financial Times*.

Brotherton, B. (1998) Developing a Culture and Infrastructure to Support Research-related Activity in Further Education Institutions, *Research in Post-Compulsory Education*, 3, pp. 311–28.

Brown, H, (1998) Nature or Nurture? Does Tutoring Increase Retention on GNVQ Foundation Programmes in FE colleges? MA dissertation, Oxford Brookes University.

BTEC (1993) *Staying the Course*. London: BTEC.

Busher, H. and Harris, A. (2000) *Subject Leadership and School Improvement*. London: Paul Chapman Publishing.

Clarke, C. (1997) Can Colleges Make any Inroads into Improving the Retention of Students on Community Courses? MEd dissertation, University of Warwick.

Cousin, S. (2001) *Improving Colleges through Action Research*. London: Learning and Skills Development Agency.

Creemers, B. (1994) *The Effective Classroom*. London: Cassell.

Crossan, A. (1996) Retention or 'Now we've got 'em, let's keep 'em'. Unpublished internal report, Ridge Danyers College.

CSET Lancaster University (1994) Quitting: A Survey of Early Learning Carried out at Knowsley Community College. Lancaster, unpublished report.

Cunningham, B. (1999) Towards a College Improvement Movement, *Journal of Further and Higher Education*, 23, pp. 403–13.

Davies, P. (1999) *What Makes for a Satisfied Student?* London: Further Education Development Agency.

Davies, P. (2000) *Closing the Achievement Gap – Colleges Making a Difference*. London: Learning and Skills Development Agency.

Davies, P., and Rudden, T. (2000) *Differential Achievement: What Does the ISR Profile Tell Us?* London: Learning and Skills Development Agency.

Davies, P., Mullaney, L. and Sparkes, P. (1998) *Improving GNVQ Retention and Completion*. London: Further Education Development Agency.

Davies, T., Bamber, R., Rudge, L. and Stobo, M. (2000) When the Going Gets Tough . . . An Investigation into Patterns of Student Withdrawals in Pembrokeshire College during 1998/99. Unpublished report, Pembrokeshire College.

Department for Education and Employment (1999a) *Youth Trainees: Early Leavers' Study*. London: Department for Education and Employment.

Department for Education and Employment (1999b) *Leaving Training for Work: Trainees who do not Achieve a Payable Positive Outcome*. London: Department for Education and Employment.

Department for Education and Employment (1999c) *Tackling Early Leaving from Youth Programmes*. London: Department for Education and Employment.

Department for Education and Employment (2000) *Modern Apprenticeships: Exploring the Reasons for Non-completion in Five Sectors*. London: Department for Education and Employment.

Elliot, G. (2000) Riding the Storm: Practitioner Research in FE Colleges. Presentation to postgraduate students in the Faculty of Education, University of Central England, 10 January.

Further Education Development Agency (1998) *Improving GNVQ retention and Achievement*. London: Further Education Development Agency.

Further Education Funding Council (1996) *Students' Destinations: College Procedures and Practices*. Coventry: Further Education Funding Council.

Foreman-Peck, L. (1999) Choice, Support and Accountability: Issues Raised from the Experiences of Non-completing GNVQ Students, *Westminster Studies in Education*, 22.

Freeman, B. (2000) Survey of Student Non-completers October 1999–May 2000. Reigate College, unpublished report.

Gill, J. (1998) Small Scale research into Student Withdrawal at Stafford College in the Department of General Education. Stafford College, unpublished report.

Gray, J. (2000) The Future of Research on School Improvement. Presentation at BERA School Improvement Research Symposium, University of Nottingham, 6 July.

Gray, J., Hopkins, D., Reynolds, D., Wilcox, B., Farrell, S. and Jesson, D. (1999) *Improving Schools: Performance and Potential*. Buckingham: Open University Press.

Hall, D. and Marsh, C. (1998) Retaining Full-time Students at Calderdale College, Interim Report. Calderdale College, unpublished internal report.

Hallinger, P. and Heck, R. (1998) Exploring the Principal's Contribution to School Effectiveness 1980–95, *School Effectiveness and School Improvement*, 9(2).

Harris, A., Jamieson, I. and Russ, J. (1997) A Study of 'Effective' Departments in secondary schools, in A. Harris *et al.* (Eds) *Organisational Effectiveness and Improvement in Education*. Buckingham: Open University Press.

Her Majesty's Inspectorate (1991) *Student Completion Rates in Further Education Courses*. London: Department for Education and Science.

Holy Cross College (1999) Raising Quality and Achievement Development Project Case Study (published at www.rqa.org.uk).

Hooper, I., Fields, E., Ham, J., Williams, T. and Wolderufael, H. (1999) Investigating Retention of Full-time 16-19 Years Old Students 1997–98. Tower Hamlets College, unpublished internal report.

Hopkins, D., Ainscow, M. and West, M. (1994) *School Improvement in an Era of Change*. London: Cassell.

Kenwright, H. (1996) *Developing Retention Strategies: Did They Fall or Were They Pushed?* York: York College of Further and Higher Education.

Kenwright, H. (1997) *Holding out the Safety Net: Retention Strategies in Further Education*. York: York College of Further and Higher Education.

Lamping, A. and Ball, C. (1996) *Maintaining Motivation: Strategies for Improving Retention Rates in Adult Language Classes*, London: CILT.

Lea, S. (2000) Improving Retention and Achievement at Level 2. South Essex Lifelong Learning Partnership, unpublished report.

Little, E. (2000) Managing Student Achievement. Middlesex University, work-based dissertation.

Longhurst, R. (1999) Why Aren't They Here? Student Absenteeism in a Further Education College, *Journal of Further and Higher Education*, 23, 1, pp. 61–80.

MacBeath, J. and Mortimore, P. (eds) (2001) *Improving School Effectiveness*. Buckingham: Open University Press.

Martinez, P. (1995) *Student Retention in Further and Adult Education: The Evidence*. Blagdon: Staff College.

Martinez, P. (1996) *Student Retention: Case Studies of Strategies that Work*. London: Further Education Development Agency.

Martinez, P. (1997a) *Improving Student Retention: A Guide to Successful Strategies*. London: Further Education Development Agency.

Martinez, P. (1997b) Student Persistence and Dropout. Paper presented at BERA annual conference in York, available at www.leeds.ac.uk/educol

Martinez, P. (2000) *Raising Achievement: A Guide to Successful Strategies*. London: Further Education Development Agency.

Martinez, P. (2001) *College Improvement: The Voice of Teachers and Managers*. London: Further Education Development Agency.

Martinez, P. and Rudden, T. (2001) *Value Added in Vocational Qualifications*. London: Further Education Development Agency.

Martinez, P. and Munday, F. (1998) *9,000 Voices: Student Persistence and Drop-out in Further Education*. London: Further Education Development Agency.

McHugh, J. (1996) Applications, Enrolments and Withdrawals at High Peak College. High Peak College, unpublished report.

Medway, J. and Penney, R. (1994) Factors Affecting Successful Completion: The Isle of Wight College. The Further Education Unit, unpublished report.

Mortimore, P. (1998) *The Road to Improvement: Reflections on School Effectiveness*. Lisse: Swets and Zeitlinger.

National Audit Office (2001) *Improving Student Performance. How English Further Education Colleges can Improve Student Retention and Achievement*. London: Her Majesty's Stationery Office.

North Tyneside College (1997) The Causes of Student Drop-out from Courses: College Executive Summary. Newcastle: North Tyneside College and University of Northumbria, mimeo.

O'Donoghue, C., Thomas, S., Goldstein, H. and Knight, T. (1997) *1996 Study on Value Added for 16–18 Year Olds in England*. London: Department for Education and Employment.

Ouston, J. (1999) School Effectiveness and School Improvement: Critique of a Movement, in T. Bush, *et al.* (eds) *Educational Management: Redefining Theory, Policy and Practice*. London: Paul Chapman Publishing.

Responsive College Unit (1998) *National Retention Survey Report*. Preston: Responsive College Unit.

Reynolds, D., Sammons, P., Stoll, L., Barber, M. and Hillman, J. (1997) School Effectiveness and School Improvement in the United Kingdom, in A. Harris *et al.* (eds) *Organisational Effectiveness and Improvement in Education*. Buckingham: Open University Press.

Reynolds, D. (1990) Research on School/Organisational Effectiveness: The End of the Beginning?, in R. Saran and V. Trafford (eds) *Research in Education Management and Policy: Retrospect and Prospect*. Brighton: Falmer Press.

Sammons, P. (1999) *School Effectiveness: Coming of Age in the Twenty-First Century*. Lisse: Swets and Zeitlinger.

Sammons, P., Thomas, S. and Mortimore, P. (1997) *Forging Links: Effective Schools and Effective Departments*. London: Paul Chapman Publishing.

Scheerens, J. and Bosker, R. (1997) *The Foundations of Educational Effectiveness*. Oxford: Pergamon.

Scottish Executive (2000) Standard Tables and Charts: Staff Development Manual. Edinburgh, Scottish Executive, and also published at www.scotland.gov.uk

Searle, A. (1998) Increasing Completion and Success Rates for Young People on Full-time Programmes. Exeter College, unpublished internal report.

Solihull Sixth Form College (2000) Raising Quality and Achievement Development Project (published at www.rqa.org.uk).

Somekh, B., Convery, A., Delaney, J., Fisher, R., Gray, J., Gunn, S., Henworth, A. and Powell, L. (1999) *Improving College Effectiveness*. London: Further Education Development Agency.

Sommerfield, D. (1995) An Investigation into Retention Rates and Causes of Drop-out of Students on Full-Time Engineering Courses within a College of Further Education. MA dissertation, University of Greenwich.

Stack, J. (1999) Investigation into Student Retention and Achievement at Bradford College. MSc dissertation, University of Manchester.

Stroll, L. and Fink, D. (1996) *Changing Our Schools. Buckingham*: Open University Press.

Strefford, D. (1999) Halton College Research Results: Interviews with Students who have Left the College. Cheshire Guidance Partnership, mimeo.

Vallender, J. (1998) Attendance Patterns: An Instrument of Management. MBA dissertation, Aston University.

Vick, M. (1997) Student Drop-out from Adult Education Courses: Causes and Recommendations for Reductions. MA dissertation, University of Wolverhampton.

Wardman, M. and Stevens, J. (19998) *Early Post-16 Course Switching*. London, Department for Education and Employment.

Wang, M., Haertel, G. and Walberg, H. (1993) Towards a Knowledge Base for School Learning, *Review of Educational Research*, 63(3).

Yang, M. and Woodhouse, G. (2000) Progress from GCSE to A and AS Level: Institutional and Gender differences and Trends Over Time. Paper delivered at British Educational Research Association annual conference, September.

18

Self-Evaluation in European Schools: Case Examples

John MacBeath with Michael Schratz, Denis Meuret and Lars Jakobsen

If self-evaluation is to be for school improvement, then it must be a participative process. Since it is designed for teachers, pupils and parents it should involve them, or their representatives, as far as possible at each stage in the process. It is important to reach agreement on what is to be evaluated before proceeding further. That was inherent in the purpose and rationale for the Socrates project 'Evaluating Quality in School Education'.

The project involved 101 schools from eighteen countries, each one with a different starting point and prior history. They had widely differing structures and diverse national and cultural backgrounds. Some were quite advanced in their thinking about self-evaluation, some less travelled down that route. In some schools self-evaluation was already formalised while in others it was informal or embryonic in development. All schools, however, joined the project to learn more and made an agreement to employ a common instrument and work with a common set of tools. How they went about it and where it led them differed immensely, but it was that diversity and ownership of the process that gave the project its inspiration and impact.

The project had a number of important dimensions – a European substructure and imprimatur; direction and advice at national level; plus three key operational features:

- A self-evaluation profile
- A set of guidelines containing a wide repertoire of evaluation tools
- The support of a critical friend.

While together they comprise an inseparable trinity, each had a unique part to play and contribution to make.

Source: MacBeath, J. with Schratz, M., Meuret, D. and Jakobsen, L. (2000) *Self-Evaluation in European Schools: A Story of Change*. London: RoutledgeFalmer. Edited version.

The Self-Evaluation Profile

The common instrument was known as the SEP or, to give its proper name, the self-evaluation profile. It is a very simple instrument, designed to help schools select for further evaluation and improvement those domains which matter most.

It consists of a set of twelve areas of school life which can be used to open up discussion about its quality and effectiveness. These are shown in Figure 18.1.

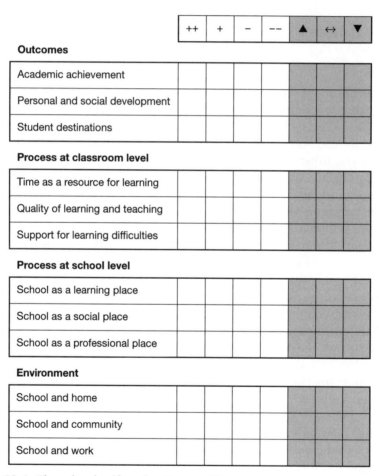

Figure 18.1 *The school self-evaluation profile*

The twelve areas were chosen after lengthy discussion and examination of the literature on school quality and effectiveness. In a sense the SEP may be seen as a 'multi-level model', encompassing processes at individual, classroom, school and community level. The areas are by no means sacrosanct and spaces have been left on the SEP for people to add their own categories. It is significant, however, that in so many different countries and school systems the twelve categories proved to be relevant and robust.

In short, the SEP aimed to:

■ Promote serious and purposeful discussion among all stakeholder groups, helping to create a culture for further inquiry and ongoing self-evaluation.
■ Get a picture of the school as seen through the eyes of staff, students and parents.
■ Help to identify and prioritise areas for deeper inquiry.

The Schools

In this chapter we consider the impact at the level of individual schools, their teachers and students. The brief accounts which follow illustrate what schools in different countries did, the issues they faced and the changes it made to their policies and practice.

The two examples are from schools in Belgium and Scotland. Both faithfully followed the suggested protocol, filling out the self-evaluation profile and selecting five areas for further investigation and improvement. In both cases, areas for further inquiry were related closely to the school development plan and fed in helpfully to future priorities for action. Both schools expressed surprise at the maturity and insights of the students and both testified to the impact of the process. In the Belgian school the head chose to be present at virtually all meetings and gained many insights from that experience. In the Scottish school the head chose not to participate in order not to influence the outcome or process of discussion. These are matters for individual balance of judgement, with the optimum scenario probably being a judicious choice of when to be present and when to withdraw. Both schools drew some similar conclusions from their involvement and offer good advice for others.

■ To follow through on the evaluation to tangible application.
■ To choose carefully the areas to evaluate in greater depth and be clear about grounds for doing so.
■ To be clear from the start how data will be gathered, analysed and used.
■ To stick with and integrate procedures into the ongoing life of the school.

The Scottish school chose to be described under its real name. The Belgian school has been anonymised by the new head in respect for her predecessor.

■ Case study: St Fiacre's School

St Fiacre's School – let us call it that – had no culture of self-assessment before it took part in the pilot project. This did not hinder it from carrying out an impressive and coherent series of investigations. As the assessment took place at a time when the school had to draw up its mission statement, it was possible to use the results to plan for the future, and the school grasped this opportunity.

From a technical point of view the evaluation was not particularly innovative: it was based mainly on the use of questionnaires and focused on those areas calling for decisions at school level rather than class level. While the various groups of stakeholders expressed a need for technical support in the development of evaluation tools, they did not really succeed in finding one that closely matched their needs. Even though an external expert paid two visits to the school, it was not seen as helpful in this technical respect. In a nutshell, the evaluation was not altogether plain sailing, but it is in dealing with the imponderables that we get a true insight into how evaluation works.

The background

The school teaches about 500 pupils aged between twelve and eighteen from a rural catchment area in Belgium. It is a Catholic school, but almost all the pupils come from the surrounding villages and choose the school because of its proximity, as a survey of parents undertaken during the pilot project confirmed. In Belgium, independent education is subsidised by the state, so parents pay virtually nothing.

When the self-evaluation project started in September 1997, St Fiacre's School had existed in its current form for only a year. It was created by the merger of two schools, a process accompanied by considerable changes in the school's culture, under the leadership of the new head.

The school started the pilot project late and in a rather unorthodox way. Instead of taking time to study the project and then deciding to apply – which is how things were supposed to happen in theory – the head was asked to take part by the Catholic Education Federation, which had recently been invited to choose a rural school to participate in the project. The head tells the story like this:

> I went down to the cafeteria and talked about it with some of the teachers. I got the feeling that they appreciated being chosen by the Federation, that it was a form of recognition after the difficult times we had been through. So I said yes. But we were entering unknown territory – we hadn't seen the document presenting the project and we didn't really know what we were letting ourselves in for.

The result of this late start was that the school only had a week or two to put together a steering group and complete the self-evaluation profile. The steering group overseeing the project consisted of the head, two teachers, a pupil and a parent. It met once a month during the year over which the project ran.

The completion of the SEP took place in two stages. First, six groups of six people met twice each for one hour to go through and score the self-evaluation profile. Each group then elected a delegate to be part of an umbrella group, and this group then selected areas to be evaluated in greater depth. The thirty-six people were all volunteers but it was not difficult to find them. As one of the two previous headteachers had been highly authoritarian, the opportunity for individuals to air their opinions was welcomed. Indeed, this was the very first time that the pupils, and even the teachers, had been asked for their views on how the school was run.

Almost two years on, the head recalls clearly what happened in these groups (which she attended regularly). She was surprised by the maturity of the pupils and their considerable interest in the exercise. She found she had overestimated what parents really knew about the school and she was surprised at the difficulty they experienced in finding common grounds of agreement.

'As the school had changed a lot in just one year', she remarked, 'some people's comments related more to the old situation before the merger, whilst other people described the new school. Some discrepancies can be explained in that way'.

Today, with the benefit of hindsight, she still believes that the process they went through really did help to improve relations within the school. The SEP process was challenging and useful although, when it came to the selection of the five areas to evaluate in greater depth, the choice was, in a sense, already predetermined: 'We went for those areas in which changes had already begun to take place. Basically, we used the project to continue what we had already started'.

One might see this as a lost opportunity, but such a judgement would be mistaken. What the school did was to build on their experience rather than venture into entirely new territory. The five areas chosen for further evaluation were not necessarily the most problematic but rather those where there was the greatest promise of success and growth. These were:

■ Pupil destinations
■ Time as a resource for learning
■ Support for learning difficulties
■ School as a social place
■ Home and school.

Not just one but several evaluations were carried out in each of these areas. These are described in a detailed and comprehensive 180-page report which was distributed to the school governors. Results were discussed with teachers at a two-hour staff meeting attended by 70 per cent of the staff, and a copy of the report was placed in the staffroom.

Pupil destinations

At St Fiacre's, final-year pupils have a special project to do (*travail de fin d'études* or TFE) which, despite its name, is not a piece of schoolwork. The aim is for pupils to trace, in their own judgement, their development during their school career in two areas: 'Self-knowledge' and 'Personal and professional development'.

A questionnaire on the usefulness and quality of the work performed in the context of the TFE was sent to pupils who had just left the school. The report notes that very few pupils in the technical and vocational streams responded, probably because answering the questions called for a high level of self-awareness plus analytical and writing skills, which made it difficult for them. Their response rate was too low for their results to be used, which is unfortunate for the few who made the effort to respond.

On the other hand, the survey of pupils in the general education stream was more productive. Teachers responsible for the TFE had done their own evaluation in September 1997. Pupils and teachers had agreed on several operational principles, for example that from the outset they should be aware of the criteria by which it would be assessed.

In addition to this, a survey of pupils who had left the school in 1991 and 1994 was carried out to ascertain what had happened to them since leaving and what they thought about how the school had prepared them for life after school. Although respondents thought that the various subjects had been well taught on the whole, they cast doubt on the efficacy of organising secondary education on the basis of rigid subjects. Some believed that the curriculum should be oriented more towards personal development and culture, while others wanted more emphasis on the technical skills needed for higher education, such as note-taking or learning to manage one's own work.

Time as a resource for learning

A two-part questionnaire on time management was distributed to pupils. First, they had to account for the time spent on various activities during a week and second, they had to say whether they were satisfied with the time spent on each activity, taking into account the usefulness and 'quality' of this time. As the survey focused on the division of time between schoolwork and other activities and did not differentiate between different school activities, the usefulness of the data was limited and a more detailed survey is planned for the future. The school also learned that planning and piloting of the qualitative part of the survey would need to be thought through more carefully in the future, with more emphasis being given to the question of precisely why the survey was being conducted.

Teachers were also surveyed, not on their periods of absence as such but on the lessons which were not taught because of absence. While the response rate was only 52 per cent, the survey showed nonetheless that many lessons were still being lost to in-service training. This raised the question: Would it be a good idea to cut the amount of in-service training? To sacrifice that many hours? To ask teachers to do more training in their own time? As a result of the survey, the issue was debated in the staff council, a body comprising members of management and teaching staff. It was decided that the number of in-service training days which could be taken out of normal teaching days should be cut from six to four.

Support for learning difficulties

Under this heading, the report assesses the school's remedial lessons and the tests taken at the beginning and end of the academic year by all first-year pupils.

First- and second-year pupils who are having difficulties receive a 'remedial' lesson every week. This is taken by teachers from the school, but not necessarily the pupils' normal class teachers. The system was initially evaluated in 1996–97, leading to a considerable improvement. However, the 1997–98 assessment yielded similar results to the previous evaluation – that is, pupils were satisfied and teachers felt that while remedial lessons had improved pupils' behaviour they had not raised academic attainment by any significant degree.

This finding left the teaching staff divided as to what conclusions to draw. Some believed that the remedial lessons should concentrate more on working methods, learning techniques and so on, while others believed that they should concentrate more on the subjects themselves.

All first-year pupils, not only those having difficulties, are tested in French and mathematics. In fact, this test is given to all Belgian pupils at the start of the year in order to test the key skills which they ought to have acquired at primary school. The report gives the results for each of the six classes at this level, but it does not give an overall figure for the whole school or provide information about the gap between the weakest and the ablest pupils, between boys and girls, or the proportion of pupils with problems in both French and mathematics. In other words, the results of this test still have to be exploited to their full potential.

Nevertheless, two very important pieces of information came out of the survey.

First, it was noted that pupils having difficulties at the beginning of the year were usually still having them at the end of the year. It was concluded that the tests were effective at identifying difficulties, and so it was decided to use them, in addition to teachers' judgements, as a basis for deciding which pupils should be given remedial support.

Second, hardly any classes showed end-of-year results representing a real improvement on the results at the beginning of the year. (As no significance test was performed on the discrepancy between the tests at the beginning and end of the year, it is difficult to say whether results are real or purely accidental.) In three cases (two mathematics classes and a French class) results were clearly lower. In other words, between primary and secondary many pupils had lost important skills, such as the ability to manipulate fractions, for example. This is perhaps because it was assumed that these skills had already been mastered. As for those pupils with the greatest difficulties, who did not have these skills when they arrived, the report shows that they evidently did not pick them up during the year. The school's development plan for 1999–2002 mentions a new activity based explicitly on the results of these tests: 'Exchange of documents and practices between primary school teachers and those teaching the first year of secondary school'.

School as a social place

All pupils were surveyed on school life, asking them what they thought of their physical environment, the school's resources, school rules, relationships with teachers and extra-curricular activities. The pupils helped to draw up the questionnaire and analyse responses. The experience has shown what could be done differently and better in the future. For example, as the questionnaire asked respondents only about their level of schooling, information about age, gender or previous school career were not available, so preventing what might have been useful comparisons among different categories of pupils. Categories chosen for multiple choice responses proved to be insufficiently discriminating with, for example, only three categories of response ('all of them', 'some of them 'or' none of them') on questions such as 'Were your courses interesting?'

Of course, pupils judge their school in terms of their own experience, and are limited by their breadth of experience and terms of reference. This does not make the questionnaire any less useful but has implications for the design and framing of questions.

The pupil responses did serve to alert the school to those areas about which pupils are very unhappy: the toilets, school rules, teachers 'whose only response is to punish'. There were complaints and suggestions from pupils in an open-ended section which merited closer attention. They alerted staff to things to which they had become so accustomed that they no longer noticed them. For example, that 'the flowers painted on the walls at the end of the playground would be more appropriate at a nursery school', or the request to place benches in the playground.

This evaluation was also followed by action. The management of the school 'tried to introduce a new way for pupils to relate to their teachers', but confessed, 'it's not easy'.

The development plan provides for benches to be installed in the playground and, according to the head, this would happen in 1999–2000. School rules are not going to be changed in the near future. According to the head 'even if we were to get all the parties around a table it would be difficult to achieve anything without first teaching democracy'. Indeed, a new activity included in the development plan – 'Setting up of a school council: learning how to be a class delegate and conduct meetings' – shows that real efforts are being made to teach pupils about democracy.

Home–school links

As an independent school which has recently experienced considerable change, St Fiacre's was concerned about its image with parents. In fact, as we have seen, the links between parents and the school were rather weak, and the school had few informal ways of finding out about its image. A parents' association was created only recently and, even now, teachers are heard to say to pupils whose parents are members, 'You shouldn't think that you can get away with murder just because your parents are in the association'!

A survey focusing on parents' reasons for choosing the school, their perception of the quality of life enjoyed by their child(ren) at the school and their opinion on certain activities, was sent to 450 families. The response rate was about 50 per cent. One significant result of this survey was that the parents of pupils in the vocational and technical streams were far more inclined than parents of children in the general education stream to believe that the quality of life enjoyed by their child(ren) at school was low.

The conclusion to the evaluation focused on three aspects – the school environment, remedial lessons and pupil participation in the life of the school. In fact, these concerns are set out clearly in the development plan. The self-evaluation proved to be very useful in deciding on the future direction of the school, not only because it improved relationships between the various stakeholders, but also because it helped them to become better acquainted with the school and better able to plan ahead.

To conclude this case study, it will be useful to summarise some of the lessons that can be drawn from it:

■ Members of a school community are generally willing to take part in an evaluation of this kind but it does creates a moral obligation to use the findings to make real decisions and, to a certain extent, to involve those stakeholders in the decision-making process. It is therefore important to link evaluation and planning, as was done here.
■ It is important to choose carefully a small number of areas to assess, taking the time to think properly about the objectives of the investigation and the best tools to use.

■ It should be decided right from the start how to analyse the data and how decisions will be taken on the basis of these data. The evaluation is, in fact, a decision-making process for everyone: the headteacher, teachers and other stakeholders.

■ This approach is only worthwhile if you stick with it over the long term. It can sometimes be a good idea to evaluate at several points in time, as demonstrated at St Fiacre's by the gradual improvement in the remedial courses following several separate evaluations. More often than not, however, an individual area will not need to be evaluated in depth every year, so that, over time, it will be possible to assess all the relevant areas one by one.

■ Case study: St Kentigern's

St Kentigern's Academy was one of the two Scottish schools involved in the project. It had previous experience of self-evaluation, as this is part of the Scottish Executive Education Department's (SEED's) policy for all schools. However, the school saw the Socrates project as an opportunity to broaden and strengthen its approach to self-evaluation and to move to a greater inclusiveness among stakeholder groups – staff, pupils and parents. The project provided the opportunity to test with more rigour and invention the question 'How good is our school?' which, in Scotland, is where the interrogation of school quality and effectiveness begins.

St Kentigern's Academy is situated more or less halfway between Glasgow and Edinburgh. It draws in pupils from the immediate village of Blackburn and a large surrounding rural area, traditionally very dependent on coal mining and heavy engineering but now facing major social change. Shifts in working patterns have created high levels of unemployment and extensive deprivation. West Lothian, the education authority in which the school is located, has the lowest rate of uptake for further and higher education of anywhere in Scotland. In this context, the school sees itself as having two key tasks:

1 How do we help our students become independent learners/thinkers to equip them to play a valuable role in society?
2 How do we prepare our students to be enterprising, confident and self-reliant?

Each year St Kentigern's admits 200 students into its first year of secondary education. These students come from ten primary schools varying widely in socio-economic background. On leaving school, the majority will settle for work in the local area. In their report on the project, the school adds this:

The opportunity to take part in the Socrates pilot project afforded an exciting extra dimension to the school's work in the quality assurance field, since it provided our colleagues with ideas from all over Europe and we welcomed the opportunity to learn from others during the project. Moreover, the possibility of building an active network with European colleagues, particularly those who had identified the same development priorities as ourselves, was a very important feature of the project.

With this in mind, the school chose to pursue learning issues in its follow up to the SEP process. This is what it did.

The SEP and after

Three discrete groups were formed to go through the self-evaluation profile – parents, staff and students. The headteacher did not have any input to this process in order not to influence the judgements of the groups. The three groups then came together to agree on a common judgement of their school and were surprised to find a very high level of agreement on their ratings. Decisions about which areas to focus on fell out quite easily from this process. These were not only identified as significant areas for all of the three groups, but closely reflected priorities incorporated in the school development plan. Three were closely interrelated and focused specifically on learning. These were:

- Academic achievement
- Quality of learning and teaching
- Support for learning difficulties.

The two other chosen areas were:

- School as a professional place
- School and home.

In the words of the headteacher, Kath Gibbons:

> It was an excellent way to begin. The self-evaluation profile provided the opportunity from the start to involve students and to create a sense of ownership among teachers and parents too.

Identifying areas for evaluation

In their report compiled for a project conference, the school describes the rationale for this choice of areas in the following terms:

> Three years ago, the most distinctive feature of the school approach to learning and teaching was passive, a culture born out of low expectations of students and staff. In terms of attainment, ceilings had been reached. The socio-economic background of the school did not encourage the concept of 'challenge'.

With a more consistent challenge to complacency and low expectations, staff believed that levels of academic achievement could be raised significantly across the school. This, it was felt, depended not simply on good or better teaching. The school culture already encouraged an emphasis on good teaching. What it needed was a closer focus on effective learning and an examination of the different contexts in which this took place. So, the focus could encompass classroom learning, learning through whole-school activities (clubs, games, projects), homework, student mentoring and study support (lunchtime and after-school sessions with a learning skills focus).

Choice of 'Quality of learning and teaching' from the twelve areas brought these disparate activities together into a common focus. Involving students and parents in this was, for the school, a new departure. While the school development plan had previously centred on the evaluation of learning and teaching, that process had not, up until this point, taken the step of involving those key players. In the words of the head:

> The ground-breaking aspect of the whole process was the bringing together of these different groups to exchange their perspectives on the key issues. In particular, the joint discussion and investigations between students and staff was revolutionary for us in St Kentigern's.

Examining the extent to which progress had been made in the five chosen areas, the school commented after the first year:

> Progress in the five areas chosen has been steady. It must be remembered that progress must be evaluated in the light of the context of the school – the predominant culture and the vision of what can be achieved by the organisation. Subsequent evaluation which records improvement must stand up to the rigorous test of evidence of improvement in the classroom.

The following are some of the initiatives that were taken within each of the five areas:

1 Academic achievement

The first-year curriculum was restructured to increase time for literacy and numeracy and the teaching of ICT (information and communication technology) through these subjects. A base tutor was given the responsibility for teaching these subjects as well as being the primary pastoral care tutor for that group of pupils. This 'base tutor' also has responsibility for study support, which is the help given to young people out of school hours – at lunchtimes and after school.

2 Peer tutoring

To support the development of reading skills, all first-year pupils with reading difficulties have a senior student to help them in the reading club which operates at lunchtimes. Parents are also involved in helping to improve reading skills and work with the learning support department. Able readers also have access to the reading club in order to encourage their private reading.

3 Homework study review

Another strand was the evaluation of homework and study undertaken out of school hours. Questionnaires were issued to pupils, parents and teachers to gather their views on homework – the time spent on it, parents' expectations and the design and use of the home/study planner. The planner was produced by parents and the cover designed by pupils and it was put into use from September 1998.

4 Examination analysis

A review of examination performance was carried out with each department of the school showing the relative performance at Standard Grade (the external examination at the end of the fourth year of secondary school), illustrating patterns of development over the last three years. Areas of weakness were then targeted by providing further resources and improved teaching materials and strategies, as well as focused staff development. While this was not a new intiative under the Socrates programme, the introduction of self-evaluation was seen as very important in giving this further impetus.

5 Professional development

As part of the Socrates project, a staff development group was set up involving a wide range of teachers from different disciplines, focusing specifically on quality assurance issues. Performance indicators used by Her Majesty's Inspectorate of Schools were discussed by staff and the staff development group drew up a 'quality features list' as a basis for determining strengths and weaknesses in classroom teaching. In addition to this, forums were set up to allow joint discussion between teachers and senior students, focusing the discussion on 'time as a resource for learning' and examining that from different perspectives.

One year beyond the end of the project, St Kentigern's has assessed its benefits in these terms:

- The quality of student-teacher dialogue has improved.
- Students have an input into school reports.
- Students are routinely asked to evaluate courses and units of learning.
- Study support is based heavily on student feedback and choice.
- Students work creatively in teams.
- Students lead parent workshops.
- Students now have a clearer focus on target setting to improve performance.
- The school now has a student council.

Summarising progress, the headteacher writes: 'One year on we haven't looked back. Having involved students in self-evaluation, we now take it for granted that they will play an active part in the planning and evaluation of our programme for teaching and learning in St Kentigern's.'

Index